T0277492

ONE GARDEN AGAINST THE WORLD

KATE BRADBURY

ONE GARDEN AGAINST THE WORLD

IN SEARCH OF HOPE IN A CHANGING CLIMATE

BLOOMSBURY WILDLIFE

LONDON • OXFORD • NEW YORK • NEW DELHI • SYDNEY

BLOOMSBURY WILDLIFE
Bloomsbury Publishing Plc
50 Bedford Square, London, WC1B 3DP, UK
29 Earlsfort Terrace, Dublin 2, Ireland

BLOOMSBURY, BLOOMSBURY WILDLIFE and the Diana logo are trademarks
of Bloomsbury Publishing Plc

First published in the United Kingdom 2024
Text copyright © Kate Bradbury, 2024
Species chapter illustrations © Abby Cook, 2024
Cover and title page illustration by Jasmine Parker

A catalogue record for this book is available from the British Library.

Library of Congress Cataloguing-in-Publication data has been applied for.

ISBN: Hardback: 978-1-3994-0886-8; Audio download: 978-1-3994-0887-5;
ePub: 978-1-3994-0884-4; ePDF: 978-1-3994-0822-0

2 4 6 8 10 9 7 5 3 1

Typeset in Bembo Std by Deanta Global Publishing Services, Chennai, India
Printed and bound in Great Britain by CPI Group (UK) Ltd, Croydon CR0 4YY

MIX
Paper | Supporting
responsible forestry
FSC® C171272

To find out more about our authors and books visit www.bloomsbury.com
and sign up for our newsletters.

Contents

Prologue

'Darling, look out of the window! Everything's fine!'

In my twenties I lived in Manchester, on the sixth floor of a block of council flats just off the A57, or Mancunian (Mancy) Way. A short walk from Manchester Piccadilly station and the city centre, it was grey, noisy and built-up. I loved every piece of it; my first stab at adulthood, at living on my own. I painted my bedroom silver and slept on a mattress on the floor and I grew sweetcorn, tomatoes and courgettes in pots on the balcony (I was 24 – of course I grew sweetcorn on the balcony).

I worked and played in the bars and clubs of Manchester's gay village and I would walk home in the early hours, keys poking through my clenched fist to protect me from would-be attackers, and I would see hedgehogs.

It never occurred to me that the hedgehogs might be in trouble, that they might not have the best time foraging beneath the ring road, beneath the noise and stench of the city. It occurred to me only that their presence was magical, and that seeing them on the grassy wastelands around my council estate, as I stumbled home from parties and nightclubs, was everything I loved about being alive.

Their home and mine was urban and gritty but there were trees, areas of long grass, council houses with messy gardens. There was a little park with cherry trees. Not much but enough. The area was unloved, had an air of urban neglect, but I soon learned that it was ripe habitat for hedgehogs, along with the birds, bees and butterflies that would visit my balcony, too.

Years later I had a job in Manchester, and in the morning before my train left to take me back to Brighton I went for a walk, to the gay village, to the bars and the clubs, and finally to the estate where I used to live. The flats had had a makeover – the balconies were now sealed with airtight windows that presumably made the flats warmer and more soundproof but which further separated the residents from the natural world. The gardens of the houses had been paved over and there seemed to be more space for parking. It wasn't just the people who would be suffering from the loss of green space; I wondered how the hedgehogs were getting on.

I posted about my trip on Twitter. An old mate, Choel, who lived two floors beneath me in the flats and still lives locally now, got in touch to say the hedgehogs were gone. The council had signed a PFI (Public Finance Initiative) with a private company to manage the area. They felled trees, paved over gardens and bulldozed the small park with cherry trees. They built the residents an allotment, but erected a huge fence around it, meaning hedgehogs couldn't get in or out. She sent me photos of entire gardens in skips, of upended trees in full blossom with bird feeders still hanging from their branches. She told me she had found 10 dead hogs, and others out in the day and underweight. Eventually, she started rehoming them, going out at night and rounding them up to take to a rescue centre, where they were fed and watered before being released somewhere they actually had a chance of living. She regrets leaving it so long before she acted; she wishes she could have saved the dead 10. But she did save seven. I'm grateful she noticed them at all.

We cry habitat loss but it's theft, really – no one is so careless as to lose their home. We call it progress, but how dare we? How many people, throughout the planning process, will have thought of or cared about hedgehogs? Or considered any of the other residents, both human and wild? The management company would have conducted an ecology survey, no doubt. But, as is often the case, it was probably done in winter when the hedgehogs were hibernating (I'm sorry to say there is such a thing as a dodgy ecologist). Did residents other than Choel and me know there were hedgehogs on that estate? Did anyone care? The council paved over the gardens to save money on maintenance. The trees and park were lost because the car parks that replaced them can be a source of income. The residents placed there by the council – many of whom are vulnerable migrants and sex workers – would not necessarily have known or thought about those habitats, making them so much easier to destroy.

Manchester City Council is not alone in its apparently wanton destruction of green spaces. In 2014, a now-infamous deal to remove nearly half of Sheffield's 36,000 trees led to public outcry and a huge campaign to save them (they saved some, and their efforts led to the formation of a city-wide tree protection group that recently earned Sheffield 'Tree City of the World' status). In 2023 Plymouth Council ordered 110 mature trees to be felled in the middle of the night. The ill-fated HS2 project is still bulldozing through ancient woodland (again, in the name of 'progress'). Then there's the London Resort theme park that was nearly built on Swanscombe peninsula, an area of nationally important grasslands, coastal habitats, scrub and wetlands that not only buffers the coast from erosion but also stores vast amounts of carbon while providing homes for countless rare and threatened species. Thanks to a massive campaign, London Resort withdrew its application, but the threat of losing the land still looms large.

There are many more micro-aggressions, micro-destructions, that go under the radar including those, of course, in our gardens. There are around 30 million gardens in the UK but the trend to lock them beneath paving and plastic grass is growing. Back in 2011, Greenspace Information for Greater London (GiGL) published a study of the changes they'd observed in London's 'garden vegetation structure' from 1998 to 2008. They used drones to look at tree canopies and vegetation and noted the colour of the ground – green for grass and grey for paving. They concluded that hard surfaces had increased by 26 per cent over the decade, equivalent to the loss of two Hyde Parks every year. As a young journalist I attended the press conference and put up my hand and asked, 'If you measured the colour of gardens from green to grey, how did you account for the replacement of living lawns with plastic grass?' They couldn't answer my question and, after some hesitation, muttered that, perhaps, the loss of green space was more than they had been able to quantify in this particular assessment.

I was sorry to have thrown a spanner in the works of an otherwise excellent study. Plastic grass was only in its infancy in 2011, having started to be used in gardens in the 1990s – there probably wasn't much laid in London between 1998 and 2008. But now? A study by Aviva in 2022 found that, nationally, 1 in 10 homeowners with outside space has replaced at least some of their garden's natural lawn with plastic grass, with a further 29 per cent planning to or considering it. That means, of the 30 million gardens in the UK, 3 million have been lost beneath plastic. Where does that leave hedgehogs?

In Manchester City Centre my old mate Choel witnessed the local extinction of a community that, 20 years previously, had made me feel alive. But everywhere we are all chipping away at the very core of life itself: housing estate by housing estate, garden by garden, paving stone by paving stone, roll of plastic grass by roll of plastic grass. And there's more now, isn't there? Among all that's wrong with the world, climate change has finally taken centre stage, as raw and destructive as a skip full of blossoming cherry trees. As if hedgehogs haven't enough to deal with, they're now dying of heat and thirst.

Habitat loss is something I know and have grown up with. I have seen it and mourned it from a very young age – the old gothic houses we used to drive past that had been abandoned and gone wild, before a developer bought them and turned them into flats; the horse paddock at the end of our road that remained for so long while the town grew around it, until it, too, was lost to a strip of new-build homes. The gradual stamping out of life and love. Habitat loss has remained the same the whole time I've known it, there's just less habitat to lose, now. (Did anyone think to plan for it to stop?)

But climate change threatens to take everything away from us, not least a stable climate in which we can grow food according to predictable weather patterns. It's already hitting the global south: in the Horn of Africa people are experiencing the longest and most extreme drought on record, causing crops to fail and livestock to die. In India, rising temperatures and droughts are reducing wheat and rice crops, while scorching conditions are preventing farm labourers from being able to work. Add to that the mayhem caused by fire and floods, in countries where there isn't necessarily the infrastructure to cope with these assaults. Here, in the global north, we are also suffering droughts, dangerous heatwaves, fire, flooding and crop losses – in the summer of 2022 UK crops of berries, peas, broad beans and salad leaves were frazzled in the heat and sun, while in winter we had a tomato shortage due to 'unseasonal' snow and ice in southern Spain and Morocco. (Yes, I know, Brexit played its part as well.) As climate scientists repeatedly say on Twitter, 'You ain't seen nothing yet.'

I have used the effects on people and food as relatable examples of climate change here because most people think of climate change as affecting people (and usually other people at that). We rarely see or focus on the ecosystems that are collapsing due to global heating, the animals that live in and are a part of them, their roles in keeping those systems functioning. On the news we see skinny polar bears clinging to ever-diminishing icebergs but what do we see of the birds and butterflies moving north to escape the heat? What of the bees that emerge from hibernation in unseasonably mild weather, only to be frozen to death a week later? What of the hedgehogs that go thirsty, the baby birds that go hungry? As the planet warms, its life systems shut down, making plant and animal (including human) existence much more difficult than we have known since the end of the last Ice Age. And it drives me nuts that most of us are just carrying on as if it isn't happening.

The thing about nature is that it has the means – to a degree – to limit the effects of climate change. Intact ecosystems such as forests, grasslands, oceans and peatlands are 'carbon sinks' – natural storage systems that remove atmospheric carbon and other greenhouse gases – and are essential if we are to minimise global heating. But they also help mitigate the effects of climate change: a bed of seagrass or kelp can reduce the velocity of waves hitting shores, and therefore prevent coastal erosion; a river system, complete with beavers, can prevent flooding in towns and cities downstream, while woodlands, peatlands and other terrestrial systems absorb and hold on to water. Gardens are human-made habitats, but they mimic the woodland edge, so they also hold on to water, slow down wind, create shade and provide food and homes for wildlife. In cities they can absorb pollution and help reduce urban temperatures. Crucially, they also link together to form vast corridors that connect other ecosystems (the woodlands, peatlands and other terrestrial systems mentioned above), enabling species to move between them, potentially giving them space to adapt to climate change. Of course, they also absorb and store carbon – in lawns, in the bark of trees, in the sludge at the bottom of garden ponds, in soil, in leaf litter and compost. Gardens are, or at least have the potential to be, an enormous but as-yet-untapped solution to the climate and biodiversity crisis. But what are we doing? Disappearing them beneath plastic and paving. Beneath weed-suppressant membrane and 'decorative' purple slate chips. Beneath cars, beneath gravel, beneath entire new homes. Beneath large stones and driftwood to make them look like the beach (my absolute favourite). We need to stop biting the hand that feeds us and we need to repair the hands we have already bitten. And we need to do this yesterday.

Climate change has happened several times in Earth's 4.6-billion-year history but it happened slowly, over thousands of years, partly because ecosystems were initially able to take the hit. What we're facing now is the rising of temperatures alongside the chipping away of the very

systems that can lessen or even slow its impact. At the exact
time we should be halting habitat loss and facilitating
landscape recovery (rewilding) for the good of all life on
Earth, we are still taking more than we are giving back – it
seems we can't stop ourselves. Temperatures are rising and
the clock is ticking.

What if the solution to these problems lies, in part, in
our gardens and other green spaces? Not that gardening
can stop climate change, but what if gardens could
reconnect us with the natural world, make us more aware
of the destruction all around us? What if we rise up, garden
by garden, park by park, balcony by balcony and do
something – anything – to help a bee or a butterfly or a
bird or a hedgehog? What would our world look like if
more of us were tuned into the life systems that support
us? Would we stop our pesticide-laden dog from jumping
into the river? Would we switch from eating factory-
farmed meat, with its many layers of pollution and trauma,
to something kinder and more sustainable? Could we all
collectively tread that little bit lighter, for the good of all
things, while still pushing for the radical change that's
needed at the top? Would more of us push for that change?
I think we would. So many people tell me they don't
bother with their gardens because they are 'just full of
pigeons and crows', and they will be, if your garden is just
decking and plastic. Bring it to life and see what else turns
up. Talk to your neighbours and see what they can attract,
too. Feed a hedgehog, identify a butterfly, stroke a bee!
With 30 million gardens, 27,000 public parks and countless
more allotments and other green spaces, not to mention
the millions of balconies, patios and rooftop gardens in the
UK, we can bring ourselves back to nature, we can rewild
ourselves. Together, we can provide food and homes for
wildlife, which is struggling as 12,000 years of predictable

weather patterns go full bucking bronco and disrupt daily life. We can create corridors to enable wildlife to travel north as the world heats. We can grow plants to provide food, nesting opportunities and places to rest, that offer shade from the sun and shelter from heavy rain. Every single plant we grow will help cool our cities, prevent flooding, absorb carbon and root us back into the world we actually live in. Every insect, bird or mammal we care for will have an extra stab at life, at survival. Every good thing we do will make us feel better and more hopeful, more determined to spread the word and, ultimately, speak truth to power. Surely it's worth a go?

I also believe our gardens can help some species survive climate change, because when it's dry we can add water to quench the thirst of mammals and birds, stop leaves shrivelling and keep flowers producing nectar. When there's little or no natural food we can offer alternatives, like halved apples for winter thrushes, mealworms for robins and kitten biscuits for hedgehogs. We can grow native plants for those that need it now and near-natives for those that are arriving here from the continent. When next door is covered in plastic we can be messy and wild; we can, at least for the time being, control some of the situations in our gardens; we can help the lucky few who have found a way to live among us. In that respect, gardens are some of the most important habitats in the world. If only more of us knew.

We are hurtling towards climate and biodiversity collapse at an astonishing and terrifying rate. I'll be honest, most of the time I'm completely overwhelmed. But I have a little garden. And every good I do in it feels like a big two fingers to the world of greed and destruction, of climate change and biodiversity collapse, of big oil giants, media moguls and ineffectual governments. Gardening helps me focus on the things I can change, helps me be hopeful about the coming year. It lifts me when nothing else does. I truly believe our gardens and green spaces have the answer to the very root of the problem that's plaguing the modern world right now: our disconnect from nature and the consequent acceptance of living in a dying world. Let's not accept, let's grow!

This book is part memoir and part call to arms. It's about waking up, noticing things and being better humans. If you're lucky enough to have a garden, this book is especially for you but it's also for you if there's a green space nearby that needs a little love. This book is about climate change and biodiversity, about gardens and parks, it's about every single leaf and blade of grass that sucks up CO_2. It's about hedgehogs, bees, butterflies and frogs. It's about a little garden in south Portslade and one terrified, angry gardener. But it's about you and your garden, too. What will you do to make a difference?

About Me and My Garden

I grew up in the suburbs of Solihull, a metropolitan borough nine miles south of Birmingham. I never really knew wildlife until adulthood. Not 'proper' wildlife. Not the sort of species you see in old Ladybird books, not big birds of prey or badgers or moles or even swallows or house martins (although my granny, who lived in the countryside, would point them out on walks near her house). I knew blue tits and small tortoiseshell butterflies, frogs, worms and moth cocoons. I knew conkers and spiders and ants, pigeon feathers, slugs and snails. I didn't really know anything wilder than that. But I've always craved it. 'I always knew you'd end up working with the soil,' says my mum.

Gardening was my way to wilder things. As a child I would lie on my belly and look deep into the thatch of the lawn, at ants crawling among the blades of grass. I would watch blue tits come and go from the tit box, I would move nearly dried-out worms stuck on the pavement, on to the soil (I still do). I have always been drawn to plants and planting, gardens, the outside. I had my first vegetable patch at the age of 10, a room packed with houseplants at 20, my first allotment at 24. But still there wasn't much wildlife, or nothing that I'd really noticed. I guess it took a while for my eyes to open.

They were opened for me. A red-tailed bumblebee made a nest in an old duvet in my ex's backyard, and her neighbours complained to the landlord. I searched online for how to move it and, with help from the Bumblebee Conservation Trust, managed to transport it – intact – to my former allotment. With just two stings to the face I fell in love, and suddenly a world opened up that I had barely known existed. I read bumblebee books, learned how to identify the different species (there are 24 in the UK), learned how they live and breed and hibernate. I would go out just to look for bumblebees, see if I could find them in early spring or still on the wing in late autumn. I would pick them up and stroke them, move them from pavement to flower. I would follow instructions on how to make a nest in the hope that, one day, a queen would return and make a nest in my garden. They never have. I've rescued and moved more nests since – nests made in walls that were being torn down or in compost bins that were tipped over, or in a bush blocking a doorway or in the ground too near a path. Many have been successful but most had already succumbed to parasites. But none has ever found her way here to breed in my garden. Yet.

I moved on to other species: butterflies, amphibians, birds, flies. I learned as much as I could, bought every book, absorbed every tiny detail of their lives and habits, their needs and … their declines. Most UK species have been in freefall since those days of lying on my belly looking into the thatch. Most have suffered the double whammy of changes in land use (building cities and towns, making farmland more 'industrial') and pesticides, including insecticides that kill insects, herbicides that kill the plants insects feed on, and fungicides that make the insecticides more potent. I made it my mission to create as many homes for wildlife in my garden as possible, to understand the needs of these species and use my position as a writer for a well-known gardening magazine to tell everyone how to do the same. I assumed that people, once they knew what was at stake, would want to help wildlife. That they would want to grow flowers for bees and erect boxes for birds. That it wouldn't be long before we had streets of long grass and bird boxes, nectar-rich flower beds, hedgehog highways and native shrubs and trees. That there would be more wildlife. Cities of wildlife. That we would have more hedgehogs and more birds, more bees and more butterflies and hell, more spiders and earwigs and blow flies, why not? That one day there would be more, not less. Not *even less*. Not ever the quietness there is now. Because we knew about the declines and we had the power and knowledge to stop them. Why would we let things get worse? Why would we let species disappear?

In her 1962 book *Silent Spring*, Rachel Carson documented the chipping away of life at the hands of those who used the pesticide DDT, which not only killed insects but was also found to thin the shells of birds' eggs, meaning few birds had successful breeding attempts. She died two years after her book was published and didn't live to see DDT banned across the world (in the US in the 1970s and the UK in the 1980s). Neither did she live to know that it's still used in some parts of the world today and persists in our oceans as a 'forever chemical'. Nor did she live to see the continued destruction of the natural world, the habitat loss, the 'progress'. I'm glad. To think her silent spring would have been so noisy and raucous to my ears some 60 years later is the cruellest irony. How would she have coped with the silence there is today?

I will never know the abundance of life my parents and grandparents knew, which they probably ignored and took for granted. I wish I could go back to see the abundance of species in childhood because, even though I saw very little, I know now how much more there was 35 years ago. I fill my garden with plants for wildlife, make spaces for only the wild things. And yet still it's quiet. Still, there are few flies buzzing around my house in summer, there are few butterflies on my buddleia. There's an eerie quietness that goes with the realisation that you can't hear bees buzzing.

Where are they? Why aren't they in my wildlife garden? I'm surrounded by concrete but some of us are growing flowers. Is it enough? Will there ever be enough?

I garden for the wild things, for my sanity, for the child with her head in the thatch. I want there to be more wildlife. I want swifts in my nest boxes, butterflies on my buddleia. I want ants and slow worms and earwigs and caterpillars. I want fat hedgehogs that are fat on beetles, not cat biscuits. I want a full clutch of tits in the tit box. I want abundance and noise and to stop worrying about every last quiet thing. Is that too much to ask?

Home is a small Victorian terrace built for railway workers, in Portslade-by-Sea, just outside Brighton. It's urban with an industrial past; it used to be called Copperas Gap, owing to the extraction of stones made of iron pyrites (copperas), which were used to make sulphuric acid. There was a windmill at the bottom of my road until the 1870s. The Victorian houses that replaced it are lovely but – unlike West Hove, which butts up against Portslade via a busy high street – there are no street trees. Now there's a busy port in place of a beach and cliffs, described proudly as 'the industrial centre of Brighton and Hove'. It was its own urban district until 1974, when it joined the borough of Hove and is now part of the city proper.

Portslade is considered by some as the slightly rough-and-ready cousin of Brighton and Hove. It's not as pretty or as genteel as its fancier relatives. But it's cheaper to live here and much, much quieter. It's close enough to the South Downs that I can walk there from my house. Plus, we have bigger gardens than those in the city centre, and hedgehogs.

When I moved here four years ago, the garden was a fairly standard 1960s design, with patios at either end of its modest 14 metres and a concrete path to one side of a tiny lawn, overgrown with enormous non-native shrubs like Japanese spindle and Californian lilac. Someone had planted a eucalyptus tree less than a metre from the back door. The small front garden was covered in weed-suppressant membrane and stones. I ruthlessly ripped out all the plants, shrubs and eucalyptus in the back, along with the back patio and concrete path. In the front I took up the stones and membrane, replacing them with a riot of pollinator favourites: viper's bugloss, dyer's chamomile, lungwort, primroses, cranesbills, knapweeds. 'Oh, you live in the house with the flowers,' say the dog walkers in the park. 'I always cross the road so I can look at them.'

While the front garden bloomed I worked on the back: I planted native trees (hawthorn, rowan and silver birch), a tiny mixed hedge of hazel, more hawthorn and things like guelder rose and field rose, and then planted more guelder rose, hazel and European spindle as shrubs in the borders. Among them I planted flowers: honesty, foxgloves, snowflakes, hellebores, primroses. I laid wildflower turf – proper turf, with lots of lovely native grasses for caterpillars to eat, and wildflowers for bees and other pollinators to feed from. I trained climbers up to the tops of the walls for nesting birds and punched holes in the bottom of them for hedgehogs to travel through. Along the entire side of the shed I made an enormous habitat pile out of the things I had ripped out, which is now home to everyone except me. I drilled holes in the trellis for solitary wasps, I made a log pile in the spaces beneath and behind the bench.

Smack in the middle of the garden I dug a pond. It's big – some might say too big – but I wanted something that would bring lots of wildlife and, as a general rule, the bigger the pond, the more species it attracts. It's kidney shaped, with a maximum depth of 60cm in the middle, graduating gently to shallow edges, as a good wildlife pond should be. It has a 'beach' of stones at either end, for birds to bathe and tadpoles to congregate, and hedgehogs to enter and exit easily. It has natural edges planted with grasses, primroses and trefoils. It has a dragonfly perch (a strategically placed stick for dragonflies to perch on) and a range of aquatic plants growing beneath, on and above the surface.

Some wildlife came straight away, and most of it came for the pond. Water bears and other microscopic life I couldn't see, but then masses of flies mated and laid eggs on the surface, followed by water beetles and backswimmers, dragonflies and damselflies. One day I came home to find hundreds of backswimmer nymphs bobbing about in the water, and I watched them grow into adults and stay to lay eggs of their own. Other days I've watched egg-laying blue-tailed damselflies, mating common darter dragonflies. I've seen a sparrowhawk breakfast on a goldfinch at the pond edge, red mason bees take pond mud to line their nests. I've rescued half-drowned male wool carder bees that were fighting for territory over nearby bird's foot trefoil and had accidentally fallen in (or been pushed?). I've seen bathing birds, from blackbirds, house sparrows and robins to goldfinches, chiffchaffs, crows and herring gulls.

One day I caught sight of a frog hanging at the water's edge, as frogs do, for insects. I was so excited. I had high hopes of frogspawn the following spring but nothing came. They took a chance the year later, spawning for the first time the night before my 40th birthday – the best present I could have woken up to. And it wasn't just a few; as if from nowhere, masses of frogs took to the water and spawned in great vigorous parties. I watched them through binoculars from the kitchen: frogs arriving to the pond and being ambushed, males fighting for females, the slow queue to the perfect spawning spot. I couldn't count the clumps. After about two weeks they were spawning on spawn, completely filling one shallow 'beach' and then starting on the other. I'd never seen anything like it.

Summer was a riot of jumping froglets. They were like fleas, hopping about everywhere, in the borders, in the grass, on the patio. I was terrified of standing on one, of disturbing them. But I was so happy they were using the garden.

There are toads here, too. The first one I found was dead, lying on its back with its tongue hanging out. I've since found them in the habitat pile at the side of the shed, and occasionally they turn up on the night camera. Once, a neighbour brought me one she'd spotted in the road and thought it 'must be on its way to your garden, Kate.' It wasn't, I popped it at the bottom of the habitat pile where it remained safe for the day, and then set the camera on the back gate to see if it would pick it up at night. Sure enough, as night fell, the toad headed out of the garden. Where was it going? There must be another pond somewhere. I scoured Google Earth to see if I could spot one in neighbouring gardens, and came to nothing.

The trees I planted were tiny whips but they have grown and now don't sway when birds and squirrels land in them. The hawthorn and rowan bear blossom and berries, the silver birch catkins and seeds – all food for different species. There are bird boxes for nesting tits, although they have nested with me only once, and there are kitten biscuits for hedgehogs. There are bee hotels and hedgehog boxes and a bat box and swift boxes. There are neighbours with paved gardens but I'm working on that.

Because it's not just my garden that matters, or my garden alone that can make a difference. I'm grateful for the alleyway (known in Sussex as a 'twitten' but you may know it as a 'ginnell') that connects my garden to eight sets of neighbours, a whole other road of gardens and, eventually, a small park. It's quite brambly in places and some people use it as a dumping ground – both those who live here and those who don't. But this is how the wildlife gets in. The hedgehogs, frogs, toads and slow worms all enter and exit via my garden gate and travel by stealth along a century-old coal route, in and out of the wider landscape.

Just one block from a busy high street in an urban, industrial port, with small gardens, many of them paved over or covered in plastic, you'd be forgiven for thinking wildlife doesn't live here. But you'd be wrong: there are hedgehogs, frogs, toads and slow worms. There are birds and there are insects. There aren't many of some species – songbirds are quite rare here, due, I think, to a dense population of cats, squirrels, magpies and crows; the nests always get predated. And I don't know how well others are doing or how numerous they are but they are here, so I can help make life better for them. In my lawn there are nesting mining bees, in my long grass and knapweeds there are caterpillars. In summer a bat catches mosquitoes over the pond, in spring and autumn the garden becomes a stepping stone for chiffchaffs and willow warblers, on their way to and from their breeding grounds. Plenty of species either don't live in the area or haven't found the garden yet but I always keep an eye out for them. That's half the joy of wildlife gardening: wondering who will turn up next.

In short, the garden is just beginning. By the time you read this it will be at least six years old, the trees and shrubs growing into the space created for them, the pond hopefully hosting a complex variety of life. I sit or stand at the kitchen window that looks out on to the garden and I watch and dream of wildlife. I imagine the space when it's grown, make plans, see what's working, laugh. Sometimes I cry and I sit on the floor, looking out until I feel better, until I see a frog or a sparrow, a butterfly, a hedgehog. The garden is a part of me as much as it is the wider landscape, and I am a part of it. We grow together but we struggle together, too. We help each other out, me providing water to keep it going, it providing life to distract me from The Big Things. I hope the wildlife will come to know my garden as a safe space, an oasis in a desert of plastic and concrete, amidst unpredictable weather and humans with their collective fist on the self-destruct button. I hope I can encourage my neighbours to do more for the species that live here, that we can all create better habitats, better connectivity and a better understanding of what is actually needed to save species and improve our world. I hope, across the whole country and indeed the whole globe, we can fall back in love with our environment and treat it better, through the simple act of tending the spaces outside our back doors. I hope, I hope, I hope.

April

My story begins in spring, 2022. So far, the year has mostly been dry and above averagely warm – we had the mildest New Year's Day on record and less than half of January's average amount of rainfall. I found my first paired-up couple of frogs on 26 January, which sent me into a meltdown because it was so horribly early, but my first snowdrop on 29 January, which is about the same as it always is. Conditions remained mild for February but grew stormy: Dudley, Eunice and Franklin all occurred within a five-day period, bringing strange purple but sunny skies, fallen trees, disruption to roads and railway networks and flooding to parts of the north. Here it brought enormous sticks for our dog, Tosca, who kept trying to bring them into the house but couldn't work out how to get them through the door. Most of the country saw above-average rainfall during the storms but in Brighton it remained dry.

Spring is a time of greeting old friends: the first hairy-footed flower bee of the year, the first great fat bumblebee queen, the first butterfly, the first flute-like call of the blackbird on the roof. I press my ear to the trunk of my silver birch and listen for the rising of sap. I marvel at the mitten-like leaf buds of my rowan. I watch bumblebee queens taking baths in the bright orange pollen of crocus flowers, great tits gathering caterpillars to feed their young. Every day there's a new friend to greet, a new bee, a wasp, a butterfly, a frog. I'm so grateful they survived winter. 'Hey bee,' I say, 'you made it!'

And so it's April. Still very dry but now cold. There are lots of bees in the garden and I'm grateful so many seem to have survived hibernation. There are fat bumblebee queens but also mining bees in the lawn and borders, red mason bees in the bee hotels, hairy-footed flower bees on the lungwort and primroses. They have everything they need in my garden, but only because I'm watering it. I'm so troubled by the lack of rain.

Spring is happening but it's muted, it's less than it should be. The ground is parched, the plants are stunted and there just isn't the volume of insects I have known before. Everything should be lush and green. Caterpillars should be feasting on foliage, beetles scuttling among the thatch. And aphids, hoverflies, leafminers and millions of other critters that most of us never even notice, should be feasting, breeding and then being eaten by species further up the food chain. And they are, but there are fewer of them than usual, and they're struggling.

The hedgehogs are struggling, too. Rescue centres are filling up with dehydrated and hungry hogs who can't find enough natural food – typically caterpillars, beetles and earthworms despite their reputation for eating slugs and snails (they do eat slugs and snails but far fewer than we would like them to). I'm keeping a close eye on them. I have a small trail camera, which I position by the hedgehog boxes or by the feeding station, or looking out over the pond or a bit of grass, or the bird bath that has become a de facto hedgehog watering hole, and each morning I drink tea and watch hedgehog videos in bed, a ritual I have come to love since moving here. I live in hope that I might spot them mating or bringing hoglets into the garden – the closest I have got is seeing a male circling a female as a precursor to mating but the camera shut off before I could find out if he was successful. Still, without mating (which, I realise, is an odd thing to obsess over at breakfast time but is a nice distraction from the weather), I can see how the hedgehogs are doing. I can watch their gait for limps, count ticks, see if their eyes are OK, see if they're drinking and feeding enough. It all adds up to monitoring the population, even if I'm probably monitoring the same ones several times a night.

There are two hedgehog boxes filled with hay in the side return, partially hidden by pots planted with hazel, ivy, wildflowers and herbs. At this time of year there's always lots of activity here, as the males search for females to mate with (often while maintaining huge erections). I watch them trundle down the path, looking in one and then the other. They use the boxes as sort of 'bachelor pads', sleeping in them for several days at a time and then moving on to another den somewhere else. The boxes are usually empty in winter, so apparently not good enough for hibernation, and I've never had a female make a nest in one. But they seem perfect for nomadic, horny males.

On the cameras today is a hog carrying dandelion leaves into one of the boxes. I can't see if it's male or female but I watch it collect leaves from the dandelion patch I left on the patio, and my heart soars. I hope it's a pregnant female, taking a chance on the bachelor pads for the first time, but if it's a male just making his home more homely that is also wonderful. I am horribly, achingly worried about the dry weather, which no one is yet calling a drought but clearly is, and the impacts this will have on wildlife, on those that need water for drinking and bathing, for raising young. I'm anxious about the rivers and the trees, about all life that is being pushed to the limits of its own existence. But the hedgehogs will be OK. These few who use my garden will have water and food for as long as they need it, and nest boxes to bring dandelion leaves into. And I can watch them — it's something I can do while we all wait, desperately, for rain.

It's sunny but cold, the sky a child's drawing of yellow ball suspended in deepest blue, the occasional fluffy cloud in the distance. Traces of frost remain on plants still in shade and ghosts of ice haunt the surface of the pond. Bees take cold nectar from spring flowers: brrrrrrr. The dog and I potter in the sun while the shade sleeps.

I plant out sweet peas and clear some of last year's stems from the border, which I had left intact over winter so insects had somewhere to shelter. I top-dress potted plants with fresh, home-made compost and water them with grey water (recycled water containing biodegradable soaps and detergents), remove weeds from some areas and allow them to remain in others. I sweep the patio, deadhead daffodils, I tie rose and clematis stems into the trellis.

I put the bee hotels out — two in the back and four in the front, of different types, made using different materials and with different-shaped holes (square or circular). The bees have their preferences but these change every year and I like seeing which ones they go for. I fill one of the release chambers with last year's red mason bee cocoons, as it won't be long before they hatch. The leaf-cutters I leave in the shed, as these can be predated while in their cocoons and it's safer to keep them locked away for as long as possible – they won't fly until June. Sometimes, if I'm working at home a lot, I let them hatch out on my desk with the window open, so I can not only watch them emerge but see them safely into the sunshine, too.

In the pond little commas of tadpoles wriggle gently on fallen willow leaves. These sit just beneath the surface and provide a microhabitat, not only generating warmth as the sun heats small amounts of water above them but also food, as they're covered in algae, which the tadpoles eat. I crouch down to watch them in their vast watery world. There is still some frogspawn left and the newest tadpoles stick closely by, some of them nibbling the jelly around their unhatched kin. Some have only just hatched and appear to lie on their leafy beds barely moving, with just the occasional wriggle of the tail. Others are older, bigger, and are using their tails more vigorously, swimming strongly in the shallows. Those older still are on the other side of the pond, feeding from algae growing on stones. All are vulnerable; it's thought that just 1 in 50 tadpoles becomes a frog, the rest are eaten by other tadpoles and aquatic larvae, by birds, by newts. There's enough here to feed everyone, enough yet to become plenty of frogs. Just as long as the pond remains a pond. I fetch the hose and connect it to the water butt and release my precious store of rainwater into their home. Just a bit. Just enough to keep a reasonable level so the tadpoles can swim freely.

Tosca growls, gently, for attention. The scruffiest of mongrels, she's a mix of 13 different breeds largely made up of border collie, Labrador, springer spaniel and Pomeranian. She looks like a skinny little collie with an enormous Pomeranian tail, black with a ridiculous white bib. She's bald on her back due to colour dilution alopecia, a genetic condition that comes from humans tinkering with the colours – the hair grows and then breaks off. She's clever and funny and makes an excellent gardening companion. Mostly she lies on the bench while I potter, occasionally coming over for a cuddle. Other times she will fetch things from the habitat pile and scatter sticks and wine corks and pieces of root all over the garden. Or she will demand that I play chase with her or drop things at my feet for me to pick up and throw for her. When she gets what she wants she gambols around the garden, like a show pony jumping high over the long grass, pretending she will ever let me catch her. She has this wonderful way of purring while growling, which she reserves specially for play. Sometimes, I'll be on my hands and knees planting or weeding something out, or lost in tadpoles or other pond magic, and she will creep up behind me and purr-growl for me to play with her. I turn around and she's holding a toy in her mouth, hopefully.

Today she has a ball, which she drops as I turn around. Her big hazel eyes look at me, willing me to play. I stop gawping at tadpoles and throw the ball for her, and she brings it straight back and drops it at my feet again. I throw it again and she keeps it. At this time of year she can run around the pond, there's not enough foliage to stop her, and so we play a futile game of chase; her leaping around the pond, daring me to catch her with the ball, and me unable to follow because I'm worried I'll fall in.

The tadpoles continue to warm up and feed from willow leaves, the bees continue to visit lungwort and primroses. The birds stay away but only until we've finished running around. I get less done when I'm in the garden with Tos but my heart is fuller. And she makes me a better wildlife gardener, she always stops me doing too much. The blackened rosehips will be pruned another day, some of last year's stems continue to provide shelter. I clear up the sticks she has scattered on the lawn and clear spent plant material into a heap, which I transfer to the habitat pile so any insects still using it can move on safely. There will be time again for gardening.

The walls of my garden are only waist high, and so trellis makes up the height to what I suppose is an acceptable level of privacy in this age of not talking to your neighbours while living on top of them. On the south-facing side the trellis runs the whole length of the garden but on the north-facing side, closest to the house, there are three fence panels that conceal the wall entirely, with trellis covering the rest of it at the far end.

The trellis supports a range of plants: rambling rose and clematis on the south-facing side; honeysuckle, hops and golden clematis, or *Clematis tangutica*, facing north (although they poke through the gaps to next door and get a fair amount of sun). Along the fence, which gets barely any light at all, I planted six little ivy cuttings that my neighbour Kate, two doors down, gave me when I first moved in.

Ivy is amazing. Self-clinging, you don't need to tie it in to anything; it will grow happily up walls and fences and it's so shade tolerant it will practically grow in the dark. It has a reputation for destroying fences and walls and it will, but only if they're damaged in the first place. Ivy will take advantage of the smallest crack or hole but if the structure it's climbing up is sound ivy can actually protect it. Studies have shown that, when growing up houses, ivy acts as natural insulation, helping to cool them in summer and warm them in winter. Another study showed that ivy absorbs polluting particles and that, when grown along main roads, it can help reduce pollution (and therefore save lives). Ivy provides habitats for anything from nesting birds to hibernating butterflies, its flowers are visited by pollinators and its leaves are used as a food plant by several species of moth, along with the summer generation of holly blue butterflies (in spring they lay eggs on holly). Its berries contain more calories, gram-for-gram, than the equivalent weight of chocolate and, because they don't mature until late winter, they help birds get into peak condition for breeding.

I strongly believe that ivy can be a significant tool in mitigating the effects of the climate crisis and indeed absorbing CO_2, that it should be grown up every house, every office block, every patch of city that doesn't have space for a tree but does have room for a small trellis. Every time I see a fancy green wall on the side of a building, with its many pockets of plants that need regular maintenance and watering, I think how much better and easier it would be if ivy grew there instead. There's no need to water ivy because it's drought tolerant, no need for feeding or tying in. Yes, it needs pruning – about once a year to stop it covering windows and growing into the roof – but otherwise it would need little attention at all. It's versatile, too: in larger gardens and wilder areas you can leave ivy to develop flowers and berries but in areas with less space you can cut it right back as a flush, lush, living wall, a wall that supports life, absorbs CO_2, reduces pollution and looks so much nicer than the bare bricks and faded fences we city dwellers are faced with at every turn.

I haven't planted ivy up the walls of my house because they need repointing, but I did plant it along the fence, which was in good shape when I moved in and remains so now. I had visions of my little cuttings growing and knitting together, of watching birds nesting in them and holly blue butterflies laying eggs on the leaves. Of letting some of it mature and bear flowers and fruit that would serve pollinators and birds, but mostly of having a well-clipped, lush green wall, something living where previously there had been nothing.

Of course, the cuttings just sat in their little soily beds and sulked for two years. I would watch them impatiently, wondering when, if ever, they would start to climb. I counted the number of fence slats above the tip of the tallest stem to measure achingly slow growth, and obsessed over the gaps between cuttings so I could track the very moment they became one. I suppose it seems like an odd pursuit, tracking the growth of ivy up a fence. But when you're obsessed with greening the grey, when you know how vital and life-giving this stuff is, there's nothing more important.

The cuttings finally started moving properly last year, and I took photos of them to track their progress. In April, a flush of new growth finally took one plant to the top of the fence, just one rogue stem reaching above a slim triangle of leaves. Astonishingly, no sooner had it reached the top of the fence than it started to become a 'habitat'. In the first week of May, as the first brood of sparrow and starling chicks hatched from their eggs, I watched their parents descend on the garden en masse, frantically turning every leaf, every blade of grass for a morsel to feed their young. I watch them do this every year but last spring was the first time they climbed the ivy, the first time they were able to rustle among its leaves and eke out tiny things – tiny snails, tiny larvae – to take back to their nests.

Starlings love snails. Last spring a whole gang of them brought their chicks into the garden and showed them where the snails were. I watched clumsy fledglings flying from the rowan tree to the neighbours' flat roof and smashing the living daylights out of their newly found treasure. The song thrush is well known for its snail-eating skills but less so, the starling. They come for other critters, too: fat leatherjacket larvae, caterpillars. I love watching starlings murmurate above Brighton Pier in winter, wondering which of them are fuelled by my garden.

Another ivy cutting has made it to the top of the fence since, while a third might manage it this year (it has just five fence slats to go). The knitting together might happen soon, too. Three stubborn cuttings remain resolutely grounded but they are growing, slowly, creeping along behind plants that will soon have leaves. I try to imagine what it will be like when the whole fence is covered in a lush panel of ivy, when more than one sparrow or starling at a time can forage among their leaves. Will a wren ever nest here? Or a robin? Will holly blue butterflies lay their eggs? Time will tell; I just wish my little cuttings would hurry up and cover the fence.

The frogs started spawning earlier than last year but continued well into March, filling up the first shallow beach and then almost obscuring the second. At night I would sit on the cold bench and listen to them croak into the night sky, listen to their splashes of frustration and possession, the scraps between males over females, the ambush of a frog that dared jump into the melee. If I moved like a whisper I could get close enough to shine my torch and see them at it, but I found I preferred not to. I found I preferred the darkness of the bench, of being alone with my senses, of honing in on every splash and croak.

One night, as I shivered quietly, I heard squeaking above the continuous rumble of croaking frogs. My ears pricked; hello! I turned on the torch and there it was, a young male toad lounging on the frogspawn like a teenager on the sofa. Common toads don't croak to attract females but squeak or peep, which is exactly what he was doing, although why was he on his own? 'Where are your friends?' I asked him. 'Where are the girls?' Over the next few days more toads arrived via the twitten from who-knows-where, and splayed out in the pond like the first one. 'Squeak squeak squeak,' they said. I put the camera on the back gate to see if I could spot females arriving but none did. Would these males squeak for nothing? Another night I swear I could hear squeaking from elsewhere, too. A greater number than the eight in my pond, but far enough away for my toads to be louder. Where was this other pond? I had no idea.

It crossed my mind to take the torch and head into the night to find out. They sounded like they were in a garden north of mine, maybe five doors down, near the neighbour who found the toad that she was sure was on its way here. Could one of her neighbours on the other side of her have a pond? Should I find out? In the end I chickened out of going to look for it; Portslade-by-Sea is not the place to be caught in a twitten looking into back gardens by torchlight; I would need to find another way.

Who do I know on that part of the road? People to nod shy hellos to: the man with a toddler called Arthur, the woman with a dog called Twiggy. Literally no one to march up to and ask if they had a pond, let alone one with breeding toads in it.

I was reminded of my friend Wayne, who, when he moved into his house, leaflet-dropped the whole road asking who had a pond (and what lived in it), who had hedgehogs, who did things for wildlife generally. Most people didn't get back to him but some did, and instantly he knew who his allies were in his efforts to save species. He also knew how likely he was to get toads in his garden. With his knowledge, charisma and enthusiasm he has built the most amazing network of wildlife gardens in his neighbourhood, with a hedgehog population to match. He's made a hedgehog box for virtually every one of his neighbours, and clubs together with some of them to buy hedgehog food. He's a hero and a credit to us all, and we should all be more like him.

I'm not quite ready to leaflet these streets, asking who has a pond, but I am ready, perhaps, to strike up a conversation with Twiggy's mum in the park. The toads have been and gone for this year, so I have a good 12 months to bring myself around to it.

In Brighton every other roof is home to a pair of nesting seagulls; herring gulls and lesser black-backed gulls, to be exact, and their enormous gangly chicks that tumble down chimneys and off roofs into gardens, and who wander around the streets among clubbers and pub-goers, squawking into the night. There are 'gull people' who keep an eye on them, who go around town with a ladder and a net, replacing fallen chicks to their roof (or as close as they can get them), who collect casualties and take them to rescue centres. Once, I spotted a herring gull caught in a kite up high in a tree, its mate waiting desperately by. I alerted the gull people and they had a team of tree surgeons setting it free within the hour. There are those who feed them and care for them in their homes, those whose house you can turn up to with an injured gull, who know exactly what to do with it. There's a whole community of people that exists only to help Brighton and Hove's seagulls, who step up during their nesting season and ensure more of the chicks survive than they otherwise would. Their lives and ours, entangled as they are, in this built-up city by the sea.

You can tell the time by the gulls. At dawn they call to each other as if greeting good morning. At dusk they fly south, zoning towards the water, the sunset reflected on their bellies. I've never managed to find out if they roost on the sea or just visit at dusk to feed, but it seems some do – certainly some fly out at dusk and back again at dawn. I've always thought how magical it must be to sleep like that out in the open, feeling safe beneath the sheltering sky, with so much going on beneath what you can actually see and feel. I have slept on dive boats a few times and felt the power of the sky above me, the mystery of what lurks beneath. But I was in a boat, with showers and duvets and a kitchen and chefs. Imagine just sleeping out on the ocean, bobbing about in the water, snuggled only beneath a blanket of stars.

They don't nest on my roof, which makes me sad, because they would be so safe here. But they do come into the garden. Herring gulls gather sticks to make their nests, take ridiculous swims around my pond. They stand guard as I set the table outside for summer meals and *Ack-Ack-Ack* to their mates if it looks like the food might be decent. Sometimes, if I leave the back door open, they come into the house, their feet slapping on the kitchen tiles as they raid Tosca's bowl for meaty morsels. I don't feed them, per se, but if the hedgehogs haven't eaten all of their food I leave the lid off the feeding station in the morning so the gulls can have their breakfast – kitten biscuits flying everywhere as they peck, dramatically, into the dish. *Ack-Ack-Ack-Ack, Ack-Ack-Ack.*

I used to say, 'You can always tell when the buzzards are around, because the gulls go bonkers.' And they would. They do. Suddenly the rooftops erupt with distressed gulls calling to each other to protect their chicks or eggs or even half-formed nests. I look to the sky and might see one or two buzzards circling above them. Or I might see a peregrine falcon, one of those that nests in the city centre and usually takes starlings and pigeons. These days I'm more likely to see the drone the bad man flies to stop the gulls nesting on his roof.

Several times a day now, the gulls launch themselves into the air, flying in circles and crying out their horribly distressing alarm calls. It's not a predator disturbing them but a drone, a drone flying too close to their nests. I thought it was a mistake at first. I thought whoever was doing this was interested in seeing the gulls' nesting. I see this at Brighton beach when the starlings are murmurating – the drones always fly too close, weaving among the birds and causing them to shape-shift into different forms to escape them. But it's born of an idiot wanting to get better footage, who ultimately likes the starlings. Sadly, this isn't an overeager gull enthusiast who can be gently persuaded to keep his distance. If only it were.

I don't like Facebook but it's best for community groups and I'm a member of a few that keep me updated with various things I like to know about (e.g. when the park is due its annual haircut so I can rescue butterfly caterpillars). There's a group for the road next to mine, which is handy for knowing if the bins won't be collected or if there are any road works or does-anyone-have-a-spare-parking-permit or did-you-hear-the-motorbike-last-night-it-was-very-loud-do-you-think-it-was-the-same-one-involved-in-the-crash-that's-been-reported-in-the-Argus?

One day someone wrote about the drone. 'I think it's being used to deliberately scare the seagulls,' she said, 'can everyone keep an eye out?' She reported the incident to the police but, without knowing who was responsible, couldn't get much done about it. A few days later she had worked out who it was – a man with a warehouse on the road behind hers, who was flying the drone at lesser black-backed gull nests to stop them nesting on his roof. She spoke to him but he was horrible. She updated the police but they still didn't come. I reported the incident to the police, too, using the same crime reference number she originally used. They wrote back and said it was being dealt with. But it's not being dealt with. The drone's still flying and the gulls are still crying and up to five times a day I feel my whole body tighten as a man sends his drone to the rooftops to deliberately distress nesting birds. Where are the police? Where is the justice? How do I get these sounds out of my ears?

My partner Emma and I head to Birmingham, to see Mum, my sister Ellie and my half-sister Anna, while Tosca has a holiday with the dog sitter. Due to Covid, it's only the second time Emma has met them, and she's never met little nephew Stanley, Ellie's partner Gareth, Anna's partner Alex or mum's husband Pete. 'Time to throw you to the wolves,' I say.

'I'm s-s-s-s-sorry for my la-la-la-la-language,' Mum stutters to Emma, and then explains she's had a brain haemorrhage, as if she'd forgotten to mention it the last time they met, or as if I'd not done so in the two and a half years we've been together. Her stutter comes and goes and she loses it as soon as she relaxes. 'I work very hard on my brain,' she says, and proceeds to list the ways, while Emma nods enthusiastically. 'Every day I do Sudoku, Wordle, Words with Friends, and then Pete joins me for the crosswords (the standard and the cryptic), and then we do "the quiz",' she says proudly.

'What's the quiz?' I ask.

'The quiz,' Mum replies. 'Pete asks the questions and I answer them.' I am, as ever, none the wiser.

'I was very surprised', says Pete, 'to learn today that your mum knows who Harry Styles' girlfriend is.'

'Who's Harry Styles' girlfriend?' I ask.

'Cheryl Cole,' says Mum, 'and she's a good fifteen years older than him.'

Emma Googles this and can't find any information to confirm or deny this 'fact'. It's something no one else in the room had ever thought about.

'And how do you know this?' I ask.

'Haven't a clue,' says Mum.

It's been six years since her haemorrhage, a Grade 4 subarachnoid bleed on the brain, after which she spent two months in hospital. ('N-n-n-n-n-o I d-d-d-d-d-didn't!' she says, 'I would have remembered!')

She bled into the front-left part of her brain, the bit where all the language and speech is. A tragedy for someone who taught literature in secondary schools for 40 years and who knows the Latin stem of everything. Who has an annoying habit of quoting Shakespeare and other random pieces of literature she thinks we should all, too, have engraved on our brains. We thought this habit had been washed away with the blood but it returned, one day, when she sprang a test on us, just like she always has.

'Nature red in tooth and claw,' she crowed, rubbing her thighs. 'Who wrote it who wrote it?'

'Tennyson,' I replied. It's an easy one, for me. It's the one everyone rolls out on Twitter whenever a woodpecker eats a blue tit or something similarly unsavoury. 'Oh it's all so brutal, isn't it? Nature red in tooth and claw!', they post. 'Yes indeed, yes it is, yes.' come the replies.

'Marvellous,' said Mum. 'Excellent daughter.'

'I haven't actually read it,' I sighed, 'it's just quite a well-worn phrase, isn't it?'

'A well-worn phrase? You haven't read Tennyson?'

We all Googled the poem and realised quickly why none of us other than Mum had read it. It has several parts and was written in different years and, 'Has anyone actually got to the tooth and claw bit yet?'

'Heathens,' Mum remarked, and we laughed.

'I'm sorry I haven't read any Tennyson,' I lied, and reminded her that I read her favourite poems to her – T. S. Eliot's *Wasteland* and Philip Larkin's *Aubade* – when she was unconscious in hospital.

'You did WHAT?' Mum spat out her tea. 'Christ, no wonder I nearly died.'

She lost her speech entirely for a few weeks and then slowly got it back, but she still forgets words sometimes. There is often such beauty in her quest to find them, like when in hospital she described the woman who 'lived on the wall opposite,' or when she got really into the wheelchair tennis but forgot both the words 'wheelchair' and 'tennis'. 'They drive around in little boats,' she said, and we all chimed, 'Golf! The rowing! Tour de France?' and she said, 'No!' and became frustrated. 'Little boats,' she said, 'little boats.' Two days later, out of nowhere, she said 'I'm really enjoying the wheelchair tennis,' and we all said 'Ohhhhhhhhhh,' and laughed for days.

She can't read books anymore, she has no concentration. I buy her poetry compilations; she can just about keep up with a poem, although she forgets about it soon afterwards. 'I'm happy sitting with Pete and doing my brain games,' she says. She makes me play Words with Friends, an online version of Scrabble but with coloured tiles and themed headdresses when you reach a certain goal (I've currently got one with frogs on it). Sometimes she beats me. Sometimes.

According to the doctors, she made a complete recovery; only we know the bits of her that have come since her injury. The part of the brain where the language is also dictates behaviour, and we were warned that she might become more volatile and impulsive. There's a switch, and if it's flicked she'll fly into a rage and there's no getting through to her. We're getting used to it and we are learning, gradually, how not to stoke the fire. There have been a few slip-ups, usually when I haven't realised that this is 'brain haemorrhage rage' rather than her just being her usual stubborn self. I spend less time with her than the others and I forget, sometimes, that these days they can read her better than I can.

She also has 'funny turns', where she goes quiet suddenly and has to hold on to something to steady herself, even if sitting down. We don't really know what that is but it comes and goes; she used to have several a day and can now go months without having one at all, but then will have one, suddenly, that takes us by surprise. It's as if there's scar tissue around the injury and sometimes messages in the brain hit the wrong bit, come to a sort of dead end and the whole brain short circuits and needs resetting. It's scary when it happens but, again, we're all used to it. Five minutes later and she's fine again, although always a bit shaken.

The sun is shining, and we sit on the front lawn together, taking in the last of the day. I notice the first red mason and tawny mining bees of the year and have to remind myself to focus on my family and not spend the entire time staring at the trunk of the tree where the insects bask. Mum asks Alex, who is very handy, to fix her water butt and downpipe, which are clogged up with moss and silt. (Poor Alex, he always gets given jobs when he visits.) Emma and Gareth keep sneaking off for 'chats'.

'Can I go to Liverpool with Gareth tomorrow to watch the football?' asks Emma.

'No you may not,' I reply.

It's been so long since I've been home I had forgotten they are under the flight path of Birmingham Airport. That being woken at 6.10 a.m. as the first plane flies overhead is quite intrusive, that conversations are interrupted, as we pause to let the noise fade, that the others barely notice it, Ellie even finds it comforting. But I struggle, as I struggle with lots of things these days, as each plane is a reminder of empty promises to reduce emissions, of the mountain of work yet to be done. I haven't quit flying completely but I do so very infrequently (although I was never a very frequent flyer). I suppose that makes me a hypocrite – taking part in one of the very things that needs to be curtailed if we are to meet our emissions targets. I drive too, but again, very little. I'm not perfect. I think it's OK to live in today's world while striving for tomorrow's. I'm practically vegan, I buy very few clothes, I drive and fly very little and walk or take public transport nearly always. You can be part of a world that needs changing and still push for that change. You can be a car driver but still campaign for cleaner roads for asthmatic children. You can eat meat while campaigning for an end to factory farming. I don't like flying and I don't want to fly but sometimes it's easier and cheaper to fly and, as with all partnerships, the decision to fly or not isn't always mine alone to make. But now, with a plane drowning conversation every two minutes, I'm faced with the enormity of what needs fixing. And it's overwhelming.

Emma, Alex, Anna and I go for a walk with Mum. 'Pete doesn't like walking,' she tells us, so it's nice that we can join her. We cross a meadow into agricultural fields and I don't know where I am. There are nearby villages I'd never heard of. There's not much in the sky; a baby buzzard mews for its parents and we stop at a big log and take photos of each other. They've had so much more rain here than we've had in Brighton; I can't believe how different the landscape is.

We pass the garden centre that closed down and was left abandoned with all the plants left on the shelves with no one to love or water them. 'I've rescued a few,' says Mum, who explains that she has been sneaking in for months and helping herself to plants that 'don't belong to anyone anymore'. Anna puts her face in her hands and we try not to laugh while reminding her she is stealing.

'It's not stealing if you're rescuing things left for dead,' she explains. 'I have given them new life.'

'What plants did you take?' I ask.

'Ah,' she says. 'I'll need your help to identify some of them, darling. But they're really coming along, the garden is looking splendid.' We are hereby complicit in her crime.

This dry spring has me anxious about the lives of wild things who live beyond my garden. I post pleas on local Facebook groups for people to leave out water but it doesn't seem enough. I have a hedgehog making a dandelion-leaf nest in my garden, but how are those in other gardens faring? And how are the foxes and the tadpoles and the birds and the worms? What is everyone doing for their wild neighbours?

How does a wildlife gardener connect with the community and help to create networks and corridors that link gardens together and to the wider landscape? How do we spread the word about species decline and habitat loss, about the amazing role gardens can have in the fight against biodiversity loss and climate change? How can we change public perceptions of what constitutes a well-maintained garden and what is considered mess? How can we help species through a drought?

Hedgehogs.

Everyone loves hedgehogs. Everyone says 'Wow' and 'Cor' and all the things you would expect from people being truly delighted by another species. Hedgehogs have a lot going for them: they're nocturnal so have an element of mystery and surprise; they have spikes, which makes them unusual; they can roll into a ball, which is basically a superpower, and they tend not to run away when they come across a human or predator, which means you can have a good look at them. They have suffered staggering declines (estimated to be around 95 per cent since the 1950s), which makes them precious. And they suffer enormously in a drought, which means we can actively help them now. To garden for hedgehogs is to garden for everyone else: they need access to the space itself as well as water and invertebrate food, and somewhere to nest or hibernate. We therefore need to open our gardens up to them, leave dishes of water or dig ponds they can enter and exit easily, grow food plants for the caterpillars and beetles that hedgehogs eat and leave wild areas where they can take shelter. If you garden specifically for hedgehogs you'll have a pretty good garden for lots of other species, too.

My garden alone is not enough for a neighbourhood's-worth of hedgehogs, and so the only way I can meaningfully help those living in my area is to reach out to the community, to engage with more people to do more for wildlife. Connecting with those who already are helping wildlife is also useful – it's good to know my allies. So I decide to set up a hedgehog group.

I email Mike, who helps run the local park group, and ask if I can borrow the park's name to create a Facebook group for the hogs of the park and surrounding streets. He says yes but why don't you launch it with a talk? I laugh and say of course I can launch my hedgehog group with a talk. 'I'll let you know when I've written it.'

I set up the Facebook group first. It doesn't have much, just a what/why/where of hedgehogs in the neighbourhood, a link to the Hedgehog Street website (a joint collaboration between the British Hedgehog Preservation Society and the People's Trust for Endangered Species that has seen neighbourhoods get together to create more hedgehog-friendly gardens) and bits of information on what to do if you find a hog out during the day. I invite a few people to join but not many will know about the group until I've done my talk. Mike was right.

I spend two days finding screenshots of hedgehogs feeding, foraging and courting in my garden, and put them together to make a PowerPoint presentation. I write a script and practise it in my head as I walk to the gym and the shops, take Tos out. I worry about the audience: will they be gardeners or not? Young or old? What if it's full of kids? I remove slides of hogs stuck in netting or with bonfire and strimming injuries, just in case, and replace them with cute pics of hedgehogs with hoglets. The aim: cheerful and easy ways to help a declining species. Not too much about habitat loss or the climate crisis. No big lectures on plastic grass and paving (although I will mention them). Just nice things about hogs and easy ways to make their lives easier, especially in a drought. I hope it will cover all bases and not put anyone off, but also that it will be the start of a wildlife-loving community that will do more for the hedgehogs and other species living in these streets.

I tell Mike it's ready and we arrange for the talk to be held in the scout hut on a chilly Wednesday evening. Someone from the park group makes a flyer and I print it out and leaflet-drop 250 houses in the surrounding streets. Mike makes a Facebook event page and invites people from local groups. In the end it's all very last minute and I worry we've left it too late for people to know about it and come. Mike, too, thinks people won't make it. I arrive to the scout hut to find he's put out 10 chairs.

'Are you not expecting many people to come?' I ask, laughing to hide my anxiety.

'Well, I don't like putting too many out,' he says.

I count in my head everyone who's told me they're coming. 'I'll add another row,' I say, hopefully. But, in the end, I have to add four rows as people keep coming through the door (about 40, I think).

I am nervous, as I always am before I do a talk, no matter how often I do them. But I get it out: the what, the why, the how. There's a good, mixed audience: tiny children who wave plastic dinosaurs at me and a handful of eight- to twelve-year-olds. But it's mostly adults. Parents of the children plus a good number who are there for the hogs. For the next couple of days more people join my Facebook group, taking the number to 54. I'm not going to save the world with my little hedgehog group but I might help make life easier for this population of hogs, which will have a positive influence on other species.

The Facebook group helps me connect with others who also feed and care for hedgehogs and I enjoy seeing their videos of healthy hogs tucking into cat food left out by kind people. I use the group to post my own videos, along with reminders to leave out water as conditions remain so dry. I hope we are making life a bit easier for them.

I also use the group to welcome new hogs to the neighbourhood, which occasionally come to my garden via my local rescue centres. Usually they are released back where they were found but sometimes they can't be – they might have been found in a garden with plastic grass or paving (so no food or shelter for them), they might have been found on or near a main road, where they're likely to be squished, or in an area with a high density of badgers, who have a tendency to eat them. Sometimes, sadly, people don't want hedgehogs back in their gardens. They don't want the 'hassle' of picking up hedgehog droppings or having to deal with their dog troubling them. They think hedgehogs should just go and live somewhere else. I don't know where 'else' is. Victims of habitat loss, agricultural intensification, pesticides and garden fences, which stop them roaming the 2km a night they need to find food, hedgehogs need our gardens more than ever. We should be doing everything but turning them away.

My first hedgehog rescue of the year is an autumn orphan. He was found in a garden as a tiny wee thing last November, being played with by a fox. He might have left the nest too early, gone for a wander and been caught out, or his mother might have abandoned the nest or been run over or picked up by someone well-meaning or otherwise, while out foraging for food. He was lucky, taken in by a woman who perhaps cared too much; she fed him up and continued feeding him through winter so he didn't hibernate, and then refused to let him be released into a garden where there might be foxes. Inevitably, she hasn't found anywhere that meets this brief and so it's April and this young male, who hasn't been outside since he was found on his first trip out of the nest four months ago, is desperate to be set free.

Foxes and hedgehogs generally get along, but young foxes can be curious and can hurt small hogs if they 'play' with them too vigorously. Foxes visit my garden and every time I catch them and hedgehogs together on the trail camera they are ignoring each other; the foxes don't even bother to sniff them. But I can imagine that a playful young fox, with all the excitement of youth, would be a headache for a young hedgehog. Hedgehogs sometimes wind up in rescue centres with bites to their back legs, which may come from young foxes or dogs. These wounds can attract flies, which lay eggs in them and lead to horrible maggoty infestations. So, yes, a young hog should be wary and perhaps even kept away from curious foxes, but for a healthy adult hog with a coat full of spines? A fox would be no trouble at all.

The message from the rescue centre reads, 'Can you take a young male hog? He weighs 1.4kg!'

Have I ever known such a large hog? The average weight for an adult is between 500g and 1kg. I have weighed hogs that came close to 1kg, but another 400g on top of that is a lot. A fox would be no match for this chunk.

'Can he roll into a ball?' I ask Pete, who runs the rescue centre with his wife, Gayle, when I pick the hedgehog up.

'Only just,' he replies.

He'd been fed a diet of mealworms, which are protein-rich but terrible for hedgehogs as they contain a lot of potassium. This, for reasons I don't fully understand, reduces the amount of calcium in their bones and can lead to 'metabolic bone disease', which causes horrible, painful fractures and often means they have to be put down. Pete keeps him in for observation for a night to make sure he is walking properly, and declares him fit. Phew! He just needs a bit of exercise, some wild ways, and an absence of mealworms. Done.

I take my new lump home and release him into the garden. It's evening, around 7.00 p.m., and the light is already fading. I have no spare boxes to introduce him to – it's a busy time of year for hedgehogs and they're full – and so I pop him at the well-used entrance to the habitat pile, and he buries himself inside. I head into the house and shut the kitchen door, and then stand at the window for a few minutes, watching to see if he will come out. There's always a pang of love for these autumn orphans, most of whom are rescued as soon as they leave the nest and have never really known the big wide world. How must he be feeling right now?

The garden is, essentially, a larger, wilder version of what he has been used to since he was found. There are no mealworms but there is a dish of kitten biscuits that I top up each evening, as well as dishes of water and a big pond to drink from (I leave out an extra dish of water in case he is too timid to travel far for a drink). There are boxes and a large open habitat pile to sleep in. There's also another box and another dish of kitten biscuits at my neighbour Kate's, two doors down, and then a dish of meaty wet food at Linda's, who lives next door to Kate and 'feeds the cats'. He has everything he needs, plus me at the kitchen window with binoculars, and at the computer watching hedgehog videos, monitoring him.

He comes out of his hiding hole within 10 minutes and sniffs his new surroundings. He finds the hedgehog feeding station straight away, and I'm pleased to see he can get in it (I was worried he wouldn't be able to), although it's a tight squeeze and he manages to move the box as he struggles inside.

'Christ,' says Emma. 'We should call him Doughnut!'

I'm pretty sure he spends the first few days in the garden. He claims one of the boxes as his own, which he leaves at dusk each evening to visit the feeding station for biscuits. He's easy to spot: 'Doughnut's on the patio, he's still massive!' says Emma, as she lets Tos out for a wee, 'Bloody hell, there's Doughnut again,' says Emma, as she fills up the feeding station, 'Doughnut's just scared the bejesus out of Tosca.' Who needs hedgehog videos when you have commentary like this?

He will lose weight gradually. There's a whole garden to walk around and neighbourhood to explore. He will find other places to sleep as he becomes more confident. A young male, he will also be raging with hormones, which will take him beyond the garden in search of females. I post about his arrival in my hedgehog group:

'Look out for a hog the size of a bus!'

Dark-edged bee-fly, *Bombylius major*

The dark-edged bee-fly is the most common of 10 species of bee-fly in the UK. Gingery and furry, with one pair of dark-edged wings, it looks like a bumblebee but flies with a hover and a high-pitched buzz, jutting out its enormous proboscis, or tongue, which it uses to drink nectar from spring flowers. It's a little furry narwhal.

It's one of the spring friends I look for as the season turns. I won't rest until I've seen one. It's a happy day when I see my first dark-edged bee-fly of the year. Nearly always, the sun is shining and the first of the primroses and forget-me-nots are in bloom. I hear its high-pitched buzz first, then there it is. 'Bee-fly!' I tell anyone who will listen.

A parasitoid of mining bees, the female 'flicks' eggs into or near nest burrows after mating and her larvae, using false legs, enter them and eat the store of pollen and nectar intended for the bee grubs. They then metamorphose into a different type of grub – a process called hyper-metamorphosis, which is rare in the insect world – and they eat the bee grubs themselves. They emerge a year later as gorgeous adult bee-flies, and hover about singing their spring song, much to the delight of gardeners.

To garden for bee-flies is to garden for mining bees – have an area of short lawn or exposed soil, plus plenty of spring flowers. Don't be sad about mining bees being parasitised by grubs with pretend legs – nature has evolved the most fascinating ways of getting by; we should celebrate all of it.

May

Despite the lack of rain, the garden has put on growth. Not quite lush but green, full-looking after a winter and early spring of being subdued and locked away. Growth is slower than it would have been if it was wetter but I'll take it. I'll take any growth, any green over grey, any new flowers. There are fresh green leaves, unfurling fern fronds, the first blooms of white comfrey, guelder rose, rowan and honesty. Next door's wisteria is coming into flower, too. 'Hello!' I say, 'hello, hello, hello!'

The sparrows and starlings have had their first brood. I can tell because there's an urgency with which they come to the garden – they have hungry mouths to feed. They descend all at once in a big mixed flock and then ransack the garden before rushing off again. They'll visit bird feeders as adults but will always need natural food for their young, and so my garden, with its meadow and its native plants and its pond and its gardener, is perfect for them. They hop around the outer edge of the pond where I've left a buffer of wildflower meadow for insects to take shelter, they climb into the teenaged ivy and peck at tiny grubs behind the leaves. The sparrows home in on leaf tips and stems for aphids, while starlings charge around, taking snails and larger prey with determined hops. I stand at the kitchen window and watch them, laughing at how busy and serious they are, compared to the rest of the year, when they are idiots.

One of the house sparrows is still being an idiot. He's decided to start a nest in one of my swift boxes. He's obviously got one elsewhere, with chicks in it, but instead of finding food for them, like the rest of his clan, he's trying to persuade them to move house. He sits in his swift hole and cheeps at them while they forage for food and they, understandably, ignore him. I'll give him a 10 for effort, for persistently trying to persuade them that my garden is the place to be, when clearly there's some resistance.

He's very welcome to the swift box, as the swifts have ignored it for three years. I've been watching him bring nesting material in, collecting grasses and sticks and other bits and pieces to build his (probably quite bad) nest. I've watched him fly in and out, to and from various posts like the shed and the hawthorn, the top of the roof, sticking his head out and cheeping like the lord of the manor. I wonder how many other half-built nests have been made in the other nest boxes on the house – the other three swift boxes and the three sparrow boxes, one of which, once, was used by great tits. If the sparrows moved in and nested in a loose colony as they are prone to do, then they could use all four of the swift boxes and all three of the sparrows'. Then there's the hole in the gable at the top of the house – eight nests. This rogue, idiot male, who's calling to his clan while they busy themselves with mouths to feed, is trying to sell them eight new homes they can move into, now, with a fully stocked garden of invertebrates on the doorstep. He's a pioneer, not an idiot. He's a leader. He has vision! They're still ignoring him. But he may have success, one day. Imagine living among a clan of eight house-sparrow families. Surrounded by cheeping idiots – I would be so happy.

The first swift of the year is marked with exclamation marks and stars, with hugging strangers in the street, with giant, beaming grins. I count down the days to it, starting in mid-April, and trip over myself for nearly three weeks, walking around with my head in the sky. I'll meet you in the pub and make you sit outside so I can watch for the telltale effortless flap of swift wings, so I might hear the hint of a scream.

'Swift!' I will say, to anyone and everyone. 'Swiiiiiiiiiiiiiiiifffffftttttttttt!' I'm really, genuinely very sorry if you're midway through talking about your divorce.

I love swifts with all my heart, with every ounce of my being. I have three swift boxes that were retro-fitted into the cavity walls of my house at the back, and a big white one at the front in case they need a bigger welcome sign. For three years I played swift calls from my bathroom window, which is said to lure them to potential new nest sites, but then a neighbour told me they were driving her mad so I had to stop. Still, swifts might find me eventually. I live in hope that, one day, my house will be full of swifts (I haven't told my neighbour this).

Like many summer migrants, swifts fly here from the Congo Basin each spring, breed and then fly back again. And, like many other summer migrants, they're declining at a terrifying rate – thought to be around 60 per cent in the last 20 years, but likely much, much more since the turn of the last century. They nest in holes in roofs in tall buildings and houses, which makes them vulnerable to home 'improvements' like insulation, new soffits or fascias, a new roof or loft conversion. These can easily be compensated for by people putting swift boxes on their homes, by councils and building developers making swift bricks compulsory, but there are no plans to do such a thing, despite petitions and pleas from nature lovers. Then there's the decline of insects, which is harder to reverse on small scales. Swifts catch insects high up in the sky and collect them in a ball in their throat, called a bolus, which they take back to their nests to feed their young. With fewer insects there's less to go around and it looks like fewer swifts are nesting successfully. Again, we can all contribute to them doing better by growing more plants that insects feed and breed on, by reducing hard surfaces and plastic, on which very little can live. Of course, most people don't bother, and so swifts continue to decline.

That swifts are declining makes them even more special, but it makes the pleasure–pain of seeing them all the more intense. There are fewer of them this year. There are fewer of them this year.

Apart from those few short weeks in which they're laying eggs and raising young, swifts are completely airborne – they eat, sleep and mate on the wing. They're so good at being in the sky that they're terrible at being on land, their wings too long and their legs too short to take off again. If they become 'grounded' they need a kind human to pick them up and help them back to the sky, often by climbing a ladder or going to the first floor of a building and holding them out on a palm-stretched hand until they're ready to take off again. Never throw a swift into the sky but wait, calmly, for it to launch itself.

Unlike cuckoos, which I also love, and nightingales and swallows and many other summer migrants that return to our shores from Africa each spring, swifts do not make for a romantic first sighting. Living in the city, if I want to see cuckoos and nightingales I have to travel to more rural landscapes. I will hear a cuckoo while tramping through cobweb-strewn pastures, hear nightingales while sitting beneath an 800-year-old oak tree. Last year, I saw my first swift flying over a bin lorry on the New Church Road. I'm not knocking it, the first swift sighting of the year remains a highlight; it's just that, sometimes, on bin day I'm reminded of them, which is a very odd thing indeed.

The bin lorry swifts are part of a colony that lives on the other side of the main road, about a five-minute walk from my house. There's a small group of swift lovers living among them, who celebrate them and have erected nest boxes. But most people don't know or care who lives in their roof spaces and would probably prefer that they didn't.

Most mornings I walk along this road to the gym, and in spring and early summer I smile and say hello to swifts that wheel among the rooftops. I don't know which roofs they nest in specifically, but if I were to hazard a guess it would be those with old roofs and wooden fascias, where slipped tiles and bowed wood make the perfect entrance holes to a small space to raise young. I wince at the home 'improvements' that take place among this colony, at the scaffolding that goes up, at the plastic fascias and shiny new roof tiles that, ultimately, make swifts homeless. Swifts are extremely faithful to nest sites and return to them every year. That's why it's so devastating when the holes are filled in, either intentionally or otherwise. The swifts are so determined to reach their nest that they will continue trying to access it, until they are exhausted and die. Sometimes they can be encouraged to nest nearby with the help of some quickly erected nest boxes and a loudspeaker playing swift calls, but only if the community rallies around to support them. It takes a community to raise swifts; it will take a nation to save them.

Sometimes, if I'm feeling brave enough, I get in touch with those who have scaffolding up and I tell them about the swifts nesting in their neighbourhood. Scaffolding provides the perfect opportunity for helping these birds; it removes the effort of erecting a nest box. You just need to pop the kettle on for a cup of tea, open a packet of biscuits and present them to your builder, along with a swift box and instructions of where you want it. 'Oh be a love and pop this box up while you're there. Thanks ever so. Jaffa cake?' Job done. Even if you're doing the work yourself, you're already up there, you already have the tools. Just whack a swift box up, under the eaves and especially under the tip of your gable, please.

In autumn, as I walked to the gym, I passed a house with an old roof and new scaffolding. Over the next few weeks I watched as the entire roof came off, as guttering was replaced, as the render was filled, sanded and repainted. I have no idea who lives there but I decided to write them a letter and post it through their door. 'Please, will you put a swift box up?'

I explained that swifts migrate here from the Congo Basin each spring, that they are on the wing for most of their lives, that the young do 'press-ups' in the nest to prepare them for a lifetime of flying. That swifts are here for only two months of the year, that they make no mess at all, that they are suffering staggering declines but that you, dear people with scaffolding, live in an area where there's a reasonable colony and that you can help them by erecting a swift box, which may or may not replace a nest that you are destroying by having your roof done. I definitely didn't use the word 'destroying', I was trying to get them on side. I was nice and gentle and said lovely things about these wondrous birds, and enclosed a leaflet about swift conservation so they could read more on this subject that they would obviously be newly interested in.

Each day, afterwards, as I walked past the house, I noted the lack of swift boxes. As the builders made finishing touches to the house and the scaffolding came down, I realised my letter hadn't worked, that they had read it and not acted, that they had not erected a swift box. There will have been a hundred reasons why they didn't want one, but ultimately they didn't put one up because they didn't care enough, and I took that very personally. I know it seems silly but I did.

This year I see my first swift in the first week of May, as I do most years. It's one of a pair, casually flying above houses in the next road, where I'm sure they are nesting, but I have found no evidence of them entering buildings. I stand with my head in the sky and gawp at them, while passers-by rush to school and work, oblivious to the wonder above them. As I walk to the gym I look out for swifts trying to access their nests in the house that has a new roof, and am pleased to see nothing at all. Lucky for them, but countless other swifts this year will be returning to nest sites to find them gone, just when they need all the help they can get to slow down or even reverse their declines. If we won't share our homes with them, where will they raise their young? They have to live somewhere.

It's raining, my god it's raining. Tap-tap-tapping on the roofs and windows and streaming into the water butt in a great noisy spout. I open the back door and stand in it, feel it. I crouch beneath the overhanging shed roof and watch it splash into the pond, hydrate the garden. Rain. Actual rain. Every single living thing in this garden is heaving great sighs of relief.

The sound of rain filling the water butt is joyous. It pours off the roof of the house in streams and rivers. I connect the hose to its tap and turn it on when the water level approaches the top so I don't miss a drop. I direct water into the pond, which needs filling up, and around the trees and tiny hedge that desperately need a drink. I have to watch the water butt closely so it doesn't empty completely into the pond and leave me with nothing when the rain stops, but also that it doesn't overflow into the drain and be lost forever. There should be an outlet at the top so water can escape into the garden only once the butt's full, but that would involve having hoses all over the patio.

I leave buckets and saucepans on the lawn, moving them around so they don't deny the grass a drink. In the front I place a bucket beneath the bit of guttering that isn't fixed properly and leaks and I should probably fix it but why would you deny yourself free water? Why would you mend something that will then direct rain into the road? I watch that, too, and empty it into the rain shadow of next door's hedge. I spend most of the day checking and emptying buckets and pans, making sure the water butt isn't emptying or spilling over, that there's no snail or snail poo clogging up the diverter, so that everything – all of it – lands in my water butt. I don't get much work done. I get very wet.

Wild Park lies on the other side of town and is Brighton's largest nature reserve. It's connected to the South Downs National Park and has woodland and chalk flower meadows, a dew pond (or at least the remains of one) and 'sweeping views across the city'. It's also home to an Iron-Age hillfort, which sounds much grander than it looks, and of course lots of golf courses. We three (Emma, Tosca and me) take a trip there for the first time. We park up in a valley, surrounded by football pitches and other playing fields, get our bearings and then start to climb, up into the woods. It's a perfect day: blue sky, big fluffy clouds, a fair bit of wind but not too much, and the odd rain shower that beats against the tree leaves while we remain dry beneath. I like these woods. I feel a magic that I haven't felt in a woodland for a long time. Is it because it's raining and I'm no longer used to it? Is it the fresh green of the leaves against old wood? Moss hangs from tree branches like curtains and sunlight paddles through the canopy, hitting the ground like disco lights on a dance floor. Our noses fill with the scent of fresh earth and new life. Oh, rain!

We come out of the woods and on to the brow of the hill, to wildflower meadows and skylarks, and indeed a sweeping view across the city. 'Look at Brighton!' we say. The first of the year's meadow brown butterflies bounce among the grasses while six-spot burnet moth cocoons hang like teardrops from grass stems. Tosca sniffs everything. I stop and look at everything. Emma wonders what she has done to deserve being saddled with such slow-moving creatures.

The area is horseshoe-shaped and we walk around the top, an escarpment if you like, before descending back through the trees on the other side. It's a funny spot, so wild and yet so urban. I could imagine boxing hares here but there are rows of houses all along the outskirts, the sound of police sirens beneath us. Boxing hares might be a stretch, although they do have. a corridor here from the Downs. But what else could there be, if I came on my own and spent time here sitting and watching, without my girls to keep me moving? I make a note to do just that.

Afterwards, we walk on the big playing field at the bottom. Tosca and Emma practise their litter-picking routine and I watch them for a bit before finding myself at a big clump of nettles, Emma's commands of 'Hold!' and 'Drop!' fading as my attention turns to other things. Almost immediately I find what I came looking for: the telltale signs of butterfly caterpillars – folded over and chewed leaves, mounds of square frass (droppings) and then, following the trail, caterpillars. There are two patches of up to a hundred wriggling together, all knitted under the shelter of silk and leaf. I think they're small tortoiseshells, which have declined by 75 per cent in the last 50 years. I realise this is my first caterpillar clump of 2022 and the first, I think, in a couple of years. I used to see two or three clumps on nettles every year and then this dwindled to one, and then nothing. But here, on this average spring day in late May, in Brighton, I have found them again.

It's funny, because I saw just one small tortoiseshell butterfly last year. It was feeding from a buddleia on the side of the road down by the port, the most unromantic of places to see a now-rare-in-these-parts butterfly. But then, on a sunny day just two months ago, in March, I saw four flying about in a local park. Four! Would they have hibernated together? Or was someone raising (and then overwintering?) them locally? Did they fly here from France? I see someone else mention it on Twitter. 'We're seeing loads of small tortoiseshells!' we say to any lepidopterist that will listen, and they would like the Tweet or respond with a thumbs-up and I supposed they couldn't really do anything with the information because it wasn't information, was it? It was two people saying they had seen more small tortoiseshell butterflies in the last couple of weeks than in the last few years, and that that, in itself, isn't evidence of anything.

But here I am now, standing in front of nettles in another park in Brighton, my girls collecting litter in the background, and there are caterpillars. I walk along and find evidence of other clumps, some of which I think may have been mown, as the trail of frass and folded leaves disappears in the same spot as evidence of recent tidying.

'What are you doing?' says Emma.

'I'm just taking a few,' I say.

She rolls her eyes. It's quite a thing, taking caterpillars, because I don't want to interfere, no one wants to meddle. I want to leave them in their own habitat. I want them to be able to feed and explore naturally, and then disperse and spend a couple of days as fat caterpillars sitting on leaves, before disappearing to pupate and then emerging 10 days later as gorgeous adult butterflies. But there's too much at stake. There are wasps and birds – natural predators, of course – and there are mowers and strimmers, anxious parents complaining to the council about nettles harming their children. Then there's bad weather – too hot and dry and the nettles will shrivel and die; too wet and the caterpillars will be washed off the leaves (no chance of that happening this year). And when you have declines of 75 per cent over a 50-year period and you know you can take them home and improve their chances of survival, why wouldn't you? I'm just so sick of never seeing any butterflies.

I take some from one of the two batches, not too many. I snap off the nettle stem with my hand and pop it in a doggy bag. Back home I set up my 'farm' (a mesh cage for kids that usually comes with painted lady caterpillars and some pelleted food so you can raise your own pet butterflies). I pop them all in the cage together, with the nettle stem I brought them home with, and watch them eat for a bit. And then I leave them to it. That's it, they're captive but not for long. I go into the garden and gawp at baby frogs in the long grass.

Later, I pop to the park to collect nettles for my caterpillars to feed on. There, astonishingly, I find more caterpillars. Older than the ones I collected this morning, they have been developing here unnoticed for a couple of weeks. I don't take them, they're nearly ready to pupate. But it's a gamble – the council hasn't been to cut everything back for a while so they must be due soon. But I take my chances. I can hear the strimmers from my house anyway.

The neighbourhood Facebook group has been busy with reports of the drone and the bad man. People have gone down to speak to him and been scared away, others have had muck from his warehouse gutters thrown at them. I observe most of this without comment, adding the odd sentence of despair when they mention how upset the gulls are. We are all upset. We are all really upset.

I'm out to lunch with Dad and his wife Ceals – a celebration of their recent civil partnership, it's only taken them 35 years. Hilariously, Ellie and I weren't invited to the ceremony; they got hitched in the registry office with just two friends as witnesses, had their photos taken with roadworks in the background. 'It's just for financial reasons,' they laugh, 'just a bit of security as we get older.' But it's still nice to celebrate. They had a boozy lunch with their witnesses and now they're here in Brighton, being taken out for a slap-up meal by me, before they head home again tomorrow. I show them how much I care by getting both the iron and the hair brush out.

'You look vaguely presentable,' says Dad.

'I do 'n all,' I say.

We have a drink before the meal and, while Dad and Ceals busy themselves with ordering, I check Facebook. In the group someone has posted a video of men on the roof of the warehouse. 'They're wearing gloves,' she says, 'and they're loading material into white bags.' I freeze but my heart races. Nests? Eggs? Small chicks? I feel sick. If flying a drone isn't a crime then this absolutely is. I read the comments: people are furiously saying they'll get in touch with the contacts they have been dealing with, that a police community support officer (PCSO) is heading down tomorrow. That this is the action we knew was coming and has finally, frustratingly happened and can now no longer be ignored by police.

We have a nice meal and I try not to be distracted. I cry only a little. On the bus on the way back I ask Dad and Ceals if they fancy taking a walk to the warehouse and they say yes OK and we walk round and the gates are closed but I can see three white bags in a skip at the back of the yard. At home I email the police again and tell them that all the evidence they need – evidence of crime – is in three bags in a skip at the address I have now given them twice. I have visions of tiny chicks suffocating in plastic, of the miracle of a police officer opening them to find life hanging in the balance and of rushing these tiny birds to a rescue centre where someone will help them *live*. Of the men being arrested and fined. Of lesser black-backed gulls being safe to continue nesting here. Of these streets being a fraction wilder. In the morning I check the Facebook group to see if the PCSO has paid a visit, if the bags have been confiscated as evidence, if anything has happened at all.

But there's nothing. The police don't come. The bags remain in the skip with whatever's in them rotting into oblivion. The Facebook group goes quiet, as does the drone, and I realise I have to let it go, I have to move on before it consumes me completely.

Sometimes I get lost in thoughts of other animals rising up. About them finally speaking out against habitat theft and violence towards them. Online there's video footage of orangutans attacking logging machines in Borneo, tales of killer whales destroying the propellers of fishing boats. Are they angry? The orangutans are, certainly. And why wouldn't they be? In our thirst for cheap palm oil we have destroyed so much of their forest home. Whale experts seem to think the killer whales are just having fun. But what if they aren't? What if they're attacking propellers to seek retribution for overfishing, which is threatening their lives? And, surely, if you have the capacity for fun, you also have the capacity for pain and anger? Surely they can see what we're doing to the sea?

One day, if climate change doesn't kill us all, a new world order will be created, where people go to university to study the languages of other species. As well as French, German and Spanish, people will study Whale, Gorilla, Pangolin. Why not? I can already speak a bit of Dog, I can play-bow with the best of them. I know when Tosca needs a wee and when she's stressed. I know when she wants to play and when she wants me to put her on her lead (I had always assumed dogs don't like being tethered but Tosca appears to feel safe, she always asks for the lead when faced with large dogs or groups of dogs, presumably so we can walk past them together).

I want to know what the whales and dolphins say, I want to know how the sharks and seals feel. How are the octopus doing, how are the dragonflies? 'It's a bit warm, isn't it?' they might say. 'Could you stop choking us with plastic?' The migrant birds that fly here each spring from Africa, what could they tell us? How could they teach us to live better? What does the robin know? I fantasise about turning on the news at night and not just hearing of human stories but those of other animals, too. Tales of the first cuckoo arriving from Africa, of the annual sad goodbye to the swifts and the swallows. On national news, on local news, on any news.

And the gulls, the poor gulls, whole streets of whom are being distracted from nest building and egg laying by one man and his ridiculous drone. What would they say about the way they are being treated? What could I say to them? If I could connect with them I would tell them to stay away from the man with the drone, to nest, instead, with me. 'You'll be so safe here,' I would say, and I would also show them where else they had allies beneath the slate roofs they call home. If their antics were on the news, beyond the usual tales of 'Gull Steals Chips'/'Gull Scares Child'/'Gull Walks into Shop and Helps Itself to Pasty', how could our attitudes change, just from being more aware of their needs as our neighbours, of the challenges they face?

Years ago, in my early twenties, I travelled to Australia and signed up to camp in the bush on a saltwater crocodile expedition, just outside Darwin in the Northern Territory. My guide was a man who had been a successful banker but had burned out and had quit his old life to take clueless backpackers into the wilderness to teach them about crocodiles and northern Aboriginal cultures. There was a group of us, all young and silly, all signed up for an 'adventure in the bush' without really knowing what it was. I was there with Kat, a student doctor I had met in a nightclub in Sydney's Darling Harbour, who randomly agreed to explore Western Australia with me in a camper van that, inevitably, was always breaking down. For three nights we slept out in the open, in outdoor sleeping bags known as swags, and ate food made on a camping stove. I don't remember the food or much of the company, the small things. I remember Kat's shoulders as we swam in crocodile-free pools beneath waterfalls, of being terrified of sleeping outside and of waking in the night to see wild boars searching for scraps among us, of the Dutch lads singing a Dutch drinking song. Mostly I remember the views and the nature, trekking up to an escarpment and watching the sun set over the wetlands, cave paintings made by long-dead people who had once shared the views that were now in front of my eyes some 20,000 years later. Mostly I remember the words of the man who had quit his old life.

He told us that Aboriginal Australians had a special way of interacting with the natural world, that they were fully a part of it. He told me they would sit, for hours, and watch other animals. That, in their observations, they learned to mimic other species; they read their body language and knew their habits. Consequently, they knew when it was safe to swim with crocodiles, because they knew if the crocs had eaten. They knew exactly how much fish to take from the river and when to take it, to protect populations so there would always be fish to eat. He told me they had extraordinary powers of sight and navigation, and could travel over huge areas of land without what we westerners would ever deem a 'proper map'. I was 21 years old and fascinated. From that point I watched as many films featuring Aboriginal Australians as possible, I visited Aboriginal museums and bought Aboriginal art (I also bought a didgeridoo, c'mon, I was 21). I felt a kinship with these people who, in my mind, had a higher understanding of the workings of life, and, inevitably, I was devastated to see what European settlement had done to them.

Weeks later, I ate curry with an English man in Vietnam, and I told him about my trip. He laughed and said Aboriginal civilisation wasn't to be taken seriously as they hadn't built any tall buildings. It's been more than 20 years but I still think about that trip, the amazing things I learned, and of the ridiculous English man who considered tall buildings – read ego – a true mark of civilisation. If only the ego wasn't the dominant force of civilisation today, what would we know? I doubt we would be hurtling towards 3°C of average global warming by the end of the century.

To connect, or reconnect with the natural world would be a thing of enormous beauty, for us and other species. To view other animals as equals, to understand and respect their needs in this world we have taken over, would be nothing short of a gift. A gift of reading the body language of another animal and understanding its thoughts and needs, its next move.

The dog jumps up for a cuddle and I say 'kisses' and she gently licks my nose. I wonder if we will ever have such kinship with wild animals, not that we need to love and hug them or teach them to give us kisses, but that we can understand each other a bit more. As wildlife gardeners we already understand the needs of others more than most. We can anticipate food and water shortages and supplement accordingly. We can create habitats that we know will be used. But if they could speak to us and if we would listen – if they could actually get through to us – what would they say?

The park behind my house is a scruffy, neglected space with a large playing field full of craters made by dogs, a children's play area, a scout hut and masses of overgrown borders. A small copse runs through the middle, where poplar trees rub shoulders with guerilla-planted cordylines and a rogue Scots pine. There are smatterings of garden escapees, helped along by those whose gardens back on to the park, along with oddities such as gnomes and a ceramic hedgehog. On the other side is more lawn, along with huge overgrown rose beds, an area of long grass and brambles, and a nettle patch. It's used by a huge community of people, including teenagers and adults without gardens, who use the space for sunbathing and socialising, people with children and/or dogs, people who feed the birds and people who don't like others feeding the birds. There are fetes, children's events, dog parties and weeding and litter-picking sessions. There are late-night gatherings and little 'balloon' dens with discarded nitrous oxide canisters scattered among the trees. There are hedgehogs and birds, butterflies and other wildlife, who are often overlooked.

It used to be better looked after but cuts to council budgets mean it now has just a few big trims a year, with no detail given to the weedy rose beds or the crater-pocked playing field. This means brambles and nettles have free rein, which is good for the hedgehogs and butterflies but risky as we never know when the council will come and cut them back. Plus, they are the source of many complaints. It's hard managing a space that is used by so many people for so many things. But we get along.

Today I'm here for the nettles, which I need to harvest daily for the caterpillars I am raising in the kitchen. I have an old supermarket shopping bag and a pair of scissors. I turn the corner and see two men in high-vis jackets, one on a ride-on mower and the other hacking into brambles with a strimmer. Of course, after weeks of nothing, today everything will be cut back, tidied up and taken away. I curse, silently. I should have taken those caterpillars.

'Hiya.'

The man with the strimmer stops his work, and I try not to look at the debris in his wake. I ask if he will be cutting back the nettles where the caterpillars are, and he says yes.

'When?' I ask.

'Within the hour,' he replies.

I tell him about the caterpillars.

'Show me,' he says.

I take him to the nettles and he tries to tell me they're the larvae of the brown tail moth, a native species with very fine hairs that can cause skin irritation and breathing difficulties in some people. I say no, these are small tortoiseshells, they have declined by 75 per cent in the last 50 years and, besides, brown tails don't deserve to die because some people, who are unlikely to ever go near nettles, are allergic to them. He sighs and says he will have a word with his colleague on the lawnmower but, really, there's nothing they can do.

I get it, I really do. The grass needs mowing and the paths need to be kept clear. And with fewer resources these jobs are done less frequently but more harshly. And the council is trying – when they mow the grass they leave longer patches so clover can flower to feed the bees. But no one ever thinks about the caterpillars.

To think I was beating myself up for taking caterpillars from nettles just two days previously. To think I had considered taking these ones and decided not to. The small tortoiseshell, a once-common and easily recognisable species, has seen populations collapse since the 1970s, and boy do we know it. If I had a penny for every 'Where have the butterflies gone?' question I'd had at talks, I would be very rich. Yet here we are, in one of the UK's 27,000 public parks, killing them. And it's not just this park, is it? It will be all of them.

Can we not dedicate areas to other species who use the park as well? Can we not manage habitats so the wildlife uses the bits intended for them and avoids those that aren't?

The first brood of small tortoiseshell butterflies lays eggs in early summer, and the offspring of this spring batch mate and lay eggs of the second brood from mid- to late summer. The egg-laying females seek out fresh, young nettles to lay their eggs on. So if they're cut and regrow they become even more attractive to butterflies. A nettle patch, therefore, which is cut in midsummer by the council, is a death-trap, an ecological dead end. I wish we could do better for our wildlife. I wish we could tell the species that make all of this unwelcome 'growth' their home, that there are better places to lay their eggs. 'Look,' I could say to them, 'Not there, it's too near the path, but this nettle patch is for you! And when you're done I will cut the nettles back and they will regrow and be perfect for your babies. Welcome!'

I start picking caterpillars off the plants and dropping them into my supermarket bag, as the man on the lawnmower gets into position. He has spoken with his colleague, he seems friendly. I resist the urge to talk to him, too, but I'm grateful for the space he's giving me to save these butterflies.

Caterpillars go through growth stages, known as instars, and with each instar the caterpillar grows before shedding its skin. The small tortoiseshell goes through five such stages. Because they hang out together, in groups of up to 100, the shed skins are very obvious – indeed, sometimes the first signs of caterpillars on nettles are not the caterpillars themselves but the ghosts of earlier instars. When I raise them in my little mesh tent I always know when they're about to shed a skin; they stop eating and move around less. I like to imagine them all crying out in Caterpillar: 'My tummy hurts! I don't feel well.' And then, suddenly, they are bigger, differently patterned and HUNGRY. 'Hello, new beans,' I say to them. 'Feeling better?'

Annoyingly, after spending most of their time huddled together, eating en masse and making collective decisions to move from one nettle tip to the next, when they reach their fifth instar they disperse, where they appear to sunbathe on nettle leaves for a few days before climbing to a suitable spot and pupating into a chrysalis. I suppose this is an evolutionary tactic – a predator would have a hard job finding them all, dispersed as they are along a huge bank of luscious leafy leaves. How do I know this? Because here I am, picking through nettles to save 100 caterpillars that are not, conveniently, in the same spot.

I walk along, methodically plucking caterpillars off leaves and dropping them into my bag. I count them as I go. The first 27 are easy to find. But there are more, I know there are. I go back to where I started, crouch down, look under leaves. I find another five, then six, seven. The man on the lawnmower busies himself with a little patch of grass by the roses. A final sweep and I have 41. That's 41 caterpillars that would otherwise have had the chop. I collect a rogue red admiral and a few mother of pearl moth caterpillars as I go, then cut nettles into the bag to sustain them all. My hands tingle with a thousand stings. I pocket the scissors, wave thanks to the man on the lawnmower and take my leave. I'll return later to assess the damage.

At home I arrange nettles in the little mesh tent, and watch Sunday's caterpillars climb on to them and start eating. I release the red admiral and mother of pearl larvae on to the nettles in the garden – my small patch will be enough for them. I recount my quarry, and am pleased that I still have 41, there were no escapees on the way home. I gently tip these into the same mesh tent and watch as they, too, climb on to the nettles, newly incarcerated but safe. I apologise to them and try to explain that they'll be free again soon. I leave them to get on with the rest of their day and make a note to buy another, bigger, mesh tent.

Later, I return to the park to see how much has been stripped back. I'm pleased to see the nettles have had the lightest of trims – possibly because I kicked up such a fuss. I walk along and find a garden tiger caterpillar wondering where its home has gone and I scoop it up to take back to the garden. The rest of the park has been scalped, one whole nettle patch has been razed completely. There will be lush new growth in a couple of weeks. Just in time for the next generation of egg-laying butterflies to meet a grisly end at the hands of more men with strimmers and mowers.

I wish caterpillars were viewed more favourably. I wish they were prioritised, like bees and butterflies, that gardeners and park-maintenance folk were as happy to see little grubs eating their leaves as they are a pollinator visiting a flower. We are trained, the world over, to see caterpillars as pests, to pick them off when we see them, to spray and squish them. We need to change our mindset, to recognise the importance of them, both in their own right and as food for so many other species further up the food chain. These tiny eating machines that grow fat and transform, like magic, into a beautiful butterfly. These fat, moist grubs that fill the bellies of baby birds, of frogs and toads, of hedgehogs. One baby blue tit needs to eat 100 caterpillars a day for the first three weeks of its life – who are we to deny them a meal?

Caterpillars represent hope, abundance, promise, new life, while butterflies are a celebration of life itself. Can you not see that, when a butterfly flies over your garden fence? Do you not yell 'Butterfly!' when you spot your first of the year? Every time a caterpillar is removed from a plant, a bit of love, hope and magic is taken from the world. This not only denies food for wildlife but also joy for people. Who are we to take that away? To kill love, hope and magic, when surely there's never been a greater need for more?

Slow worm, *Anguis fragilis*

The slow worm is not a snake but a lizard without legs. A lizard that has eyelids and can blink. Males are a dull brown and females are golden, often with go-faster stripes down the sides. They bask to warm up in the morning, beneath the shelter of logs or other items (some people lay down slates or corrugated iron for them to rest beneath). They eat slugs and other small invertebrates but, if you're a gardener, the most important thing you need to know about slow worms is that they eat slugs. They eat slugs!

They are common across the British Isles except for the Scottish islands and the whole of Ireland. I rarely see them in the garden but when I do, they are resting beneath the old roof slate I have laid down for them at the back of the border. They also like the habitat pile and the log pile beneath the bench. They venture out, in late spring, to look for a mate. I have found slow worms trying to cross the road, slinking across the lawn, heading out of the garden down the twitten. Mating looks uncomfortable but who are we to know? The male clasps on to the female's neck and holds fast while they roll around together, for up to 10 hours. In common with two other lizard species, the common lizard and sand lizard, slow worms incubate their eggs internally, which then hatch out while still inside their mother so she appears to 'give birth' to her young. She seeks out warm places to bring her young into the world, such as the top of plastic compost bins and the toasty centre of open compost heaps.

To garden for slow worms is to open up the space for them, ensure they can come and go as they please. Compost your kitchen and garden waste, either in plastic bins or open heaps (or both!) and avoid turning it until early autumn. To see if they're living among you, the best way to find them is to lay down a piece of slate or corrugated iron over long grass or straw; they won't be able to resist.

Slow worms are often found, and tormented, by cats. Ensure, then, that they have plenty of hiding places to escape to, that the log pile, compost heap and piece of slate are distributed evenly around the garden. If they can nip to safety quickly they have more chances of survival. The cats will have to play with something else.

June

I steal a few hours, alone, in the garden. It's unusually quiet, the neighbours must be away. But the borders are quiet, too. There's a few bees but not many, and I wonder if the cold, dry conditions a few weeks ago hit them just as they were starting their nests, or if the dry conditions generally have been too much for them. It's eerie. There are few hoverflies and other insects, too, there's none of the 'hum' of life that I would expect in early June, when things typically start getting noisy. But there is some life and I hold on to it, hard.

The pond is fuller since we had rain, and covered in duckweed, which I can't remove because the tadpoles are too small to deal with the onslaught of being hoofed out and then chucked back in again (I can do this from July). I focus on other things: I tie clematis, honeysuckle and hops into the trellis, trim off wayward stems and check them for caterpillars – nothing. I trim the hedge, which has only just started looking like a hedge, and check the prunings for

caterpillars – nothing. I cut back bindweed that's allowed
to live in the twitten but is not allowed to grow through
the gate and strangle my hedge. Two caterpillars! Phew.
But, sorry. I fetch a clothes peg and carefully attach the
leaves to some living bits of bindweed so the caterpillars
can eat them, instead. I check everything again and then
throw my clippings on the habitat pile between the shed
and the wall, where everyone lives but me.

The garden starts to look completely wild at this time of
year. I mow the 'lawn' until May so the mining bees can
use the short grass, and then set it free. It took a while for
things to gather pace this year because it's been so dry but
it's picking up speed now. The grass is knee-high in places
and the borders are busy – ornamental poppies rub
shoulders with foxgloves and alliums, along with the last of
the honesty.

I collect seeds from white deadnettle to scatter elsewhere.
I reduce the height of the knapweed around the pond so I
can still see the pond. I 'Chelsea chop' the dusky cranesbill,
(*Geranium phaeum*) so it flowers again, and the white
comfrey so it doesn't produce seed. I find baby frogs and
photograph them. Hi!

I make tea and lie on the bench, a treat I rarely allow
myself. In the sky I count 10 swifts flying overhead and far
above them a buzzard being escorted away by six of the
finest herring gull bouncers. Herring gulls are such good
parents, such fine neighbours. I think of them, happily, as I
fall asleep, and wake 10 minutes later with a jolt. More
gardening? Why not?

I planted the front garden to be a riot of colour and
wow! People stop to comment on it. It was covered in
plastic and pebbles when I moved in and now provides
food for pollinators all year round. There are primroses,
crocuses and lungwort for the spring bees, then mountain

cornflowers, Macedonian scabious (*Knautia macedonica*), dyer's chamomile and viper's bugloss for the summer crowd. Purpletop vervain (*Verbena bonariensis*) and rudbeckia for the autumn stragglers and a bit of winter honeysuckle for anyone who wakes up or is disturbed during the cold months. It's a succession of pollen and nectar, carefully managed, not too tidy. Except there's a problem.

Honeywort (*Cerinthe purpurascens*) is a beautiful hardy annual with fleshy, glaucus leaves and purple tubular flowers. A member of the borage family, it produces good levels of nectar, plus being Mediterranean, it's used to dry conditions. It's therefore a brilliant bee plant and the fact that it still produces good levels of nectar in periods of drought makes it extremely useful for dry gardens (or newly dry gardens due to climate change). Most flowers stop producing nectar in drought so honeywort can help them through. When bees visit its blooms they make a tinny buzzing sound, which makes me happy. Lots and lots of bees love honeywort, which makes it produce lots and lots of seed, which makes it produce lots and lots of new plants, which attract lots and lots of bees. See where I'm going here?

It would be an understatement to say the honeywort is extremely happy in my front garden, indeed, it's completely taken over this year and nothing else has been able to grow. I've removed a few plants but, knowing how much the bees love it, I haven't taken too much; it's not nice to cut down plants when you know the bees love them and you know they will carry on feeding the bees when others won't, especially when conditions are so dry. Instead I vowed to cut the plants back after they'd flowered but before they'd set seed, which seemed like a reasonable compromise.

I can tell when honeywort starts seeding as the leaves lose their beautiful blue hue and the seeds are huge – you can see them a mile off. It's not a bad time for it to go: the hairy-footed flower bees, which are active from March to May, have pretty much finished for the season and the bumbles, if there were any, have plenty else in the garden to feast from. But still, it never feels good. I climb over the short wall and start chopping. The lack of bees makes the job easier, and soon I have a large pile of plants. I feel like I'm chopping down a forest – it takes a good hour and then five good armfuls to clear it through the house to the habitat pile at the back. But what I'm left with is heartbreaking; I was expecting to find little stunted clumps of chamomile and catmint beneath it, desperate for a bit of light. The plan was to give them a good drink so they could grow and fill the space left by the now-absent honeywort. But there's barely anything at all, just some viper's bugloss and Macedonian scabious that have seen much better days, and a few clumps of lungwort. The rest has died under the shadow of blue glaucous leaves. There's no honeywort, and now there's barely anything in its place, either.

To add insult to injury, as I pile it up at the side of the shed, a bumblebee finds it and starts taking the last of the nectar from its flowers. I sit, deflated, on the hedgehog feeding station. I'm being oversensitive because of the lack of rain; I'm taking it personally as if I were the dry garden, as if I were the empty skies. But the reality is that I've just removed a potentially important source of nectar during a drought and have nothing to offer in its place. I feel awful.

The bee takes her fill and buzzes off, for the last time, because the flowers will have dried out by tomorrow. I remind myself of all the things in bloom in the back, which I'm hydrating with grey water. There really isn't a shortage of pollen and nectar in these parts. But the front garden is a mess, with virtually nothing growing in it. I'm sad but also mindful of an opportunity: what can I do with the space now?

The park caterpillars have started to pupate already. I knew they would, it's never that long after they've dispersed. They seek out the perfect pupation spot like a dog sniffing out its next wee. I watch them crawl, with purpose, to the top of the tent, and stop. After a while they start to wriggle, uncomfortably, and then they hang down from the roof by a hooked tip known as a cremaster, a little silk pad holding them in place. Initially hanging in a straight pole, they seem to relax into the process and then curve up into the perfect, chunky comma. They might hang like this for a day or two before their skin splits for the last time and a chrysalis is born. Sometimes, despite much wriggling, the caterpillar skin stays whole, suspended from the bottom of the chrysalis. Other times just the gruesome remains of its old head are left.

Pupation is an interesting process; it's when I start to see which caterpillars have been successful or not. First, there are those that don't manage to pupate. Something happens during metamorphosis that stops them in their tracks. They hang and hang but never curl up into a comma, instead dying as a rigid, withered pole. Then there are the parasites. *Sturmia bella* is a parasitic fly that arrived here from continental Europe a few years ago (thanks, probably, to climate change), and is thought to have contributed to small tortoiseshell declines. It parasitises small tortoiseshells, peacocks and occasionally red admirals, the adult female flies laying eggs on nettle leaves and the unsuspecting caterpillars gobbling them up. The eggs hatch inside the caterpillar and the grub eats its host from the inside, eventually persuading it to pupate at the same time as its siblings. Then, while the others gradually turn into a butterfly, the *Sturmia bella* grub chews its way out of the chrysalis and drops down from a silken thread, hiding under leaf litter (or kitchen paper if you're in Kate's little mesh tent). There, they pupate into hard, wine-coloured pupal cases, and hatch out as adult flies a week or so later.

There are other parasites, too; tiny wasps that lay eggs in eggs and first instar caterpillars, their larvae bursting out of their unsuspecting host just before pupation – these caterpillars don't pupate but wander around aimlessly until, eventually, they seem to explode, yielding their grubby secret.

Those that survive pupation then have other problems. In the wild parasites might lay eggs in the chrysalis or a park gardener might come along with a strimmer and squash them flat. When the butterfly is ready to emerge (eclose) from the pupa, it's an extremely perilous time because it emerges with small, wet wings and it needs to hang upside down for a few hours to pump blood into them and dry them off. If conditions are windy or if the butterfly suffers a knock or it catches something while coming out of the chrysalis, it might get stuck or it might not be able to pump blood into its wings. This results in a crumpled butterfly, complete but deformed, which will survive for only a day or so. Men with strimmers are just one of so many dangers – can they not just stay at home?

These 41 from the park are lucky. If I hadn't found the other batch, I wouldn't have noticed these ones and I wouldn't have been out gathering nettles into a plastic bag. The nettles would have had a bigger trim and the caterpillars would have been lost. I watch them crowd to the top of the tent and start to change, wishing they were doing so on the park nettles but grateful that they're in my kitchen.

I'm very good at raising caterpillars because I have been very bad in the past. I took my first batch (from a clump of nettles that had been sprayed with weedkiller) nearly 10 years ago. I raised them in my bedroom, in an ice cream tub without a lid, from which, of course, they all escaped. I would gather nettles on the way home from work and then spend an hour searching for and then returning the adventurers to their ice-cream home. Then, one day, I came home to find a large number of them had pupated under my duvet, and I spent all night carefully teasing them off (remember they stick themselves in place with a silken pad), and it was long after I also wanted to be beneath the duvet that I had managed to prise them all off and reattach them to the kebab sticks I had arranged, like fishing rods, from my bookcase. They all turned out fine but, as well as pupating under the duvet, some pupated behind the wardrobe, another on the mirror. When they eclosed, which they tend to do together over a period of two to four days, they all flew around my bedroom and seemed reluctant to fly out of the window. I would then find surprise butterflies that had pupated in mystery places (the wardrobe, the mirror), which also had to be caught and released outside.

Another time, as I walked past men with strimmers attacking the communal paths of a local park, I gathered hundreds of caterpillars that were about to lose their homes, and transferred them to the nettle patch in my garden. Of course, every wasp in town was extremely grateful because I had essentially served them a very easy meal, all on one big plate. The whole lot had gone within a few days. Butterflies go about their business in the way they do for a reason. We are fools to ever forget that.

So it was with sadness that I realised that, if I was going to 'save' the caterpillars, I needed to do so at home, with the right kit. I searched online for some sort of mesh tent, only to learn there are such things designed exactly for the job in hand. I bought one designed for kids, a beginner tent if you like, and have been raising one or two batches a year in it ever since.

After a few hours, most of the Park 41 are hanging like chunky commas from the tent roof. I lose two of them to rigid withered pole syndrome (unofficial term). I keep an eye on them while cooking my tea, and watch a few wriggle themselves a new form. Looking after caterpillars is the easiest thing in the world. I wish more of us did it.

I see them as soon as I walk into the kitchen to make the day's first cup of tea, four box-fresh small tortoiseshells hanging from their empty chrysalises in the little mesh tent, the blood-like spatters of meconium decorating its sides. Four of the 41 saved from the park, four little lives that otherwise wouldn't have made it. My heart soars. 'Hey, gorgeous things!' I say, as the kettle boils. They've been there a while, all are dry with their wings perfectly expanded, ready for take-off. It's 5.45 a.m. I open the kitchen blind and the day is dry and still but the sun hasn't come around yet. I take tea back to bed, give them an hour.

Later, when the sun has moved round and I can be sure there's no wind, I release my butterflies, one by one. I choose the front garden to release them, the hedge keeps everything protected and the sun is strongest here at this time of day. The tall stands of viper's bugloss make the perfect release spot for them – each of the (now six) butterflies can have its own station on the same plant, and how marvellous they will look as they stick their tongues into the blooms for their first-ever sip of nectar.

I reach into the mesh tent and pop a finger in front of the legs of the one nearest the opening. It climbs aboard and then I transfer it to the other hand, which can take up to four butterflies at a time, for the short journey to the front door. I fish out three more, each one obligingly stepping on to my finger to be transferred to the other hand, to be carried to the door. Although their wings have fully dried, it's still a vulnerable time for them, so I have to be careful. Outside I move my hand beneath the flower and let them climb on to it, where they settle themselves and open their wings a couple of times before moving into position to hang some more. The sun makes everything glisten. Today is going to be a good day.

I spend the next few hours popping my head out of the front door to see how they're getting on. They move around, some visiting other flowers or other stations to hang from, before disappearing completely. I release another five butterflies from the little mesh tent, a total of nine that made it from caterpillar to adult, despite the efforts of the council.

It's not rained for a month. Everything is struggling, and not just in my garden. In the park the playing field is yellow, the soil is sand. The tall poplar trees planted around the edge are shedding leaves but otherwise seem OK. The young trees are doing less well – three silver birches I planted in the copse have died, there's a young hawthorn that's seen better days and a couple of newly planted trees that desperately need water. At the edge of the playing field is a lone chestnut-leaved holly, its once-glossy leaves faded and brittle, the earth around its roots rock hard. Chestnut-leaved holly is a good tree for a changing climate because it does well in hot, dry conditions but doesn't mind a lot of rain, as long as the soil doesn't become waterlogged. Its leaves don't hold much value for wildlife but its flowers attract bees and its berries feed birds. But it doesn't become drought tolerant until it's 'established', which means it's too young to cope with this heat and lack of rain. It, too, could die.

I've been trying to keep these trees alive with grey water, which I decant into old 5-litre shampoo bottles that I bulk-buy my shampoo in, and take to the park when I walk Tos. Each day a different tree gets its 5 litres and when I've done them all I move back to the first one – that's roughly 5 litres a week, per tree. It's clearly not been enough, I've already lost my three silver birches and probably one of the newly planted trees near the edge. Now it looks like we'll lose the chestnut-leaved holly. I can't do this on my own, I can't keep everything else alive as well as my garden. So, finally, I ask for help.

There's a Facebook group for the park, plus my hedgehog group and another for the road next to mine. There's also a huge network of dog walkers, connected by a WhatsApp group. I start with the dogs – we all take water to the park for our pups and most of us tip the bottles on to the grass as we leave. What if we tipped the leftover water on to the chestnut-leaved holly, instead? I text the group and some people respond positively while others suggest it's the council's job. It is, but the whole city is bone dry, they don't have the resources to go around watering every tree on top of everything else they do on a skeleton budget, and what would they be watering with? Fresh drinking water?

This is our community and our trees, we can look after them. I gently suggest they drop their leftover dog water on the chestnut-leaved holly as they leave the park, and post photos of the tube that takes water directly to its roots. Some of them will, some of them won't. It's a start.

I write much the same message in the Facebook groups and get much the same responses – some people deride the council for not doing enough, others fill watering cans and old pop bottles with water and take them to the park to douse the tree's roots. I know this because they post about it on Facebook, and I feel happy. I am reminded, once again, that it's the community that will save these trees, not me. I'm reminded that community is everything.

I spend four days releasing butterflies into the garden; some into the front, where the viper's bugloss provides the perfect sanctuary, and others to the buddleia in the back. I release a total of 27. I write this figure down in my notebook, which reminds me that 12 were parasitised by *Sturmia bella* and two didn't manage to pupate. That's not a bad emergence rate, and probably better than if they had remained wild. Certainly better odds than they would have had if they'd been strimmed. It feels good. It feels good to do good things.

The original caterpillars, that first batch I collected from Wild Park, are not far behind. They started to pupate just a couple of days after this batch and it won't be long before they, too, are set free in the garden. Meanwhile the patch of nettles that was completely destroyed two weeks ago is ripe with the freshest of new growth. I check them most days, when I walk with Tos around the park. Surely it's only a matter of time before I find more caterpillars on them?

   I wonder if the lack of rain is causing, or contributing to, all of these caterpillars? We are, apparently, not yet in drought but I can't see how. The grass is yellow, the plants are withered and dying, the pond is disappearing before my eyes. And yet it will be faring better than wild areas because I'm keeping it hydrated (well, as hydrated as I can). I'm showering into a bucket and keeping washing-up water and the dog's bath water, which I know only contain eco-detergents, and am reusing it in the garden. Are more butterflies coming to gardens and parks because they're less parched than the food plants in the countryside? Maybe.

   I buy a new mesh tent. It's bigger than the child's one I've been using for the last few years. It's taller and wider and has a large door that takes up one side of it, which makes it easy to add plant material and clean. I could stand a vase of nettles in there if I wanted, to save me having to fetch new material from the park so often. It will be just my luck that I don't need to use it, now that I've had my fill of caterpillars for this year. But something tells me there will be more.

Common backswimmer, *Notonecta glauca*

The backswimmer is so called because it swims on its back, using its oar-like legs to propel itself through the water, like a rowing boat. It's also called a water boatman but so is another species, *Corixa punctata*, which is smaller, vegetarian and swims on its front. The backswimmer is a fierce predator that attacks prey like tadpoles and small fish, using its forelegs to grab its next victim and its 'beak' to stab it with poison, to kill it. Gruesome, yes, but a sign of a healthy pond environment – if yours can sustain backswimmers it means there's plenty to eat.

Backswimmers have a large, silvery body covered in fine hairs, which they use to trap air when they come to the surface, so they can breathe below water. They are light brown with large, reddish eyes.

The backswimmer was one of the first species to colonise my new pond. One day I came home and found lots of tiny crab-like things bobbing in the water. These, I discovered later, were backswimmer nymphs, which grew through the season and eventually metamorphosed into the large adults that took a chance on my pond and laid their eggs. The second generation also laid eggs, and suddenly I had a family – large adults that would glisten as they swam to the surface for air, little nymphs that gradually shed their outer skin and grew into adults. One day I found a shed skin and kept it as treasure.

To garden for backswimmers is to have a pond where lots of species can live, so the backswimmers can eat them. It's a backswimmer-eat-tadpole world, and I like it.

July

I work away for a week at the Hampton Court Flower Show, where I have a nature table and chat to children and adults about the amazing natural finds you can display in your home. I have skulls and shed snake skins, a hedgehog 'pelt', a bit of bumblebee nest, a couple of hatched birds' eggs. All from home. Throughout the week I find other bits and pieces: a ladybird pupa that ecloses on the table, live caterpillars that eat nettles, tadpoles, green parakeet feathers. It's a week of hanging out with my treasures and talking to people about how great my treasures are.

'What's that?'

'It's a COYPU skull! Isn't it great? Look at its orange TEETH!'

It's a busy week, in which I stay in a tiny bedsit and walk to work every day through the straw-like grassland of Bushy Park. I crave my home life, the garden, my girls, rain. But it's worth it. On the last day, a young boy begs me for my fox skull and I give it to him but ask that, in return, he always looks out for the wild things. We strike a deal and he takes it home. Another child has the grass snake skin and many others take feathers. By the end of the week, everyone wants a nature table, wants treasures as precious as mine. It feels good.

I arrive home to a dried-up garden and an even drier pond. I should have known. The grass here is also straw, the plants are wilting, the flowers devoid of bees. I crouch down at the pond edge. Brooklime, curled pondweed and duck weed lie on the bottom like deflated balloons. The mud is still muddy and I hope things have tucked themselves in here, waiting out the drought. Maybe not: I also track hedgehog and bird footprints – what dying morsels have they been helping themselves to? Everything, by the looks of it. Tadpoles, certainly, there were hundreds a week ago. Backswimmers? Neither the adults nor the wingless nymphs are here, the adults will have flown elsewhere but the nymphs – which hatched from eggs laid in May – will be in the bellies of other beings. No dragonfly or damselfly larvae, no whirligig beetles, no pond skaters, no caddis flies. What have I done? I lie on my belly, my head and arms in the 'hole', and root around the deflated balloons. There's not even dead tadpoles, no sign they were ever here. I turn leaves and stems to reveal the occasional pond snail, some leeches and water hoglice missed by truffling hedge pigs. But nothing else. Welp.

It's not just hoggy footprints in the pond that gives them away but also the wet, muddy footprints I watch them leave on the trail camera at night. I catch up on a week of videos in which there has still been no rain, but suddenly moisture and mud as hedgehogs cross the patio with bellies full of dead pond. Some of even them have bits of plant material caught between their claws.

I'm pleased they and the birds have had a good meal, it's not like things have been easy for them. But all of that work! Three years old, nothing special, but the beginnings of something, a solid ecosystem. Now we have to start again. Will the backswimmers return? They were some of the first colonisers of the pond and some have spent their whole lives in it; I'd catch their silvery bodies glinting in the light as they surfaced for air. Where are they? Will the common darter dragonflies return, the lone red male defending his territory from the stick I've wedged into mud by the side of the pond and romantically called a dragonfly perch? The damselflies, the little brown beetles that hung around the edges, the mosquito larvae, the non-biting midge larvae. Where did they go? If garden ponds are drying up, you can bet those in the wild are, too. So where did they go? Rivers, which are full of human excrement, nitrogen run-off and pesticides? What a choice.

Drying out is a perfectly natural thing for a pond to do. So-called 'ephemeral' or 'vernal' ponds dry out every summer in the wild – some studies have shown that this can put species like frogs at an advantage over fish, as frogs need ponds only until summer, when the froglets leave for the land, while fish live in them all year round. And fish eat frog tadpoles, so a pond without fish is better for frogs. The area of mud that's revealed as the water level drops is known as the 'drawdown zone' and can be the most biologically rich area of the pond. Lots of species can survive here for several months, with some even laying eggs here. But I wonder if the drawdown zone is as biologically rich when there are hungry hedgehogs snuffling around? When the pond dries out in early July? When there's nowhere for flying insects to escape to as other bodies of water will be in the same state or too polluted to live in?

I'm cross with Emma for not noticing that the pond was drying out, for walking past it every day to top up the hedgehog bowl but not being awake to the other things going on around her. If she'd mentioned it I would have asked her to keep it topped up, not completely full but partially, so the tadpoles and other aquatic species had somewhere to continue living. It's not her job, and she has plenty of other things to do. But how could she not have noticed?

I take the opportunity to clear some of the plant material, which was starting to take over the pond, and which I had earmarked as an autumn job. I rake it, gently, to avoid scraping the muddy layer, which holds so much carbon, and scoop it out of the hole. I sift through it, looking again for signs of tadpoles or other life – nothing but the leeches, snails and hoglice I had already spotted. I leave it piled up at the edge so they can crawl back in. I fill the watering can with tap water and leave that at the side, too, so I can start topping up the pond tomorrow. A few inches will be enough for thirsty mammals, at least.

It rains in the night. Blows in on the wind and smashes against the bedroom windows. I lie awake listening to every drop, feel the earth cry with relief. Its tears run off pavements and into gutters; a brief, unexpected five minutes in the darkness. I think of hedgehogs getting wet for the first time in weeks. Do they run to shelter or embrace it? I think of dust washing off leaves, of raindrops disappearing into baked earth. I think of tumbling out of bed and into the garden, naked, to dance in it. It stops as instantly as it had started but there has been just enough of it for the smell of petrichor to waft in on the breeze.

In the morning the water butt is still empty. A fat slug had been sleeping in the pipe that connects the downpipe to the water butt and I didn't have the heart to evict it, is it still there? I pull the pipe out from the butt. A bit of sludge comes out on my hand, followed, eventually, by the slug's little inquisitive face. 'Hey, slug.' It shrinks back into its pipe, where it will no doubt wedge itself in and block more rain from entering the water butt. I curse myself for being so soft. But there's no more rain forecast and, I have to admit, it's the perfect place for a slug to sit out a heatwave.

It's day one of the anticipated two hottest days ever in the UK. I spend the earliest hours outside, throwing grey water from the shower and washing-up bowl around plants that need it the most, adding precious fresh water from the tap, and therefore from our chalk aquifer, to the bird bath. I worry about the chalk aquifer. Local news reports tell me we're in a good spot here in Brighton, as the aquifer, rather than human-made reservoirs, holds our drinking water, and levels are still good so we can carry on as usual. The chalk acts like a sponge and holds on to water beneath the ground, which is pumped out for the city to drink and bathe and wash cars and windows, and waste to our hearts' content because there remain no restrictions on it. Chalk aquifers feed chalk streams, which are already under threat from pollution and climate change. So shouldn't we be limiting our water use? Chalk aquifers are also extremely vulnerable to pollution, as the water that runs into them can be contaminated by anything from nitrates from farmland to oil and tyre pollution from roads. The Aquifer Partnership (TAP) was set up to promote the protection and cleaning of Brighton's water. TAP promotes using less water while doing more to slow the flow into the ground so it's less polluted by the time it reaches the chalk, with time, sunshine, plants and microbes playing their part in breaking down pollutants. How do you slow the flow of water into the ground? Gardens, plants, water butts. Funny how everything is connected.

Why are news reporters encouraging us to carry on wasting water? Why are people still washing their cars and patios and why is the man in the estate behind me power-washing bollards of all things? Bollards. I ask him to water the estate's three silver birch trees that stand, wilting in the sun.

'It's not my job,' he says, 'I'm here to clean the bollards.'

'Please, just a bit of water, just throw it in the direction of the trees while you walk past them on your way to the next bollard. It's not rained for weeks,' I plead.

'You'll need to email the garden management team,' he says, for he is not budging on the matter of his water being only for bollards. Meanwhile I'm using manky bits of grey water to hydrate shrivelled plants so I can keep the garden alive, keep the park's trees alive. How many teaspoons have I lost watering the garden from the washing-up bowl? How many bits of spaghetti are draped over frazzled plants? The injustice of it all. Of all of it.

I try to work, with the news on for temperature updates. There's an air of catastrophe, of Covid-esque anxiety. The streets are empty and I don't want to go outside. It feels like those early days in March 2020 when we didn't know if we'd be put into lockdown, and what to expect if we did. When will it hit 40°C and where will it hit first? What will it feel like? For us and the wildlife? Will the birds fly? Will the hedgehogs wake up thirsty and go searching for moisture in the heat of the day? Will it be like a solar eclipse? The last decent eclipse was in the summer of 1999. I was 18 and Mum, Ellie and Anna were away so I had the house to myself. When the eclipse came I sat in the garden and felt the shade draw in, felt everything dull and quieten, tuned in to the silencing of the birds. Then, after a few minutes, everything started up again. I don't know why I'm thinking of the solar eclipse on a day where the sun is anything but eclipsed. Will everything fall silent? Will it all fall silent?

I feel drowsy and fall asleep on the sofa, there's nothing else to do. I wake to more of the same: obsessive reporting of rising temperatures across the country, but not yet 40°C.

The garden is in shade now so I venture out in it. The earth is cracked and sore, like chapped lips, the worms a distant memory, hopefully safe somewhere in the furthest depths of it. Who eats worms? Birds, hedgehogs, frogs, badgers. And where are the caterpillars and beetles? The living things? I have nightmares about moles. I imagine cross-sections of earth with stuck, roasting moles waiting to die. Instead, I know they're coming to the surface in search of food and frazzling in the sun.

I need to do something. My wonderful wildflower meadow is yellow straw. It's a fire hazard. My neighbourhood is so built-up that one spark from a nearby barbecue could set the whole lot in flames. I get on my hands and knees and check it for wildlife. There's nothing – no frogs, no slow worms, no caterpillars, no grasshoppers. Where are they? Did they perish? Did they not exist in the first place? Literally nothing is living here.

With shears I chop bits of it in front of the pollinator border, smoothing each piece over and checking again for hogs and frogs, although I know this process is pointless. The dust hits the back of my throat as I work my way through it. I leave a strip on the left that has not been bleached by sun and another around the pond that has benefited from its proximity to water. I plump up border perennials over cut grass stalks, give nepeta and geranium some room to spread out.

In its fourth year the meadow has lost much of its floral diversity. Only the strip beside the pond is still packed with flowers, the rest is grass. Grass is an important food source for many species of wildlife but it's not as pretty as it could be and, besides, this year it's dead. Perhaps it's the attention from the animals, or the soil is too rich, that makes the grass grow faster and stronger, out-competing the wildflowers. I've sowed seed and planted expensive plugs of yellow rattle, a semi-parasite of grass that limits its growth so wildflowers can thrive. Such attempts have failed. But in the front garden, which was covered in plastic and stones for many years, and was then swamped by a forest of honeywort, the soil may be less fertile, better for wildflowers. It gets more light and – perhaps – has less footfall from heavy mammals. Well, at least Tosca doesn't rampage through it. This is one of many reasons that I have decided to move the meadow into the front garden for next year and keep most of the back short. It's not an easy decision. Most years the meadow is home to all sorts of things: bees, butterflies, grasshoppers, frogs, slow worms, caterpillars. And the hedgehogs love to party in it, of course. But with the partying hedgehogs, the playful foxes and our own little bouncy canine, it gets a lot of 'attention', and that doesn't seem to be good for the production of flowers.

The front garden will be a proper meadow, with different types of grasses along with perennial favourites like red clover, ox-eye daisy and knapweed. These will join the few survivors that managed to live beneath the honeywort: the viper's bugloss, lungwort, primroses and Macedonian scabious. Perhaps I'll throw in some field poppy seeds to make more of a display of it. The bulbs, too, will look nice in spring before everything else grows. Maybe.

I save grass seeds from yellow stalks, combing them through my fingers into a bucket, where tufted vetch and greater knapweed seeds wait for their moment in the soil. I dig up self-seeded ox-eye daisies and red clover, both from the patio and the pavement outside the front, and plant them in pots to move to their final growing place, when it's not so hot. I do the same with ribwort plantain, red, white and bladder campion, evening primrose and sweet rocket. I water them with precious grey water and store them in the side return, in the shade. I buy more yellow rattle seed, to sow later.

The day ends with us just shy of the 38.7°C record set in Cambridge in 2019. This will be broken tomorrow. I try to focus on the new phases of the garden, of where the front garden plants might go now they will be replaced with meadow. I focus on the small things, or try to. The big things are just too big today.

We wake at 5.00 a.m. and check the weather forecast for the temperature.

'It's only 20 degrees,' says Emma.

'I'll take Tos out,' I reply. It makes sense; the ground will be too hot for her little paws within a few hours.

We head out into the early light, to blue skies and a fresh breeze that's almost cooling. To a stretch of the Downs closest to my house, which I can walk to and from in a 10km loop. There's a world of 'city' before we get to the country: a mass of car dealerships, a ring road, a giant supermarket. Yet we trek from this to corn buntings and yellowhammers, to six-spot burnet moths and brown-banded carder bees – it never ceases to amaze me. I wait impatiently as Tosca stops at every lamp post.

I like the world better at this time of day. There are fewer people and more birds, or at least the illusion of such. No one to bump into. No fumes from the road or traffic to wait for before we can cross. No bubbling rage as I pass people sitting in their vehicles with their engines on, polluting the atmosphere for absolutely no reason at all.

The scrub in the shadow of the Downs is as frazzled and yellow as my garden, but the thistle flowers are the brightest pink against the blue sky. I am grateful for them. Everything is dusty and dry but there is just a hint of hope, of freshness, here, that I wouldn't have realised had I stayed at home and sulked.

'Isn't this wonderful?' says Tosca's little face. 'Isn't everything great?' We will hit 40°C today, somewhere in the UK, and I will cry. But, for now, I savour these precious, peaceful moments with the dog.

There's not much wildlife to ogle, few singing birds and not many insects, although this patch of Downs isn't as flower-rich as it could be and I don't take Tos on the nature reserve. There are a few buzzing bees, making the most of the cooler early-morning temperatures, there are caterpillars still dripping from nettles that haven't yet been chopped down. We stand at the highest point and look over Brighton, over dry fields and scrub, over lush, watered golf courses, over the glistening sea. 'Where are we headed, with all of this, Tos? What will happen?' She looks at me with her giant hazel eyes, and then moves her gaze to my pocket, where the treats are. I throw one for her, returning my gaze to the sea. I am so broken by all of this, for god's sake could I not just cheer up for the dog?

I break the rules and throw her ball on to the empty golf course. Her feet are horses' hooves on the ground as she races after it, returning and dropping it in my hand each time, for half a treat. I kneel down to give her a drink and a kiss. 'Our little secret,' I whisper, as the first golfers arrive and we move on.

We make our way back, down the hills, my boots echoing on hard ground, through another golf course and the supermarket car park, back to the sticky heat of the city. It's not yet 8.00 a.m. but I check the paving with the back of my hand and try to walk in the shade as much as possible. Eventually I panic and pick Tosca up and carry her the last sunny leg of the journey. I will not let this heat burn her paws.

At home she sleeps, contented, and I switch on the rolling news, again, to torment myself. It quickly gets hot and becomes too hot to do anything. I have all the windows and doors open to encourage a breeze, I lift the hatch into the attic so the hot air has somewhere to escape to. I try to work from the sofa but am distracted by the weight of everything. I can hear sparrows but I can't enjoy them. How are they coping? Is there enough food for their chicks? How can there be, when the grass is straw, when the earth is cement? How many dead chicks lie in dusty nests?

If you're a bee, or a hoverfly or a mole or a stag beetle, and you nest in the ground, you need that ground to remain as you found it (permitting, of course, the changes that come with the seasons). If it bakes and cracks, you're dead. If there's a fire, you're dead. If there's a flood, you're dead. A mole might do better than a stag beetle larva, on account of being more mobile and therefore having a larger stretch of land to escape to, but these extremes of 'weather', which we have been warned about for *years*, are pushing already-declining species further towards extinction. What scientists call 'change of land use', *i.e.* turning wild places into cities, giant industrial farms, golf courses and shooting ranges, have already made us one of the most nature-depleted countries in the world. Hedgehogs, birds, butterflies, bees: all dead or dying. Other species whose numbers we simply don't know about because they haven't been studied. Wasps? No one cared to count them until a few years ago. Hoverflies? It's complicated.

Beetles? Hmm. The World Wildlife Fund (WWF) suggests that one in seven native species faces extinction in the UK and more than 40 per cent are in decline. Add in a cocktail of flood and drought and fire and you quickly see why people are gluing themselves to motorways.

The irony is that as the world warms, many species, where able, will be travelling north in search of cooler temperatures. We Brits could, as a nation, be their ambulance. We could help French bees and butterflies cross the Channel, we could bring food plants from southern Europe to help them adjust. We could save species that may, one day, if we pull our socks up, return to the habitats they came from, when and if they cool down again. But we're not going to do that, are we? Some species have already arrived on their own – European bee-eaters are nesting in Norfolk, swallowtail and long-tailed blue butterflies are breeding in Sussex, several other species are arriving in Scotland, a country that was once considered too cold for them. These are climate refugees and we should be doing everything we can to help them, along with the human refugees we are also, shamefully, turning away. Instead we cover the land in paving and plastic and turn rivers into soups of pesticides, algae and human excrement. Oh, and just a few more coal mines, they say. Just a bit more oil.

That soil, which needs to remain a certain way for the species that live in it? We need it too. It's where we grow our food.

Outside I top up the bird bath, throw a bit of water in the pond so there is something in the bottom, so the mud doesn't become cement. I check the hedgehog feeding station and assess which frazzled plant is most deserving of manky washing-up water today. (Astilbes. It's always astilbes.)

At one point I have a craving for cold spaghetti bolognaise. Cold bolognaise! Of all things. I sit with the craving for a while and then get up and make it. I fry onions and garlic, add carrots, courgettes, vegan mince, tomatoes and masses of fresh oregano. I boil a pan of spaghetti. The kitchen becomes uncomfortably hot but I keep going, still with this craving for cool food that I am making myself hot to create. I let it cool naturally initially, then plate it up and put it in the fridge.

The 40°C record is set in late afternoon, somewhere in Lincolnshire. I sit on the sofa, spooning cold bolognaise into my mouth, and cry. How is this happening? How are we letting this happen?

The thing about experiencing drought during climate breakdown is that, while I'm a nervous wreck due to the breakdown part of the story, others remind me, 'It has been hot before.'

'Is this another lecture about 1976?' I ask my mother, on the phone at some point during the hottest week the UK has ever experienced.

'Darling, it was boiling!'

I know this, of course. I know that temperatures reached 32°C for 15 consecutive days across much of southern England, peaking at 35.9°C. I know some regions had no rain for 45 days straight. In some parts of the country they ran out of drinking water and had to use a standpipe at the end of the road. I know that everyone was encouraged to water their gardens with bath water, that many were bitten by a 'plague' of ladybirds.

'The world didn't end,' everyone says.

I ask them if they know that most butterfly populations crashed in 1977, thanks to the drought the year before. That it took the common species 10 years to build their numbers back up but that rarer, more specialist butterflies have never recovered, thanks, of course, to the combined assault of habitat loss. They fall quiet. Of course, no one thinks of climate affecting other species. They didn't notice.

They didn't notice that plants didn't flower, that leaves shrivelled up and grass crunched underfoot like fresh snow. They didn't notice that the hedgehogs starved, that birds were abandoned in their nests, that frogs died of desiccation. In 1976 the heat generated masses of aphids, which boosted ladybird populations but then at the end of summer, the ladybirds went hungry and started biting people in huge, locust-like flocks. It was this that made the papers.

'What was 1976 like, Mum?'

'I was my sister's bridesmaid,' she says.

I can't bear it. I can't look after the garden, I don't have enough water to keep it going. I'm sick of taking my miserable washing-up bowl of manky water to see which plant is most deserving of it, which is more wilting and shrivelled than the next. The leaves are scorching, the flowers just aren't appearing. How did I get to the age of 41 and not realise that some plants just don't produce flowers in a drought? Lots of drought-stressed plants flower quickly and then bolt (run to seed), which seems more of a sensible path, in terms of attempting another generation. But refusing to bloom entirely? Lamb's ear, no flowers; ruddy clover, no flowers; penstemon, no flowers. The bumblebees emerge earlier and earlier each day, trying to survive, but the pavements are littered with the dead. Butterflies, which I suspect have flocked into our gardens to escape the wider countryside suggest a greater abundance than there really is. There have been ringlets and meadow browns this summer – two records for the garden but probably for all the wrong reasons. I find two batches of large white butterfly eggs on the tattiest, most mildewed charlock, which had self-seeded next to the 'pond' and then bolted. Friends on Twitter post of similar apparently desperate attempts, of butterflies laying eggs on already dried-up plants seemingly because they had no choice but to. I collect the large whites and keep them in my little mesh cage with a handful of cauliflower leaves my neighbour Kate gave me. (I hope they don't mind sharing the space with the dead frog I am drying out, which Kate also gave me.)

As the shade descends I do a stupid thing, which is to say I attempt to garden. I need to do something. On a whim, I decide I no longer like the Kilmarnock willow that sits at the far end of the pond, and whose drought-stressed leaves are dropping into the empty pool as if it, too, dreams of autumn. I saw its head off, which I stuff into the gap between the shed and the garden wall, and then dig up its roots, adding its long, bent stem to the log pile. I feel bad for chopping down a 'tree', but it was on its way out anyway and it was taking up so much space that could be used to grow other things. Its carbon will remain locked away in its stem and branches for many years, and there will be more growing in its place, of course.

I dig the soil, which isn't as big a challenge as I thought it would be – the shade cast by the umbrella of Kilmarnock branches will have protected it from the sun's baking rays. I rake it over a bit, but not enough to make it level and certainly not enough to remove 'weeds', and then take my spade to the front garden and start digging things up: agapanthus, ruddy clover, lamb's ear (they definitely won't flower now), lavender. I hoof salvias and geums out of pots and rescue a privet-leaved ageratina (*Eupatorium ligustrinum*) from the clutches of black horehound – both of which have seen better days. I carry everything through the house to the back, tangled roots scraping against white walls and clods of earth falling on to varnished wood. I'll never learn. There are pots of buddleia and scabious left over from a photoshoot, which I commandeer also. I arrange the plants in order of height as they are now, and then again where I anticipate how they will be in the future. I space them evenly but probably too close together, as I always do. I plant them, one by one, with no compost or other food in the planting hole, no moist soil, no teasing of roots. I firm them in, fluff around the edges, shift a couple of things around that I planted and then didn't like. I deadhead the lavender, salvias and geums, as they'll need to divert that energy to repair the roots I just damaged as I pulled them out of bone-dry soil. I fetch my half-full washing-up bowl and pour grey water over two plants, and wish the rest good luck.

Why am I doing this today of all days? Why must I do this now? Emma comes home to a woman possessed, a woman on a mission, who can't sit still and has to be busy. To mud-scraped walls in the hallway and clods of earth on varnished wood. It can't be nice for her, coming home to this. She sits me down and hands me a beer. She's absolutely loving the sunshine but daren't tell me as she knows it's destroying me, while I try (badly) to keep the worst of my anxiety from her. 'Shall I bathe the dog?' she asks, gently. 'You can use the water on the garden.'

The aim of the new border, while created on a whim on the hottest day the country has ever seen, is to establish a continuous display that spans the length of the garden, from the patio to the shed. Before, the border went as far as just beyond the bench and then dropped off, as the soil space that curves around the far edge of the pond, next to the wall, is so small and dry that very little grows there. Then there was the Kilmarnock willow, which looked alright for a couple of years but soon outgrew its space to the point that it became a giant green boulder that sat in the way of nice flowery things and drew your eye straight to it as a lump in front of the shed. Now, freshly bedded in with Tosca's dirty bath water, the border will sweep around the pond and create depth and interest and all the things garden designers talk about when putting things together. There will be a succession of flowers from March to December, there will be different heights, there will be plants in the narrow space between pond and wall (I haven't worked out what yet, and the soil is too dry to attempt planting), there will be colour. And oh, can I not just have something new?

It's a bit mad, though, to have done this today. But I am mad, I am frantic and anxious and not thinking straight and my god will it just rain? I try to persuade Emma to eat cold bolognaise for tea and she pulls a face that says absolutely not, and so we eat it, warmed, while watching the news, while watching fire after fire, scorched earth, unsafe houses, terrified firefighters. Afterwards, as the day fades, I sit on the bench with the garden. My rain app tells me rain will start in 15 minutes but it won't, will it? The garden stills and rustles, the rain cloud moves over me but it doesn't rain. It's too hot to rain, the water is evaporating before it can leave the sky. I stare at shrivelled plants taking a breather as the temperature cools. Please, please, can we just have some rain?

Wool carder bee, *Anthidium manicatum*

The wool carder is an angry little bee, chunky and black with wasp-like yellow bands or spots on its abdomen. The male has a set of spikes at the tip of his body to fight with other males, but also to ward off butterflies, bumblebees and giant dragonflies from his territory. Once, I had one nesting in my bee hotel and I kept its precious cocoons so I could sit with them as the new bees hatched out the following year. They emerged in a frenzy of angry buzzing, the cocoons spinning around before the bees chewed their way out and headed straight to the window to be free. If wool carder bees were human they would be short and stocky with a broken nose and a black eye, permanently wearing boxing gloves. 'C'mon then! C'mon!'

The females 'card' hairs from hairy-leaved plants to knit a woolly sock, into which they lay the eggs of next year's angry boys. They favour lamb's ear, which is easy to grow and should be in every garden. The males install themselves at patches of lamb's ear and claim it as their own, so they can be ready for passing females checking the territory. They also favour bird's foot trefoil – indeed the year they nested with me was the only year I've had masses of it, which was draped, like curtains, around the pond (bird's foot trefoil has a habit of disappearing, which is annoying). Every day I would fish wool carder males from the pond which, I suspect, had been pushed in by others. I took one dead individual into the house to dry off, for my nature table, and it came back to life some hours later.

If a wool carder bee nests in your bee hotel you have reached the Holy Grail of bee hoteling because they so very rarely nest in them. Some suggest the hotel should be placed high up, that you need a ladder to fix it to your wall. But mine nested at head height and the following year, although laying only two eggs, a wool carder nested just one metre from the ground.

To attract them to your garden grow lamb's ear so the females can make their woolly sock nests, and grow bird's foot trefoil so the males can fight over it. You might not get them nesting in your bee hotel but you will get the best spectacle a bee lover can imagine – angry bees fighting over flowers and knitting woolly socks. Tell me, what is there not to love?

August

Back in the day, as a 'jobbing' journalist, I would attend trade shows and meet people who would try to flog me things or, worse, try to get me to write about the things they wanted to flog in the magazine. My shoulders would ache with the weight of leaflets and I would come away with free things I didn't need or want – sometimes really odd things that I would use for years before finally accepting that I didn't like them. Sometimes I would get really good things like a tool sharpener or a great pair of scissors. Always I would ask difficult questions, such as the time I asked a company why they were launching a butterfly 'throw and grow' mix with peat-based compost. Peat bogs are vital carbon sinks that lock away carbon and are essential to minimise global heating – globally, they hold more than twice as much carbon as the world's forests do. But they also provide a home for lots of species of wildlife, including now-rare butterflies. Couldn't they see, at the very least, that they were stealing from rare butterflies to create food for common ones? Everyone else flocked to get their hands on a free sample of quite average flowers that would bloom and then disappear in one season, during which time they would, perhaps, attract butterflies while their rarer cousins died and more greenhouse gases were released into the atmosphere, and I would stand there, resolute, refusing to be greenwashed. Harumph.

All of these events merge into one, but there are two occasions that are burned into my brain for ever: watching the slug pellet marketer eat slug pellets to 'prove' how wildlife-friendly they are (instead of using, I don't know, science), and the woman from the water butt company who told me that people only install water butts in summer, when it's dry. 'They should install them in autumn, when it's wet,' she said, 'and then they wouldn't run out of water in summer.' If only she knew I think about her every day.

When I redid the garden I installed one water butt. An expensive one, it's attached to the wall of the house so it doesn't take up valuable ground space. It connects to the downpipe from the house gutters and fills up quickly and, before this summer, it never stood empty for long. In hindsight I should have bought a bigger one or bought two and connected them, but one seemed enough at the time and no one really wants to spend their money on water butts. So I didn't, and now I'm spending my summer with the words of the woman from the water butt company in an endless loop in my brain: 'No one installs water butts when they should.'

I grit my teeth and buy another expensive one to connect to the original. It holds 160 litres, which will double my water-storage capacity when the sky eventually yields rain. I fix it to the wall myself (not quite level but never mind), and connect it to the other water butt myself, and then sit and look at it, empty, by myself. Will two be enough? What would the water butt woman say? I think she'd suggest more water butts (of course she would, she sells water butts).

The shed has a roof, of course, so it could be another candidate for keeping me sane next summer. But the overhang is too great for traditional gutter brackets and, so far, I have ignored its potential to store water and hydrate the garden. But I return to it now; surely someone has invented a way of connecting gutter brackets to vastly overhanging roofs? Will I have to erect fascias? Will I need to get a man round? Surely there's a bit of plastic for the job? I google the very thing and indeed someone has invented what I need – a bracket that clamps on to the roof and holds the gutter in place, albeit, I realise later, not very securely. Of course they are four times as expensive as regular gutter brackets but I have no choice if I am to save winter's water. I buy some online and then head to my nearest DIY store for gutters and downpipes and two cheap water butts that I hope I will eventually be able to conceal with plants. I set it all up just in time for precious, life-giving rain.

A few weeks ago, during some of the driest, hottest weather we have ever seen in this part of the world, a woman spotted a hedgehog out during the day as it was climbing into a drainpipe on a busy high street. She acted quickly and grabbed the hedgehog before it could get stuck (it would never have been able to get out again), and took it straight to the rescue centre where it was found to be dehydrated and starving, along with all the other hogs that had been taken in since very early spring.

The little hog was weighed (400g), sexed (a female) and named (Minnie, as she was so small). She was given water and food in gentle doses, so as not to overwhelm her little system, and her own cage filled with soft bedding. She settled into the hoggy hospital well. Some hogs hate it and resist every attempt to care for them; they remain very firmly Wild. But Minnie seemed to know what was good for her. 'She's a delight,' says Ann, who brings her round to be released into my garden. 'She's a little darling.'

Wildlife rescue centres are jam-packed with hedgehogs this year; they seem to have struggled more than most in the hot, dry weather. Hedgehogs come out of hibernation in early spring and refuel on juicy caterpillars, worms and beetles, rehydrating from puddles and ponds. It's all timed so perfectly – after winter dormancy, the longer days and warmer temperatures encourage leaves to unfurl and flowers to blossom. Some of the year's first insects feed on the blossom and others lay eggs on the leaves, while the warmer soil brings worms to the surface. April showers provide moisture but not too much, just enough for seeds to germinate but not enough to wash caterpillars off leaves. Just enough for a little puddle to form but not enough to completely saturate the soil. Spring, it's the uncoiling of everything. It's a little bit of bounce. 'Hello,' says everyone, blinking in the spring sunshine. 'NOM,' says the hedgehog. 'NOM,' says the baby bird. 'NOM NOM NOM NOM NOM NOM NOM NOM,' say the wasps and the badgers and the slow worms and the bees, who are all bouncing, uncoiled, too, with the sudden abundance of everything.

But take away the showers, and the leaves unfurl but then shrivel, the eggs are laid but the caterpillars don't develop. Do the worms come to the surface? No. Do puddles form? No. Without rain, spring is only half uncoiled, it's an aborted bounce, more of a slow roll. Add to that fluctuating temperatures and tired animals that should have been conserving energy in hibernation but actually kept waking up because temperatures were so mild, and you end up with dehydration and hunger. To start the season dehydrated and hungry is one thing, but to struggle through to August? Imagine being so desperate you're searching for moisture up a drainpipe.

Minnie is lucky. She was spotted by someone who knew she needed help and she was given that help. Too many people see hedgehogs out during the day and just take photos of them, such is our detachment from the natural world. They post the pics on social media. 'Oh isn't it cute, oh how lovely!' Old Boring Pants here chimes in with a gentle 'They shouldn't actually be out in the day. Could you go back out and find it, pop it in a high-sided box and take it to a rescue centre ASAP? Thanks.' I hate ruining the party but Christ.

I chat to Ann as she scoops Minnie out of a cat carrier and strokes her, gently, looking reluctant to let her go. 'She really is lovely,' says Ann, and I nod in response. Weighing 600g now, she's still small compared to the chunky boys I catch on the camera at night. But she'll have all the food she needs here.

'But wait,' I say. 'She'll mate with one of the boys and have babies…' I count the weeks '… in mid-September.' Hedgehogs emerge from hibernation in spring, feed themselves up to be in good breeding condition and then mate, the females giving birth to their first brood from late spring to early summer. They often have a second brood in September, but the hoglets from these second broods tend to struggle as there is less natural food available and they are unable to gain sufficient weight to survive hibernation. These babies are known as 'autumn orphans' and they rarely survive winter. Hedgehog ecologists suggest a weight of 450g is necessary for successful hibernation, anything less than that and the hoglets won't make it. After a summer of (usually) dealing with hogs injured by strimmers or fixing a nasty cough caused by lungworm, rescuers like Ann turn their attention to feeding up little babies that can't put weight on. The hoglets often spend all winter in their care and are released in spring.

'She'll have autumn orphans!' I cry.

'They'll be fine though, sweetheart, they're well looked after here. Just keep doing what you're doing. Keep feeding them.'

Ann pops Minnie down at the entrance of the box I cleaned and filled with fresh straw, and the hog crawls in. It must be strange to give an animal so much care and love and then say goodbye to it like that. I promise to update Ann on any activity I catch on the cameras, and add an extra pile of kitten biscuits to the bowl in the feeding station and fresh water to the 'bird bath'. Ann leaves to go and look for three hoglets that were spotted on Shoreham beach, and I head to bed. Minnie, almost certainly, has a lot of fun on her first night of freedom.

The rain comes early in the morning. It wakes me with a tap at the windows, and I get up and run into the garden, stand in it, watch it fall on leaves, kiss the pond. It's light at first and then grows heavy as the darkest clouds roll in and throw down their water. I take shelter beneath the shed roof, which juts out just enough to protect me, and breathe in great lungfuls of petrichor. It's raining. It's finally raining!

The ground has been so hard it had started to echo like stone when I walked on it. Now, small puddles form as the compacted earth struggles to absorb moisture. This is how flooding starts; hard ground resists rain and so the water pools on the surface or finds a slope to roll down to join other puddles, to form a stream, a river, a flash. My little puddles will be fine and the pond could take a fair bit more if the ground remains stubborn, but I wonder how neighbours' paving and plastic grass are looking. Wet, I imagine.

I obsess over my new water butts – the one on the house that connects to the original one, which takes water straight from the roof, and the two I installed on either side of the shed. I watch droplets pool and fall from shed roof felt into gutter, lift water-butt lids and check for trickles. Can it not pour in? Will you please pour? Some of the roof felt is missing the guttering so I'm losing vital drops. But it's 6.00 a.m. and I'm in my dressing gown, now's not the time to climb on to the roof and adjust gutters. The house butts are better but too much water is sneaking out of the downpipe, into the drain. I fill the kettle for tea and, while it boils, fetch a plastic bag and block the downpipe so every last drop is directed into the water butt. I lift the lid – more than a trickle but it's not pouring in. Not yet.

I take tea to bed and drink it while watching rain through the windows. I listen to cars drive through puddles, rain gurgling into the downpipe. I look at my rain app and it says there will be a lull, with more to come in half an hour, which means I have a small window to take the dog out. We go to the park, partly so we can run home quickly if there's a downpour and partly so I can be with the park as it rains. Does that make sense? I want to hold its hand somehow, maybe feel its relief as the trees finally get a good drink. That little bit of rain, will it, could it, have made a difference already?

Tosca hates rain. She rushes out of the door and then backs up, wants to be indoors. 'Give over, it's only spitting,' I say, and give her a treat for stepping out again. I once read that rain – or post-rain – is exciting for dogs as it washes all the smells away so all new smells are NEW, but I think we'll need more before that happens. I wonder how much will be needed to rid central Brighton of its residual stench of beery piss.

In the park the grass is short straw but the earth is wetted and there are no puddles – must be all the holes dug by dogs. We have the place to ourselves. We walk the perimeter, me picking litter, Tosca sniffing. I have forgotten her ball.

I realise I am cheerful. I tell Tosca she is the best dog in the world, throw treats and watch her bound after them. I am excited, bouncy, pleased. As humans we so often cast rain as something miserable and 'bad'. Try living without it. This water, which falls from the sky and which we all take for granted in the British Isles, gives and sustains life. That I am so cheered by it is the most basic of human responses. I want to dance, I want to sing, I want to spend all day just being in it. I wonder if I can take the day off work, to hang out in the rain.

We walk past the big privet hedge and a wren stutters to life, a machine-gun killing the silence. Further on, there's a great tit 'tee-cher'ing around the corner and a blackbird gurgling his sub-song. Could it be? No. The rain? I try to think when I last heard birdsong. Can't. Birds moult at this time of year and keep a low profile so it was more likely moulting that made them quiet, and that now has come to an end. And, besides, their song is a statement of territory rather than joy. But it's quite the coincidence that they're singing now the rain has come. When did it last rain? A flash of hope half dreamed on the warmest night and before that, early June. Perhaps, and more likely, I have been so consumed by drought I just refused to hear them.

Tosca sits down and raises a paw that says, 'Please, Mumma. Home now.' I remind her that it might rain all day and she won't get another walk. She looks at me with her great big eyes that say, 'I have no idea what you're saying.' I throw treats and say, 'Find it!' and she finds them but with none of the usual enthusiasm. The paw comes out again. 'OK then.' We head back, the long way around so she can get more sniffs in, tire herself out a bit. We're just in time – the heavens open as soon as we get in and we both stand at the kitchen window, transfixed, looking on to the garden.

I can't stop checking the rain. I want to watch raindrops fall to earth, see the pond fill up, hear the smacking of droplets on leaves. I check water butts. Inside, I have the window open so I can hear them fill. In Zoom meetings I lose my train of thought as the intensity of the rain changes and I am drawn to look outside. The pond fills like a huge bath and I want to jump in it. I stand at the window and watch leaping frogs.

The rain has softened the soil so I set to work on moving the meadow to the front. I start by digging up winter honeysuckle and other bits and pieces still in the ground, and hoeing away honeywort seedlings, which I have to do often, before raking the soil. In the back I dig up meadow cranesbill and divide the rootball into three pieces, along with a bit of meadowsweet that has grown away from the main rootball and was ripe for picking off and moving elsewhere. I bundle them into a bucket along with my pots of ox-eye daisies, red and white clover, knapweeds and yarrow, and thickets of grass that I dig up from gaps in the patio. I take it through the house into the front and plant it all, haphazardly but with some sense of order – daisies will look nice here; yarrow will survive better there. I scatter my saved seed of greater knapweed, grasses and ribwort plantain from the garden, and wild carrot and salad burnet from up in the Downs. I chop heads off the echiums and lay them in spots where they haven't yet colonised. Finally, I plant the winter honeysuckle and some rooted ivy cuttings in the gap on my side of next door's hedge. The honeysuckle should fill the gap while providing winter forage for bees. The ivy should, eventually, grow through everything, adding diversity and perhaps even slowing the growth of the existing forsythia and Japanese spindle (a girl can dream). I imagine it's quite hard to slow Japanese spindle growth, but if anyone can, ivy can. As ever, I have high hopes for my little cuttings.

I water everything using grey water saved from the dog's bath, which I collect into the watering can and walk down the stairs in many, many visits. It looks terrible, little scrappy bits of this and that surrounded by mud and dying honeywort. It will be a while before it pops up and greens over, before it grows into itself and starts to look like a meadow. In a few weeks I'll scatter seed of red poppy, which will brighten the display while the perennials get going. And then yellow rattle, the semi-parasite of grass, which should subdue grass growth and allow the wildflowers to flourish. I have my eye on seeds of this and that growing beyond my garden, which I can legally take small amounts of to bring a piece of the wider landscape home. It will be good, eventually, I know it will. Just not now.

Or anytime soon.

In the back I work around the pond, which had become so overgrown the sparrows had stopped bathing in it. The Kilmarnock willow (RIP) had grown so big it was shading out a large portion of the pond while the meadow, although completely dead across the rest of the garden, had made a comfortable buffer zone for itself around the pond edge, its yarrow, red and white clover, ox-eye daisies and knapweed making the most of the extra moisture available. The beach area – stones laid over mud to deter plants from growing – has all but disappeared under seedlings of water figwort. It needs a good haircut.

With the meadow plants safely ensconced in their new front-garden home, I can see the shape of the pond edge for the first time in ages. I sink big rockery stones into the mud and weed out one of the beaches before re-laying the stones in a much less orderly way than they had been laid in the first place. I sink my hands into the water and retrieve stones to add to it. The other beach has been colonised by bird's foot trefoil and I quite like it, so it can stay, I can live with just one pond beach. I fill holes made by removing plants, smooth mud around the top. I empty pots of old compost on to the grass around the edge and tamp it down to make it level. Finally it looks better, finally it resembles a pond.

It's still quiet compared to previous years; there have been no dragonflies or backswimmers recolonising the water, few midge and mosquito larvae. The habitat has returned but there's little living in it. I so hope they return next year.

Hummingbird hawk-moth, *Macroglossum stellatarum*

The hummingbird hawk-moth is a curious thing, a day-flying moth that hovers with wing beats so rapid they hum. If it stops for long enough you might notice its brown, white-spotted abdomen, brown forewings and orange hindwings. It has a long tongue, which it uses to probe flowers such as buddleia and red valerian, as it darts from bloom to bloom. To the untrained eye it looks just like a hummingbird, hence its name.

A resident in southern Europe, it used to be a rare migrant to the British Isles but has gradually become more common. It usually arrives in June, where it mates and lays eggs before dying, its young returning to the Mediterranean in autumn. It could not overwinter in the UK. But in recent years it has proved that it can, and in spring I spotted a newly emerged and mated female laying eggs on my cleavers.

To garden for this climate-change refugee is to grow flowers with plenty of sweet-smelling nectar – buddleia, red valerian, honeysuckle, jasmine. But you could also grow food plants for its caterpillars to help it breed. These include lady's bedstraw (*Galium verum*) and wild madder (*Rubia peregrina*), but cleavers do just as well, so the easiest thing to do would be to avoid weeding them out. The caterpillars are chunky and green with a yellow stripe down each side, and like all hawk-moth larvae they have a 'tail horn' at one end. They pupate in leaf litter near their food plant, so letting leaves accumulate in corners would also do well for them.

September

Sometimes I sit in the garden at dusk, waiting for the hedgehogs to come. I perch on the hedgehog feeding station itself, which is sturdy enough to take my weight and which, I think, the hedgehogs don't mind me sitting on. I bring my knees up to my chest so the box takes the whole of me and I wait, quietly, as the sky reddens and dims, as the birds hurry to their roosts, as seagulls fly overhead, like fighter planes, to the sea.

I don't like dusk so much. There's a nervousness, an anxiety, about suddenly not being able to see. My eyes struggle to adjust to the changing light and my world feels smaller, somehow. But there's an unfolding quietness that I love. Suddenly you can hear snails scratching over leaves. A gentle rustle in the border reveals a frog or a distant bark tells me the foxes are about. If it's damp I might be drawn to a worm pulling a leaf into the soil or a field mouse popping its nose out to see if the coast is clear. It's never long before the hogs come, it's never fully dark. They charge through the borders like elephants, always one from of the hedgehog boxes near the house, another from the habitat pile to the side of the shed, and sometimes a neighbour coming through the hole in the wall from next door or under the gate from the twitten on the other side.

I'm sure they can smell me. I'm sure they know I'm sitting as quietly as I can on top of the wooden structure in which they find kitten biscuits. They don't seem to mind, 'Oh there's Kate,' they seem to say, 'the one that fills the bowl.' They trundle along, climbing the big stone step to get up to the station, sniffing the air constantly. Are they sniffing me? What can they smell? They squeeze themselves into the cat-proof hole beneath me and I wait for that first, tentative *crunch!* Sitting in near-darkness on a box in which a red-listed mammal is eating kitten biscuits beneath you is really quite something.

On the wildlife camera I have picked up Minnie, who is smaller than other hogs and has helpful birthmark-like growths on her nose that make her easy to spot. She is, inevitably, always followed by a gang of males, who push each other around while sniffing out the new girl. I don't get to see much on the camera but I know Minnie has found the feeding station and 'bird bath' (and presumably the pond, too). I know she hasn't strayed far from the garden and I know she's getting a lot of attention from the males.

One male started to join her in her nest box, and so she moved to the other box and is now busy collecting leaves to add to the masses of straw I had packed in there. It's highly likely she's pregnant but she could just be gathering leaves for hibernation. Either way, Minnie has settled in. I text Ann, who thanks me for the update.

I can rarely identify the hogs when I'm outside with them; they always seem so much smaller than they do on the cameras. Even Doughnut appears to have lost enough weight to have blended in with the others. I don't pick them up or touch them to find particular identifying marks; I stay out of their way as much as possible. To spend time with them like this, crashing through the borders as snails scratch over plants and worms steal leaves into the soil, is all about the magic of being among them. And I love it, hanging out in near-darkness with the hedgehogs. I love it.

The pond is full now and there are water butts on standby to fill it up when it threatens to disappear again. I squat at the edge. Kelp-like curled pondweed has started to recolonise, while little sprouts of water soldiers are popping up in the margins. I see a ramshorn snail move slowly across the clay bed. There are mosquito larvae, water hoglice and tiny whirligig beetles. Life. There are still no backswimmers, no dragonfly larvae. I'll have to wait until next year for them. At night, frogs sit at the edge and catch flies.

The garden looks better since the rain, the grass is green again and thin new shoots are starting to fill gaps. But it's still not great. Gardens can look wonderful in September – a last burst of colour and light before everything dies back again. The existing border is OK but a bit gappy and the new border is too new for it to do much. Still, there are things I can do. I make notes and then take them to the new garden centre up near the woods.

The new garden centre has a walled garden you can walk around in, which I do, for 'inspiration'. There are pollinator beds and dry beds, a rain garden and an 'all seasons' garden. Of course, I am most impressed by the compost bin in the middle, which is sturdy yet handsome, and full to the brim with garden waste that smells, richly, of autumn. It's made from wooden slats and has three bays, presumably for successional turning. I have always coveted grand, centre-of-attention compost bins, and one day I will have one. Some people aspire to driving around in fancy cars, living in a detached house. Me? A really big, sturdy set of compost bays, please, ones that I can walk into and fork the waste from one into another. Wheelbarrow access a must, perhaps separate bays for leaf mould. The bays would be central to a 'composting area', a whole space dedicated to decomposition. I once tried making my own, using old pallets I'd collected in the street and dragged home. But the ground wasn't level and the pallets were different shapes and, besides, I could never get them to stand up straight. There was no room for a wheelbarrow, let alone me. So I took it all apart again and settled for inferior plastic (just the one) with other waste making the habitat pile between the shed and the wall. It's a fine system. But one day... one day ...

I buy new plants – a *Rosa rugosa* called 'Jam-a-licious', which has nice single open flowers for the bees, big hips for the birds, floppy leaves for leaf-cutter bees and autumn colour for me; a big Shasta daisy and a couple of lady's mantles for the shade. I bring them home, water them and try them out in various places before planting the rose at the side of the pond near the wall, where it should grow into dead space next to the ice plant. I chop the Shasta daisy in two with my bread knife, planting one half next to the new rose and the other half in a gap in the existing border. I move things around, weed out honeywort, replant bulbs I dug out last time and forgot to chuck back in the soil, and tickle the earth so it looks nice. It already looks better. It already looks ready for next year: buddleia at the back, ready to hide the water butt, salvias and geums ready to wow with their purple and orange combo, lamb's ear for the wool carder bees; honesty for the orange-tip butterflies. I think it will look alright but I won't find out for another nine months. Oh, gardening.

Like the Shasta daisy, one of the lady's mantles has a rootball that can be easily divided; essentially two plants growing in the same pot. My bread knife comes out again and I saw the rootball in half, and then plant the separate pieces beneath things on the shady side. Now the grass will be shorter I need to add more depth to the borders – a few low-growing things here and there will do perfectly. I bury them in the soil and water them in, along with a foxglove that had seeded into the patio and deserves a better spot. I mow the lawn and empty the clippings into my small, plastic bin.

In the front the new meadow is slowly taking shape. I coo over seedlings of bird's foot trefoil, ox-eye daisy, viper's bugloss. I weed out honeywort seedlings into a bucket; there are so many of them they make a soft pile up to the top. I make a note to remove the last of the ornamental plants that I have yet to find a home for. I make a note to buy snake's head fritillary bulbs. I make a note to summon the energy to cut my side of next door's hedge.

I go in, make tea, put my feet up. Everyone says summer gardens are made in autumn, that autumn is the real beginning of the gardening season. They're right. Some things are still flowering, eking out the very last of the growing season, but there are seeds of change elsewhere that I'm excited about. I am gardening in a still-temperate climate, pottering with plants and soil. There's rain in the water butts, there are bees in the borders, a whisper of hope for the new season. If you grow plants, there is always a future.

For the last few weeks there has been a chiffchaff in every tree. I've caught glimpses of them in the park, heard their telltale short, sharp *hweet* everywhere from the seafront to supermarket car parks. I know they've been in the garden. They fly like Tinkerbell, moving around in graceful, giddy circles, here one minute, in next-door's wisteria the next. They don't generally stay still long enough for me to get my eye in. Finally, today, one hangs around in the garden long enough for me to gawp at it through the window of my study when I should be writing.

It flies into the garden with a leap, and then flies out in an instant, in a great arching circle, landing somewhere next door. Brownish but not a sparrow. Brownish but followed by six sparrows that fly in directly and land on the bird feeder and make me doubt myself. Am I mistaken? Is it a sparrow? I wait. It comes again, arching over the fence and back up into the climbers – completely different behaviour to any sparrow. 'Chiffchaff!' says my heart. I stay put and watch as it seems to pluck up courage to take a sip from the pond, darting down and then back to the safety of the climbers, a little olive yo-yo. I run downstairs, padding on the floor as quietly as I can, careful not to appear as a lumbering shadow against the window.

In the kitchen I stand and scour the garden. Where is it now? The sparrows remain on the feeder. After a minute it appears from behind a clump of grass at the pond edge. It has been having a drink! A chiffchaff has been drinking from my pond! I grab my binoculars and adjust the focus. From the pond it launches into the hawthorn tree, then the guelder rose, then the shrub rose, which has a long, rogue stem jutting out above the rest of it. I had been meaning to cut it back but it's now sacred.

The leaves of the rose are on the turn, yielding the first autumnal hints of russet and amber. Through the binoculars the chiffchaff is the perfect yellow–green and the combination of the two has me awe-struck. I curse myself for not having a fancy camera but remind myself I am looking in real time through binoculars. Savour the moment. I watch, intently, as the chiffchaff picks aphids from the underside of the leaves, moving delicately up the stem until its weight causes the stem to bow down and it flies up, startled. It does this a few times, before I wrest myself away and back to my desk.

The chiffchaff (*Phylloscopus collybita*) is a summer migrant, a small, insectivorous warbler named after its repetitive summer call, which sounds like it's saying its own name over and over. It doesn't *chiff chaff* at this time of year, though, it *hweet*s, from every tree.

Its scientific name (*Phylloscopus*) means 'leaf seeker' because it likes to eat insects such as aphids, caterpillars, gnats and midges from leaves, like my roses. This is why, as I keep telling anyone who will listen, we shouldn't remove insects from our plants, we should always celebrate the fact that they are food for other species. What would the chiffchaff have to eat if I had removed the aphids? Or worse, what if the chiffchaff ate poisoned aphids that had been sprayed but not removed?

It's olive green, with a pale eye stripe and a darker 'eye brow'. It's almost indistinguishable by sight from the willow warbler; they're much better told apart by their different songs – the willow warbler has a watery warble rather than the obvious *chiff chaff*. Their contact calls differ too, the willow warbler's is more of a *hu-weet* than a *hweet*. I see and hear willow warblers in the garden, too, but they are gone by this stage of autumn.

Both species breed in the UK in summer, and overwinter in southern and western Europe, southern Asia and North Africa (although more recently, thanks to climate change, some chiffchaffs avoid the long journey to overwintering grounds and remain here). Birds of wilder spaces, I see them only in spring and autumn, presumably just after they arrive and again before they leave – on country walks I hear them calling from the tops of trees but never catch a glimpse of them. My garden is a stepping stone, a place to spend a few days after making landfall following a long journey, and again to fatten up and gain strength before heading back. These fairy-like birds, which glide from tree to bush and make calls I usually hear only in the countryside, mark the seasons.

There have been other migrants of late, too – swallows and house martins in their hundreds. I watch them flying over the garden, in the park, on the high street. Like the chiffchaff, they also head south for winter, travelling great distances to reach their African wintering grounds. House martins do sometimes nest in the suburbs, but swallows, like chiffchaffs, are countryside birds. It's strange watching them now, in such an urban setting. Strange watching them above the traffic and noise of the urban sprawl of Portslade. What are they doing here? The same as the chiffchaffs – flying south from wherever they nested in the UK; Brighton is the last bit of land before they cross the Channel. They need insects to fuel their journeys, they need our gardens with leaves and trees and an absence of bug sprays; we gardeners can help them on their way. In the park, with the dog, I watch a lone swallow quarter above ground, navigating around children playing football and dogs being idiots, a random dumped armchair, the scout hut, litter. It goes round and round and round, jerking left here and right there, avoiding this and that or moving suddenly for a morsel of food. Tosca and her best friend Alfie gambolling in the background, Alfie's mum Rhi and I chatting about our days. I think about the land the swallows used to find here. Before the park was a park it was a landfill site and before that 'waste land', a brick pit, fields. When did this parcel of land last have nesting swallows? Last have nesting chiffchaffs? Will it ever again?

Little nephew Stanley has discovered the allotments in his village. He and his mum, Ellie, walk past them on the way to the park and he asks to stop and look at the vegetables before playing on the swings and slides. Ellie texts me a video of him wandering around the beds, pointing out 'pumpkins' (winter squash), runner beans, a large white butterfly laying eggs on nasturtiums.

'Where are the tomatoes, Stanley?' Ellie asks.

'I think they're over here,' he replies, running off. 'And here are the big pumpkins,' he says, which of course are a different species of winter squash. 'They're beautiful!'

'Get off the mud, please, Stanley,' says Ellie. Three years old and already in love with an allotment? No chance, sis. Absolutely none at all.

Stanley's fondness for 'pumpkins' led to his parents taking him to a pumpkin farm to harvest his own Jack-o'-lantern for Halloween. I'm not sure how he managed it but he came away from the farm with eight pumpkins, one of which he carried around with him for three days.

'Stanley's in the bath with his pumpkin,' texts Ellie. I beam proudly.

'He's one of us,' I tell Dad on the phone a few days later. 'He's got the gene.' Dad wasn't around for long when I was little, but when he was it was me and him on the veg patch, me and him harvesting runner beans and puddling in leeks, me and him adding sticks to the bonfire on late summer evenings, me and him against the world. Suddenly Dad and I both know exactly how we're going to spend our time with our little green man: outside, loving what we love, together.

Ellie doesn't have that 'gene', the calling for the outside that Dad and I have. Just two years younger than me, she had every opportunity to develop the same love and wonder for the natural world as I did but it never happened. She feels inadequate about it but she needn't, it just isn't in her. But it's in Stanley, which is both hilarious and wonderful.

'Sis, how am I going to support him in this when it's so alien to me?'

'You'll work it out,' I tell her. You can develop an interest in gardening without being completely consumed by it. It doesn't have to be all or nothing. You can learn enough to take joy from it yourself while helping to feed your child's obsession. It needn't be your everything, you don't even have to be good at it.

They're moving house soon and Ellie promises me Stanley will have his own vegetable patch.

'Remember he's only three,' I tell her, and wonder how much Mum can be relied on to water things I plant for him. Or indeed if Ellie, pregnant with nephew number two, would know how to keep plants sated, if she even had the time to do so. It's times like this I wish I lived closer. Or they did.

She sends videos of the new garden, which is mainly lawn but has a small greenhouse at the end and a sunny bed overrun with hypericum and euphorbia, which could make a nice spot for pumpkins. 'Can we grow runner beans?' she asks, 'and sweet peas?' We agree for me to go up one weekend in spring and set up some sort of veg patch. There are also roses to prune and a hedgehog highway to create, plants to identify. Mum has claimed the greenhouse as her own, which is a blessing as she will teach Stanley how to water, feed, weed and pinch out, and she will keep an eye on his veg patch when I'm not there. He'll grow into a fine gardener yet.

Common darter dragonfly, *Sympetrum striolatum*

The common darter is a dragonfly that regularly colonises new ponds. Males are rusty red and females are more of an ochre, fading to a dull red as they age. They are narrow-bodied and 'dart' out to collect prey, which they take back to their perch to eat. The male will tend to use the same perch from which to defend his territory – if you sit and watch you will see him jump up to scare off a bumblebee or butterfly, before settling back down again to guard his space.

Climate change is, at the moment, working well for British dragonflies, which thrive in warm weather. The *State of Dragonflies in Britain and Ireland 2021* report states that 19 species have increased their distribution since 1970, compared to five that have declined. We have gained eight new species since 1995 and two others have reappeared after a long period of absence. Most species are moving north and west into areas that were previously too cold for them.

The common darter appeared in my garden within weeks of me digging the pond. The following spring I conducted pond dips and found the chubby nymphs in my net, along with those of skinnier damselflies and mayflies. The nymphs eat tadpoles and other aquatic larvae before climbing up the stem of a plant growing out of the water and completing their final stage of metamorphosis into an adult.

When mating, the male and female form a 'wheel' where the male holds on to the female by the back of her neck with claspers at the end of his abdomen. If she likes him she will lift her abdomen up to the base of his thorax to allow him to transfer his sperm. They then travel together to the pond, where he holds on to her as she dips eggs into the water.

October

A call from a wildlife rescue. 'We have a young male hog here, would you take him?' I say yes, of course. I clean out one of the empty boxes and fill it with fresh straw, and drive up with another box of straw to carry him home in.

He doesn't have a name. He was found in someone's garden with two siblings, both female, in summer. It looked like the nest had been abandoned by their mum, as sometimes happens, and the three hoglets were out and about far too early to survive. They were scooped up and taken to my local rescue centre, where they were fed puppy formula until they were big enough to be released.

'We didn't want to release the boy with his sisters,' said the centre worker. 'They're not the brightest, are they?'

The females go back to the garden where they were found and the male comes to live with me. He was the smallest of the three, weighing just 43g, about the same as a small egg or two tablespoons of butter. He weighs over 700g now (two cans of pop or a loaf of bread), and with the recent warm, wet weather, the gardens are having a second, pseudo spring. The lawns are lush and green, the trees and shrubs are putting on new growth, there are caterpillars and beetles breathing a sigh of relief after the long hard summer. It's unseasonably, scarily mild but if you're a young hog needing to cut your teeth on the big wide world before settling down to hibernate, it's pretty perfect.

I call him Tiny, even though he isn't anymore. I scoop him into gloved hands and whisper a gentle 'Welcome' before placing him in front of the entrance to the hedgehog box. I have been taught to do this – never place a hedgehog in a box but at the entrance hole to it, so they can enter of their own accord. Sometimes it can take half an hour before they go in, but they are nocturnal mammals and they will always seek darkness over light, or so I have always been told. Tiny won't go in. I stand with him for 30 minutes and he refuses to budge. I wonder if the box smells of bigger, scarier hog or if, as a rescue, he's not as nocturnal as he perhaps should be. I have released many hogs into this garden and none has behaved like this. I head indoors and stand at the upstairs window, instead, to see how he gets on.

Tiny has absolutely no intention of going in the box. As soon as I leave he starts exploring. He sniffs all around the edge of the box, around the wider vicinity of the box, and tries to climb on to the box. I stay watching him; it seems irresponsible not to. Suddenly he rolls on to his back and starts self-anointing, a process in which hedgehogs salivate and lick the saliva on to their spines, perhaps as a way of familiarising themselves with the scent of whatever they're in contact with (no one really knows). They mostly do this when encountering new things, of which everything is right now. Imagine being Tiny, found the size of an egg on your first foray out of the nest and then raised in captivity with your siblings. Then, suddenly, there's a huge world to explore, starting with a New Box. Little teenaged Tiny, finally set free. Anything is possible.

Except he should be sleeping.

He shuns the box I prepared for him and, instead, enters the box opposite, which doesn't have a resident but which I haven't cleaned out and filled with fresh straw (there is old straw). I wait for five minutes and he doesn't come out. I wonder if the other box is more homely to him, smells more of sleeping, safe hedgehog. I wait another five minutes and he still doesn't come out. He's settled then, finally, nearly an hour after I brought him home. I relax a little and get back to my work.

Later, Emma comes home with Tos. Tos asks to go outside and I check for signs of Tiny first, before letting her. She runs out, as she always does, to the end of the garden, but stops in her tracks as she picks up Tiny's scent, and does a big sniffy U-turn to the boxes. Like Tiny, Tosca sniffs and sniffs, taking in messages I couldn't begin to imagine. 'Yes, we have a new hedgehog,' I tell her. 'You done? Come on now.' She reluctantly leaves the boxes, then continues with her existing mission of Seeing-Who -Has-Been-In-My-Garden-Since-I-Was-Last-Here, growling at the two exits to ward off any would-be intruders, and doing a wee. Eventually, she comes to a stop next to the compost bin and sits down, giving me what I can only describe as a withering look.

'What?'

[Hard stare]

'What? Do you want to show me something?'

If Tosca could talk I think she would tell me how sick she is of me bringing new animals into the garden. How much she hates the foxes, how annoying the squirrels are, how those stinky little spiky things are the bane of her life and how dare I make homes for them and feed them. How the newest spiky thing is sleeping under the pallet that the compost bin sits on.

'I've had enough,' say her eyes. 'I've had enough but you should know the thing you think is in the box is not in the box. It's here.'

I get on my hands and knees and use a torch to look under the pallet, and sure enough there's Tiny, fast asleep. It's a mild, dry day so I'm not overly concerned he's curled up with no bedding, but it's no place, really, for a hedgehog. I thank Tos but lock her inside and retrieve a sturdy plant pot and fresh straw from the shed – if Tiny decides to make this his den he must at least have the means to make it comfortable. I set up the trail camera in front of the compost bin and head inside.

Tiny is free now, and he's a wild animal. If he wants to sleep under a pallet he's perfectly within his rights to do so. There are some rescue centres that insist on a so-called 'soft release', whereby you release the hog into a box within a cage (I have a rabbit run), so they can familiarise themselves with their surroundings for a few days before going into the wide world proper. I have done this before, but prefer not to, and most rescues these days choose to just let them go. There are studies that suggest this method is less stressful, at least for the hog, although not the human watching them having a party through a window.

I wonder if a soft release would have been better for Tiny as it would have stopped his excited wanderings, but it's too late now. He's not where I intended him to be but he's wild and he's asleep during the day, as hedgehogs should be. This is enough. He weighs 700g and will no doubt find the dish of kitten biscuits on his adventures around the garden tonight. He's a young, excitable thing, he'll be OK.

Later, I check the trail camera and it tells me Tiny continued his adventures. He woke from his slumber beneath the pallet and headed back to the box (no, not the one I prepared for him). He found the kitten biscuits. Over the next few days, I see that he is using the garden as his base but adventuring down the alley and hopefully into other gardens. This is good news, he's settled in well.

Emma comes home, shouting, 'Where are you? I have something to tell you!'

I head downstairs and she tells me she's just bumped into our dog-walking friend Vicki, whose kids Stan and Minnie have just seen a hedgehog in the park.

'They thought you should know,' she says.

It's dusk. 'When did they see it?' I ask.

'Just now.'

'What was it doing?'

'It was sitting beneath the zip wire in the children's play area,' she replies. 'Are you not excited? They saw a hedgehog and thought to tell you!'

But it's dusk, which is neither day nor night. And it's autumn, which is when food starts to become scarce. And it was… sitting beneath the zip wire? A hedgehog out during the day at this time of year is in trouble. A hedgehog just sitting there is… odd. It's Friday. We have beers and a takeaway to order, catching up to do. I find a box and a pair of gloves and head out into the night.

I enter the play area and walk around with my box. There are teenagers and dog walkers in the distance, but no one I could ask about the whereabouts of a hungry hedgehog. It's no longer beneath the zip wire. It's not in the play area at all, and it's too dark to go venturing into the wooded area. I search the whole park and find nothing. I go home and post in my hedgehog group: 'Please look out for any hedgehogs out during the day or at dusk.' I open beer, I order a takeaway, I have my Friday.

The next day I bump into Stan and Minnie, who tell me it was not only sitting beneath the zip wire but that it had its nose in a packet of crisps.

'How big was it?' I ask.

'Small,' says Stan.

'Medium,' says Minnie.

'And it was eating crisps?'

'Skips! Do hedgehogs eat Skips then?'

'Erm…'

I ask them to keep an eye out when they're next in the children's play area, and I spend the next few evenings patrolling the park with Tosca. If anyone knows where a hedgehog is, it's Tosca. It's probably fine, dusk is dusk and many hogs do come out as soon as night falls. I just worry about the small ones, and the ones that feel the need to nose through a packet of Skips. I'm worried it might be my excitable little Tiny.

I wake early and take Tos to our favourite patch of the Downs. By the end of the road she knows where she's going; we've walked past the park and we haven't crossed to go up to the beach. As soon as she knows where she's going she tries to drag me there, as if I don't also know where we're headed.

'Tosca!' We fight our way to the first patch of green space.

I let her off the lead when we get to the playing field at the supermarket, and throw treats into the leaf litter. She sniffs in circles, then zones in on the scent with zig zags, her snout working overtime, close to the ground. When she gets really close she snuffles like a pig until she finds her quarry – the tiniest plant-based 'W' – and snaffles it up.

The path is gorgeous at this time of year. At some point someone planted masses of broad-leaved cockspur (*Crataegus prunifolia*) and their bright red berries shine like beacons against bright yellow foliage. I laugh at pigeons gobbling them up and marvel at the beauty of what is, essentially, municipal planting at the edge of a supermarket car park. There's a chiffchaff *hweet-hweeting* in every tree, the occasional *chak-chak-chak* of fieldfares. A cold blue sky. It's all so beautiful.

The berry-laden path takes us round the back of the supermarket, to a patch of scrub known as Benfield Valley that's at risk of 'development'. This smallish patch of land used to belong to the supermarket chain but was, ironically, gifted to the council on the proviso that it would be for the community to enjoy indefinitely. Word on the street says one of the previous councils sold the land lease to a property developer, and now planning permission has been granted for a new housing estate. I wonder if some of the same councillors who sold the land are now fighting to save it, either trying to make up for what they've done or knowing the quest is futile but using the debate to score points against the opposition? Politics is a dirty game.

This bit of land gifted to the community was probably a bit underwhelming initially. But over the years, trees have grown – mainly hawthorns, ash and sallows, complementing thickets of long grass and banks of thistles, teasels and other wildflowers. In spring we walk among clouds of hawthorn blossom and now, of course, there are berries. There's a song thrush here that sings his heart out from the top of a tree. There are chiffchaffs and whitethroats in summer. This little patch of land behind a supermarket is actually an important stop-off for migrating birds as they hit land after journeying here from Africa – a stepping stone to wilder parts. I don't come here at night but it's the perfect scrubby habitat for hedgehogs to make a home, for bats and dormice and other endangered species to carve out an existence in an otherwise completely urban setting. Bookended as it is by the Old Shoreham Road and the A27, with the slip road from one to the other running to one side, I find it amazing that so much lives here. Traffic roars while the song thrush sings. Lorries thunder while butterflies feed. Dogs play here, people see nature they would otherwise have to travel to find. Isn't that worth something? And yet most people, and most councils, view scrub as wasteland, comprising thickets or 'bushes' in a great tangled mess. Ancient woodland it ain't, nor does it have the time-honoured romanticism of a wildflower meadow. But it's absolutely brilliant for wildlife. It's a rare and much undervalued habitat, certainly the only bit I know of within walking distance of my house. Scientists suggest more than 450 rare and threatened species of plant, insect and bird are associated with scrub, although it's unlikely that many of them will be here. But there are plenty of the commoner things. Commoner things that have been squeezed out of the city because they need a wilder land. And all of them, all of them, will be bulldozed.

Residents have formed a group to try to stop the development. They've organised litter picks and nature days to show the world how much they care about this little patch of scrub, organised protests and walks with MPs and councillors. Some councillors have voted to build on it without ever having seen it, without knowing its value to people and wildlife. It's a green lung of the city, it's a rare and precious habitat. Yet, apparently, it's not even worth looking at before signing it away.

I joined the group for a protest outside the town hall when the council was making its final decision on whether or not to build on it. Around 50 people turned up, all with banners depicting butterflies and bees, birds, green space, nature. We spoke to councillors as they entered the building, begged them not to sign our scrub away. 'There are nicer places,' said one. 'There are nicer places than Benfield Valley.'

Brighton is a growing city with a small amount of land to grow into – we can't build on the Downs. So small green spaces, which mean so much to its residents, are constantly under threat. We need to build more houses, say the councillors, and they must go somewhere. Yet a report sent to the council showed that some 3,000 properties across the city were unoccupied, with a large proportion used as second homes or Airbnbs, while a government report suggests that one in every 37 homes across Brighton and Hove lies empty. But, sure, we need to bulldoze homes for wildlife to build more houses for people, who may or may not actually live in them. Sure we do.

We cross the road, before starting the climb into the Downs proper. I tune in, instantly, to yellowhammers and corn buntings as the sound of cars, of humans, fades. We climb further, up a steep path at the edge of a field of corn stubble, skylarks yo-yo-ing through the autumn sky.

We have perfected this walk to avoid golf courses (Tosca is scared of golf buggies) and farm animals (Tosca is scared of cows and sheep). We stick to the path, always. We reach the top of the hill where, for less than a mile, we hear no traffic at all. I relax into the sound of the countryside, of birds and wind and the crunching of chalk underfoot. Little pants from the dog. I stop to look at yellowhammers through my binoculars and she woofs impatiently. 'Stop your whingeing,' I reply. I am happy here. Sometimes my peace is ruined by golfers, lawnmowers and young lads racing around on quad bikes, but not today. It's just us and the birds today. Us and the birds and the fungi and the berries and occasionally other dogs, some of which Tosca is also scared of.

We loop back, past Benfield Hill Nature Reserve, past golf courses and back over the A27, down to threatened land and back through the supermarket car park. The roads and car dealerships are still here, the traffic louder now it's later. I wonder will we ever stop building? Will we ever learn? The fight to save Benfield isn't quite over yet and the dog and I will continue our walks there. But this land is tainted, there's an air of lost hope. At home I check the hedgehog bowl to see if the biscuits have been taken. I hope the new residents of Benfield Valley housing estate will do the same.

Batman hoverfly, *Myathropa florea*

Myathropa florea is known as the Batman hoverfly because it has a mark on its thorax that looks like the Batman logo. It's a common species, flying from May to October, and is often found in gardens, where it hangs around compost bins and drains, or the stinky comfrey solution you're making as an organic liquid feed for your tomatoes. I think it's beautiful, all fresh yellow abdominal bands with black anchor-like markings, a yellow face and its whole body is covered in fine yellow hairs. It has quite a high-pitched buzz and always joins me when I open the compost heap or turn my organic comfrey solution. Why? Because it wants to make more Batman hoverflies.

Most gardeners think of hoverflies as aphid eaters: the adults eat pollen and nectar but, after mating, the female lays eggs on aphid colonies and her larvae eat aphids. Hoverflies are therefore considered a gardener's friend, as 'natural pest control'. But only around 40 per cent of British hoverflies lay their eggs on aphid colonies; others lay eggs on plants, in rotting wood, in bee or wasp nests or the sap of trees, while some prefer mud or stagnant water. *Myathropa florea* is in this last category, but she's quite adaptable. She will lay eggs in stagnant water or mud but also my compost bin, if given half a chance. Known, affectionately, as 'rat-tailed maggots', her larvae are 'detritivores', feeding on bacteria from the decaying organic matter in the water or mud they have been laid in. (The 'tail' is actually a breathing tube, which they use like a snorkel.)

The female Batman hoverfly is not alone in her egg-laying choices; many other species also breed in stagnant water and mud, including the common drone fly (*Eristalis tenax*), the tapered drone fly (*Eristalis pertinax*), the footballer hoverfly (*Helophilus pendulus*) and the thick-legged hoverfly (*Syritta pipiens*). These are all common species that are regularly found in gardens but there are rarer ones, too, which lay eggs in puddles of water in the roots or forks of trees where leaves and other debris accumulate. These are (again, affectionately) called 'rot holes'. Rot holes of rat-tailed maggots.

Hoverflies that lay eggs in mud and stagnant water are vulnerable to climate change because mud and small bodies of water dry out quickly in a drought. Next time you're walking in woodland have a look at holes in tree roots and at the fork of two branches – are they holding water? If not, where are the hoverflies breeding? Is the ground moist or cracked? Has is rained lately? Where are the hoverflies?

Luckily, some species, like *Myathropa florea*, are adaptable; that's why they use gardens in the first place, they have adapted to live alongside us. That's why the females buzz around me as I'm sieving or turning compost, that's why I often lose my comfrey solution, because a hoverfly has sneaked in and laid eggs and I can't drain the liquid now, they'll die! She'll be buzzing around you, too. You could give her a helping hand by leaving your compost bin open a fraction, so she can get in to lay her eggs. Or, even better, you could make her a Hoverfly Lagoon.

A Hoverfly Lagoon is a rot hole in a bucket, a pretty unappealing replica of a beautiful woodland habitat. It's easy to make: simply fill the bucket with grass clippings or leaves and then add water and sticks that reach the top so the hoverflies have something to land on when they lay eggs, and the larvae can climb out to pupate. Providing a layer of leaves or other plant material around the bucket will ensure the larvae have somewhere to go to pupate, but you could just let grass grow around it. You can make one using something as small as an old 5-litre (4-pint) plastic milk bottle but I like to go the whole hog and give them an old water butt to lay eggs in – it attracts hundreds and hundreds of the things. It can get quite stinky as the plant material rots down, so keep it at the end of your garden, but don't forget to top it up when the water level falls. Keep an eye out for your first Batman hoverfly. She will buzz around you, politely, and then get on with the business of making more Batman hoverflies. Whether she does or not is up to you.

November

It's raining again. I head out in the near-darkness of dawn and empty the water butts into the pond. Each one has a hosepipe connector on its tap, and I move from one to the other, connect it up, turn the tap and stand beneath the shed roof to watch the water stream out. As the water in the butts recedes, the trickles from the downpipes start up again as they immediately refill. I could listen to them all day.

I have a rain garden of sorts. A fully functioning one would not have a gardener running around in her pyjamas, turning taps and connecting hosepipes, but it would collect water in much the same way. Rain gardens are designed to hold water, with no need for drains to take it 'away' into rainwater drains or sewers. Plants are chosen to cope with being waterlogged for a couple of days, and rain is directed from sheds, greenhouses and house roofs into pools, which gradually recede as the water soaks into the earth. There are usually also green roofs to further slow the flow of water from sheds and other outbuildings, and a limited amount of hard surfaces like patios and paths, which enables more water to soak into the ground and prevent 'run-off', which can lead to flooding.

I have the big pool of water (the pond), I have minimal hard surfaces, and I have lots of plants with thirsty roots. But, when the water butts connected to the house become full, the rain is directed back down the downpipes into the drain. I could easily drill holes into the top of the butts and run hoses from them into the pond to take the excess, but I'm not sure I want pieces of hose as visible, permanent features of the garden. To bury a pipe from the house downpipe, I would need to dig up the patio. So I'm stuck, obsessively fiddling with water butts in my pyjamas, releasing water as they fill to prevent rain from being taken out of the garden. I quite like the process. I say hello to frogs, marvel at mushrooms, listen to birdsong. We don't often get out into the rain, so we miss things; I like the excuse to be out. I get wet, of course, but I like that. Besides, most of us don't have the money or inclination to install a fully functioning rain garden, but we might have water butts we can empty from time to time. We can all be weird little gardeners in our pyjamas.

We've had a lot of rain in recent weeks, but I'm still not over the drought. I think back to July, when the garden was so parched the plants had wrinkled leaves and I recycled the dog's bath water just to keep them alive. When I stopped using the dishwasher so I could hand-wash dishes and throw the water on to the lawn. I can't go through that again (I know I will have to). I want to hold on to as much water as I can, here, in the garden. So I keep every drop, savour every puddle. And when my tanks fill up, I release the water into the garden – sometimes into the pond, sometimes around the trees and little hedge at the back – so they can fill again, so the garden can be full again.

There are reasons beyond being obsessed with water and wanting to keep it as my friend. 'Surface run-off' is caused by too much water landing on too many hard surfaces. The water collects and runs down the nearest slope, where it gains energy and meets other water, more and more of it pooling together and flowing faster and faster downhill. Eventually it surges into drains that can then back up and cause flooding. Sewers become 'overwhelmed', and their contents are discharged into the sea by water companies, who claim they are doing so to prevent it from backing up into the streets. I live near a sewage outlet pipe and have lost count of how many times raw sewage has been discharged into the sea I swim in due to 'heavy rainfall'. I see it and I smell it; I watch lifeguards warn people against entering water full of human excrement. It's disgusting and I hate it.

Most houses have both rainwater drains and wastewater drains. The rainwater drains take rainwater directly to rivers and the sea, while wastewater drains take grey water, along with 'foul' or 'black' water from toilets, into sewers. In older houses, thanks to renovations and corner-cutting, these separate drains can have the wrong type of water flowing into them, with rainwater draining into sewers and grey water flowing into rivers and the sea. Even black water, from toilets, might not be headed for the sewers. Add to that water from roads, which ends up in the sewers, and water from driveways and paved front gardens, which is usually directed into the road and therefore the sewers, and you have a lot of rainwater entering the sewerage system. Roads plus people plus paved gardens equals more hard surfaces. Climate change means more moisture in the atmosphere and, therefore, heavier bouts of rain. Hard surfaces and climate change mean more flooding and – currently – more sewage in our seas. It doesn't have to, of course, but when you add privatisation into the equation, you soon realise where the money is that could have helped prevent these problems and see how we've ended up in the shit we're in (pardon the pun).

UK water companies were privatised in 1989. I don't understand why public services were ever allowed to be put into private hands because there will always be shareholders to direct profits to rather than the services themselves. The companies tell us they have poured billions into fixing leaking pipes and improving a system worthy of twenty-first-century levels of rainfall and excrement, but they are failing. When it rains, the systems can't cope and our rivers and seas end up full of shit. (There has been public outcry, of course, but our government voted to let this continue anyway, of course.)

I don't believe I am responsible for the shit that ends up in the sea. But I can do my own small thing to reduce the amount of rainwater that flows into sewers and the likelihood of sewage being discharged into the sea. Anyone with a garden can help slow the flow of water into drains and sewers. Anyone with a garden can help save our rivers and seas. And maybe, just maybe, if our gardens hold on to more water, they might cope better with drought. Their own little water tables might take longer to recede, the plants might remain hydrated for longer. And so the worms might continue to work the soil, the moths and butterflies might have plump leaves to lay their eggs on, and the birds might have caterpillars to eat. The ponds might take longer to dry out. Isn't that worth doing? For our sakes as gardeners, as well as those that live among us in our garden, such as the frogs and the birds and the bees, which all went hungry this summer?

It is. I am telling you, it is.

The ground is a sponge. Tree roots are a sponge, and ponds are a sponge. When rain falls, it lands on leaves and trickles slowly into the soil, where it gently seeps into the earth. A pond will fill gradually and then gently spill over the sides, percolating into the soil and plant roots around it. Plant and tree roots absorb water; lawns hold water, and water butts, bird baths and buckets store water. You might notice puddles on your lawn, but they disappear quickly. It might be soggy underfoot, but usually not for long. Our gardens are sponges. Let's use them.

I visit Dad and Ceals in Suffolk for a few days of walking, catching up and helping Dad on his allotment. They're not so good at walking long distances these days, and so I set off on mini adventures each morning before they get up, see what I can find and learn. The first day I head east to Southwold beach, cut along it and then up through the dunes, round the back of Dad's allotment and then home. It's nice to say hi to places I haven't been for a while. But I need more. I look at a map: why have I never explored the estuary?

On day two I set out at 7.30 a.m. I trample the damp, dark pavement as streetlights flick off and gulls return to the rooftops from the sea. I cross the road and head down a footpath along the side of a school and then get lost in the half-light among bracken and fences with huge KEEP OUT signs. I walk between chain-link fences for a while and then become cross; I am not here for chain-link fences! I return to where I started, make a right turn instead, look at the horizon for the estuary. There it is. Through the gate and on to a ridge above marshland, where longhorn cattle graze their breakfast and a lone barn owl seeks out the last of the night's prey. Barnacle geese fly in great, noisy skeins overhead, chaffinches scatter in the gloom, reeds rustle as the wind picks up. I don't know what I'm looking for. I don't have my binoculars. What's that? I think… I think I hear curlews.

Have I heard curlews? Could I have heard curlews? The most wondrous birds with the most beautiful, eerie calls, I have never seen them or heard them before. But I know them. I've watched videos of them. I am mildly in love with them without being acquainted with them. Mournful wading things with long, gently curved bills used for probing sand and moist soils for invertebrates. They nest on the ground, often in farmland, which rarely ends well for them. I have watched videos of curlew mothers flying in circles and crying as their chicks have been destroyed by farming machinery. I have donated to curlew conservation funds. This once-common bird is yet another victim of 'modern farming practices', of human expansion and disregard. And oh, its call! Its haunting call. If we ever really look at ourselves and see what we've done to the world I hope it's to the soundtrack of the curlew's call.

I head further towards the estuary, through mud trampled by cows' hooves. At the water's edge I look out to a flat expanse of sand and marshland, which I later discover is the perfect habitat for overwintering curlews. More geese. More flying things with different calls that I manage to record and send to a friend who tells me they are wigeon. More eerie calls that could be curlews. I need to know more about curlews. I need to be back at Dad's by 9.00 a.m. so I can shower and have breakfast before going to meet his friends. I set off, through mud, across the ridge, keeping one eye out for the barn owl, two ears out for curlews. I shower, eat breakfast, see Dad's friends then return, much later, to my room to rest for a few hours before heading out again to do a talk for Dad's allotment society. I return to bed, again, feeling exhausted.

I text nature friends about curlews, and read about overwintering versus nesting habitats, spring calls versus autumn and winter calls. My nature friends text back and tell me that, if they are curlews, they will make brief calls as they take off or come to land, that they call for longer during the breeding season. I tell them: 'Tomorrow I look for curlews!'

It's my last morning here and I wake at 5.30 a.m. It's now or never. It's dark and cold, it's raining and has been raining all night. I creep down to make tea as quietly as I can so I don't wake Dad and Ceals. I drink it in bed as rain pounds the windows. Of course it does. Should I just not go? I wait for half an hour, make another cup of tea. Eventually it eases. I head downstairs to find Dad in the kitchen. 'Did you find the binoculars?' he asks. He points at the door. I grin. 'You'll get wet,' he says. 'I will!' I reply. 'But that's OK.' I make my escape, 20 minutes before sunrise.

I am ill prepared; badly dressed in running shoes, tracksuit bottoms and a jacket made of recycled plastic bottles that is neither wind- nor waterproof. I cross the road and join the footpath that is now one long puddle, and splash my way through it as the wind whips the bracken against the chain-link fence. I turn right today. There's a blackbird, followed soon by two wrens, not remotely impressed by the figure splish-splashing clumsily towards them.

On to the ridge, where today there are few cows and no barn owl. I push on to the estuary, the only sounds are the rain tapping the hood of my jacket and the squelch of my shoes in the mud.

A sound muffled by my hood sounds like my phone is going off. I pull it down and catch the end of what I think is curlews. Two figures fly overhead with swooping wings, but fall quiet before I can confirm who they are. I keep my hood down so I don't miss them again and plough on to the estuary. The rain is horizontal and now whips my face and ears. One arm is completely soaked through. Through Dad's binoculars I can see a figure feeding in the mud. It has a long bill but is too far away to see it clearly. Curlew? Barnacle geese fly overhead again, plus lapwing and the wigeon I met yesterday. Curlews?

I walk on, to the estuary proper. I scan the muddy flats with binoculars. There are wading birds with long bills; I can just make them out in the half light. There are bubbling calls overhead. If I can't make out the curlews on the ground I can make them out in the sky. There are curlews, there are curlews! I wish I could stay longer. I wish my coat were waterproof, that my running shoes were wellies. I wish the curlews would make more calls. But no matter all of this. No matter because I met the most wonderful birds on the most awful of mornings. I can't wait to come back to see them again.

My favourite thing about the natural world is how it surprises me. How it can be one thing in one moment but something altogether different the next. How it's just there, getting on with itself, but if I spend just five minutes exploring it, it can change the fortune of my day. It can lift me, excite me, throw me and educate me. It can send me down a research rabbit hole where, for the next three days, Emma will ask what I'm doing and I'll say, 'I'm reading about black redstarts.'

The male black redstart is a gorgeous bird. A dunnock dressed in the finest velvet suit, his black face and chest graduating to a grey-white belly and an orange tail. Smart grey cap. He's exquisite and he knows it, the white patches on his wings like two fingers to anyone gawping at him. He's a silver fox, a dapper gent, he's debonair *and* sexy. And he turns up EVERYWHERE. How do I know this? Because I spent three days reading about them. Because I lifted binoculars to my eyes expecting to see a pied wagtail and—

Oh.

My.

GOD.

There's a black redstart on that roof.

It was a filming day. Filming days are busy and hectic but also involve lots of hanging around, which I take as a gift to look at the garden. I always find new species: the first yellow-faced bees in the bee hotel, the first aphid wasps, a funny-looking female damselfly that spent the whole day laying eggs in the pond and which I later learned was a *rufescens-obsoleta* form of the blue-tailed. Mining bees nesting in the lawn, a comma caterpillar under a hop leaf, the first ever ringlet butterfly. And today, as the cameraman got his cut-away shots of seed-bearing plants, I watched a bird gambolling about on the roofs of the houses opposite. I thought it was a pied wagtail, due to the slight wagging of his tail. But as I lifted the binoculars I found someone else entirely: he on someone's roof and me at my kitchen door, meeting for the first time. Hi! He continued to gambol about for a bit, circling roofs and hopping up and down the roof tiles. Sometimes he'd sit and stare out to sea (or so it seemed). I wasn't sure who he was at first but made a note to look up redstarts. I drew a picture: a child's drawing of a bird with a white patch on each of its wings and arrows pointing to 'dark face', 'long orange tail'.

'Are you going to post that on Twitter?' asks Blake, the director, laughing.

'No, I'm going to find out on my own,' I reply petulantly. And I do, the next time Ed the cameraman needs to film cut-aways I look up redstarts, and I find my silver fox.

The black redstart, *Phoenicurus ochruros*, is a rare bird in the UK, with less than 100 breeding pairs. It can be found all year round in some parts, including London and other cities, brownfield sites and industrial areas, but there are 'passage migrants' in autumn and spring, which can turn up anywhere, especially on the coast. Well, here we are.

They traditionally nest in rocky outcrops but have adapted to urban areas astonishingly well. They need crags or holes in buildings to nest in, and rocky or stony, sparsely vegetated ground on which to find their invertebrate food. Populations boomed in London after the Second World War as they moved in to bomb sites, which earned them the nickname of the 'bomb-site bird', a veritable Mother Courage profiteering from war. Now they nest on green or rubble roofs high above the city, but also down the road from me, on the cliffs in Hastings, where the first record of them breeding in Britain was made in 1923.

They sing a hurried warble, followed by a scrunching sound that some suggest is like a bag of marbles being shaken, and then finish with a burst of ringing notes. They feed on insects and their larvae, but also earthworms and small snails. They take fruit and berries in autumn. The female is not quite as sharply dressed as the male, a duller brown-grey with a rusty rump and tail. But still gorgeous.

After mating, the female builds a cup-shaped nest of grass and moss on a ledge or a crack in a wall, which she lines with wool, feathers and hair. She incubates up to six eggs alone but both parents feed the chicks. The black redstart is one of the few species that relies on brownfield sites and is at risk from development of these areas, which is why green and rubble roofs can offer them a lifeline. Every building in every city should have a green or rubble roof. I want to shout this from the rooftops. I want there to be more black redstarts. Everyone would, if they just stopped for a moment and spent five minutes exploring the natural world. Why wouldn't you want more black redstarts?

My silver fox will be on his way to the Mediterranean for winter, perhaps from northern Europe. It's unlikely that he'll return with a mate, although the nearby port and sparsely vegetated, stony beach could pass for an ideal habitat. I have cracks in my walls, little black redstart. I have insects and spiders. I have a heart that is full of you and your gambolling ways. For you, I will throw stones on my neighbour's flat roof.

I lie on the sofa with tea and biscuits and an unopened book, watching birds feast on sunflower hearts on the other side of the window. It's a drizzly Sunday and I have no urge to be outside but I like looking at it. I like being snuggled and warm while the outside entertains me. I like being in and out at the same time.

I watch house sparrows, mostly. Occasionally a robin will turn up or a blue tit or even a wren (the wren picks up spills from the tray). But mostly, it's house sparrows. There are so few songbirds in these parts.

I feed the birds but am conflicted about it. Ultimately, I wish I didn't have to. I wish there were enough habitats and insects for them to feed themselves in mine and neighbouring gardens. I wish climate change wasn't dealing almost constant blows of too-hot or too-cold, too-wet or too-dry weather. I wish my Twitter feed wasn't full of images of starving chicks in spring.

But it is, and so I'm compelled to feed the birds.

The production and sale of bird food is a multi-million-pound industry. The food is grown on land that would once have been wild – which habitats have been lost to produce it, and which species are suffering as a result? It's usually grown using pesticides, which harm the land and wildlife where it's grown, but then may also harm the birds that eat it (is bird food ever tested for pesticide residues?). It's flown halfway across the world to fill single-use plastic packets we mostly buy in the supermarket to compensate for a lack of insects in our gardens. Why is there a lack of insects in our gardens? Because we mow, chop, weed, spray. We literally empty our gardens of natural food and replace it with food grown on land elsewhere – land presumably emptied of its own natural food to do so.

There's more: the filling of bird feeders brings greater numbers of birds into smaller spaces and so bird diseases are passed between species that wouldn't usually interact with each other. Trichomonosis was passed from pigeons to finches and is responsible for the huge crash in greenfinch and chaffinch numbers in recent years. Avian pox virus affects tits, dunnocks and pigeons. Then there are leg lesions, feather abnormalities, 'general malaise' caused by salmonella. All of these diseases are spread at bird feeders and bird baths. Keeping these vessels spotlessly clean will help prevent the spread of disease but what if we didn't use them? What if we all focused on creating more natural habitats and used supplementary food only when natural food was in short supply? I love watching birds on my feeders but not as much as I love watching chiffchaffs pick aphids off my roses, or blackbirds gobbling my rowan berries. I love watching house sparrows strip grasses of their seeds, goldfinches taking knapweed seed. I laugh at gulls dancing on the lawn to lure worms to the surface.

There's more still: recent studies have shown that feeding birds in rural and suburban areas gives advantages to more common birds over rarer ones. For example, a review of the impacts of bird feeding (in the journal *Biological Conservation*) by Jack Shutt and Alex Lees at Manchester Metropolitan University linked burgeoning populations of dominant garden and woodland birds with declines in subordinate woodland species. The dominant birds, with their bellies full of peanuts and suet, steal nest sites and monopolise food resources over the more timid species, which are less likely to visit feeders. Great tit numbers have increased by 40 per cent in 25 years. In the same timeframe the marsh tit has declined by 50 per cent.

The sparrows bring their fledglings to my feeders every year and I watch them fill gaping mouths with sunflower hearts, often from the comfort of my sofa. They're doing well, there seem to be more of them each year although I'll have no way of knowing how they fared during this year's drought. House sparrows mostly feed aphids to their chicks, which puts them at an advantage over tits and other species, which prefer caterpillars, which tend to struggle in hot weather. There have been good numbers of aphids this year.

Until 2022, Ukraine was the largest global producer of sunflower seed, but sunflowers are grown all over the world, with countries such as Russia, Argentina, Romania and China producing the largest crops. Sunflowers and other seed-producing plants are, of course, grown for a variety of uses, but what of the insects grown to add to suet mixes? And the cows used to make that suet, where did they live? Did they have a nice life? Did they breathe fresh air and feel grass beneath their feet? Where are the mealworm factories?

I miss the hum and buzz of insect life. I miss seeing clouds of insects, feeling the sigh of flying things scatter as

I brush past the plant they're resting or feeding on. This year has been particularly bad and there may be better ones. But, on the whole, things are only going to get worse. Global food supplies are faltering and, with them, so will supplies of bird food. We all need to do more for birds at home.

I have long grass and native plants, berrying shrubs, seeds. I water the ground so the worms don't retreat quite so far beneath the soil surface. I keep my pond topped up. Next year, I'll grow sunflowers. Lots of them, a whole pack's-worth if I can. If I can grow my own food to harvest and store for use later that would be better than relying on global food industries, wouldn't it? I realise not everyone can do that. I can't promise I won't buy another packet of sunflower hearts or mealworms, that I won't buy fat balls at the sight of desperate birds in desperate weather, but I can try. That's all we can do, isn't it?

Each winter a robin comes to the garden, a gentle soul that seems at home here among the house sparrows and starlings, the seagulls and the occasional wren, tit and blackbird. I see him only in winter; in summer there are other robins but they are scarce and spend little time in the garden, and never use the hanging bird feeders. This one is always here and has crafted the art of taking sunflower hearts from the seed hopper, balancing on little perches and dashing back to the climbers to eat his quarry.

Robins are a migratory species. Most people think the robin in their garden is the same individual all year round but many hold their territories in summer only, flying south for winter. 'South' could be anywhere: Leeds if your summer residence is Edinburgh; Brighton if you're from

Birmingham. Some fly to the UK from Scandinavia or fly from the UK to overwinter in France. Never underestimate your individual robin, or the individuals you think are your one robin.

This one spends every winter in and around my garden. He sings his song, eats sunflower hearts and bathes and drinks in my bird baths and pond. When I stand in the kitchen looking out on to the garden I know he's there, even if I can't see him. He will be on the ground beneath my tiny hedge or in next door's wisteria, waiting for the perfect moment to nip out and grab a sunflower heart. He also seems to like perching from the rowan tree and I hope he arrives in time to eat some of its berries before the blackbird and starlings gobble them all (I make a note to keep an eye out).

On the night camera I watch him drink and bathe in the pond at dusk, his big eyes enabling him to stay out later than other species. I don't know where he sleeps; one evening I was outside after dark and he arrived, suddenly, on the fence, his little feet landing with a scratch. I stood still and watched him for a moment before he flew off again, to who-knows-where.

I always miss him when he leaves, there's no one to fill his boots when he's gone. There's a pair somewhere in the neighbourhood but I don't think they have much breeding success so I rarely see them in what must be a large and lonely territory. Neighbours have told me robins have nested with them a few times but their nests have always been predated by magpies. Others have told me about the squirrels that got their blackbirds and the cats that took their goldfinches. On top of predation there's less invertebrate food (caterpillars and insects), thanks to increasing amounts of paving and plastic and, these days, any food that is here is often destroyed by too-dry, too-cold, too-hot, too-windy springs that neither the invertebrates nor the birds have evolved to deal with.

So the landscape here isn't good enough for the robins, the weather isn't good enough for the robins and the ratio of predator to prey seems to put the robins at a disadvantage. The same goes for the blackbirds, goldfinches, tits and wrens, all of whom I see so little of in the garden.

The predators do well. That's the problem with compromised habitats: the clever, adaptable species will be clever and adapt. Domestic cats are fed at home, but crows and magpies have a varied diet that includes food scraps thrown away by people, and crows won't think twice about ripping open a bin bag to reach food to feed their young. In dry springs they manage because they take food from bins and soak it in water (often my pond) so their nestlings have moist food to eat. It's probably not very nutritious – white bread and pastry, crab sticks, bits of fried chicken from the high street – but it appears to be enough to get their chicks through, while other species struggle. I've seen crows swoop in to steal treats from dogs in the park, and raid next door's solar panels for pigeon chicks that were nesting beneath them. Numbers of songbirds are decreasing while numbers of predators are increasing. So the predators are outcompeting but also eating the songbirds. What hope do they have?

Starlings and house sparrows do OK because they nest in holes in our houses, of which there still seem to be plenty (in other areas they're not so lucky). But anything that nests in a hedge, tree or wooden bird box seems to be at a disadvantage, both here and in all urban areas. Which is yet another reason why we all need to work hard to make these areas wilder.

Common wasp, *Vespula vulgaris*

The common wasp is one of the most misunderstood insects on the planet. Like honeybees and bumblebees, it's a social insect, forming massive colonies run by a queen in which hundreds of sterile female workers gather food for their siblings as the queen lays more eggs. Bees are vegetarian and eat pollen and nectar, but wasps are carnivorous and eat caterpillars, aphids, thrips and other insect 'pests'. If it were not for wasps, the leaf munchers would eat all the leaves, including crops we need for food. No one notices wasps from April – when they emerge from hibernation – to August – when they become annoying – because they are so busy patrolling our plants for invertebrates to return to the nest. It's when there is no one to take food back to that we start to notice them. Why?

Common wasp nests are annual. The queen creates her nest in spring and starts laying eggs, and the nest grows and grows throughout summer. Towards the end of summer, she stops laying eggs and the nest begins to die down. The workers, who have been collecting insects to feed their siblings, have less and less to do.

There's more: during spring and summer, as the workers feed their siblings with grubs, the grubs discharge a sugary solution, which the workers eat. The solution is a reward for their work but, as they become redundant, the sugary treat dries up. So they seek out sugar elsewhere: your beer, your open jar of jam, your ice cream. They also take nectar from flowers (they are efficient pollinators), but so too will they find grapevines and plum trees and can destroy whole crops. Then, when the fruit falls and ferments, the wasps eat it, and some suggest they get 'drunk'. Along comes the human, flapping the wasp away – of course, you are a huge threat.

Towards the end of the season, the queen starts laying the eggs of daughter queens. Like social bees (bumblebees), these wasps mate before entering hibernation. Research has shown that they don't hibernate alone – they carry yeasts in their abdomen. Yeasts present in the air throughout summer disappear in autumn and reappear in spring; it's one of the reasons why your sourdough loaf takes longer to rise in winter. For years, scientists couldn't understand how the yeasts would disappear as temperatures dipped and reappear when they rose again. But now they know: yeasts sleep and wake with the wasps. That we have bread, wine, beer and all other things made using yeasts is partly due to wasps.

To garden for the common wasp is to give it space. Let it live! They make paper nests in sheds, lofts and underground. If you can, give a nest a wide berth throughout summer or remove it early in the season so the queen can find another spot to start again. Wear light clothes and stand still if one flies around you. Leave wasp nests in your roof, keep your eyes peeled in early summer for wasps gathering caterpillars and aphids from your plants, and marvel at how hard they work. Then, as the season fades, let them have a bit of jam. Go on, it's a nice thing to do, a kind thing, and it might just save your plums.

December

I greet the first frost, like the first rains after the drought, with the biggest, happiest grin. It's absolutely perfect: crisp and clear, with no biting wind to dampen the newness of it.

I head out in it, to the gym, at 6.30 a.m. It's still dark, with a nip in the air I've felt for the first time today. I'm wearing gym leggings and ankle socks, but a jumper, coat and hat for warmth. I stride into the beginnings of a bright orange sun. I am cheerful; it's cheering when the weather behaves as it should.

People always say, 'What climate change?' when the weather behaves as it should. As if to say 'See? No problem! The world isn't ending. Carry on!'

I reserve the very hardest stares for these occasions, because it is always the same people who failed to notice that it didn't rain for the entire month of April, who don't see the vanishing bees, the hungry hedgehogs, the caterpillars clinging to life on shrivelled plants. They notice only the weather that affects them – and here, now, it's inconveniently cold. Of course, they love the milder winters that climate change has so far brought us. To them, this cold snap isn't evidence of a further changing climate but of a return to normal: cold. And they don't like being cold.

When I can, I tell these people about the Gulf Stream, and how its collapse will trigger longer, colder winters closer to those of Siberia than southern Europe. But the fact that we don't know when this will happen makes it an empty threat. At least to them. 'But not in our lifetime,' they say. 'Just be present,' they say. 'I wish I could,' I say.

I look at weather maps posted by meteorologists on Twitter. I see that northern Europe is freezing while southern Europe is extremely warm. Is that weather behaving as it should? An invisible line crosses France and Germany; to the north of it are Arctic winds and freezing temperatures, to the south it's practically summer. I read about subtropical depressions, the North Atlantic Oscillation, a wind named Sirocco. I learn about blocking patterns that mean certain weather conditions remain stuck for weeks on end. Or do I? It's all so complicated. How do I know what's 'climate' and what's just plain old 'weather'? Is any of this normal?

What I do know is that the first frosts should be in November, not December. That they knock plants back, stop them flowering and hasten leaf fall. They 'stratify' seeds, a necessary process for some species, without which they wouldn't germinate in spring. They kill 'pests' like slugs and snails, they break up clay soils, they ensure hibernating species remain hibernating. The first frosts signal the beginnings of autumn, not winter. The beginnings of a pause of growth, of death before rebirth. Everything starts to shrink back. In the garden in winter, I watch plants rot into themselves, gradually turning into skeletal stems and seedheads, which new growth supercedes in spring. Yet every year they remain intact for that little bit longer.

If frost puts the earth to sleep, and it doesn't get that sleep, does it become tired? Does the ground need sleep like other living things? A winter reset? If bumblebees and hedgehogs wake from hibernation they can waste energy in search of food, which puts them at risk of starvation. Does the land work in the same way? Do plants? I think of those still flowering in my garden: the shrub rose, the perennial wallflower, the sowthistle, the cranesbill geraniums and geums. Are they exhausted? Do they need a rest? I'm grateful they're getting it, whether they need it or not.

And what of those that aren't used to frost? I realise I have forgotten about my lemon tree. Normally it spends winter indoors, but now it's butted up against the south-facing wall, which is warm to the touch from winter sun. I decide it's better off where it is but it's a gamble, with temperatures so low and predicted to sink lower with no end in sight. I gather bits of fleece from the shed and wrap them around the pot to protect the rootball – if the plant loses a few leaves then so be it but if the rootball freezes it will die. I turn the pot around so more of the crown is close to the warm wall.

It remains bitterly cold for a week, each day getting harder and harder to bear. I walk to the gym for the first few days and then fall ill and stop going altogether. I allow myself a modest amount of central heating, and wear my tank suit (designed to keep you warm in a tank), woolly hat and gloves around the house. I obsess over closed doors and gaps in curtains, the electric blanket and hot-water bottles.

Baked potatoes and beans. I try not to look at the smart meter. A wind picks up and the beautiful freshness of the first few days of frost are gone, it's just horribly, bone-chillingly cold.

Everything becomes a struggle: for Emma, who works in a draughty warehouse, for me and Tosca on our walks, for the birds. I pick up a routine I'd forgotten about for years: each morning I break ice on the bird baths and top them up with fresh water. I scatter seeds on the lawn and in the borders. I stand in the kitchen, sometimes busying myself with emptying the dishwasher or making tea, and watch the birds descend: the little robin that steals in from the edges to take a sip of water, the herring gulls that stamp about on the shed roof, the chattering starlings, the crows that shoo them away. Then the pigeons, always a few pigeons. And finally, when all is quiet again, the blackbird and wren come to finish off what's left.

The sparrows, of course, have their hanging feeders. I have two up but I'll take them down in late spring. I used to feed birds all year round but the threat of diseases now is so great I'd rather not be part of it. There are berries and seeds on plants that will only provide more berries and seeds as they grow. There are tufts of long grass sheltering caterpillars that will come out for a feed on mild days. There are fallen leaves sheltering a host of invertebrates that the birds will find as they pick through them, again when it's milder. But, for now, there are scatterings of seed and a full and fresh bird bath, sustenance for all.

We have snow and ice, ground temperatures of -8°C, and the Met Office confirms we have had the coldest day in the UK for 12 years – all that within a week of that first, precious frost. I'm still grateful for it, but it's anything but normal.

A member of my hedgehog group messages me on Facebook to tell me the remains of a hedgehog have been found in the children's play area of the park. My heart sinks. It must be the hog that was found with its nose in the empty bag of Skips, the hog I searched for and didn't find. I feel responsible, I should have searched harder. I meant to go and leave kitten biscuits for it in the undergrowth but I never got around to it. I have dead hedgehog blood on my hands.

It's the worst possible timing for such grief – I have just got off the train at Mum's and am walking up the path to her house. The woman tells me she's called the council to have it taken away.

Hurriedly, I text Emma:

'Dead hog in the park.'

'In the kids area… please will you get it?'

There's a pause, for a fraction of a second too long. Then typing:

'Where?'

'And put it where?'

I ask her to leave it in the shed. It's so cold nothing will happen to it before I return. I greet Mum, drink tea, swap Christmas cards, show her photos of Tosca.

In the time it takes me to drink one cup of tea and politely decline an invitation to join Mum and Pete for the crossword, Emma has been to the park and not found the hedgehog. She leaves me voice notes that I don't hear until it's too late:

'Where exactly is it?'

'It's cold…there are children still playing.'

'I feel like a weirdo.'

In the next message she tells me she's befriended the parents of the playing children and that four adults have scoured the play area for the hedgehog's remains and found nothing.

'Perhaps someone put it in the bin,' she suggests, and I resist the urge to ask her to search the bins.

'Perhaps someone dumped it in a corner so it didn't upset the kids.'

I wanted to see it because I wanted to know if it was Tiny, the hog I released into the garden just two months ago. He was this year's baby, brought up in a rescue centre, and knew little about the dangers of life. A little adventurer, it would be just like Tiny to have set up home in the park and forgotten how to get back to my garden, where the bowl of kitten biscuits remains topped up. It would be just like him to come out at dusk and nose through an empty packet of Skips in front of perplexed schoolchildren. It would be just like him, he who rejected the straw-filled box I prepared for him and settled under the pallet beneath the damp compost bin, to be caught out, hungry and cold, in the children's play area of the park. And, I don't know, if I could just see him, maybe I could identify him. Maybe I could identify the cause of death, or perhaps there would be something that would suggest it was another hog, Captain Prickles or Branston Prickle, maybe? One of my hogs. One that's fed in my garden, slept and mated there, a hog that I have seen and known. A hog that deserves more than being collected for the council incinerator.

The woman sends me photos of the remains and they are just that. I see why Emma and her four new friends didn't find it. 'It looked just like a pile of leaves,' the woman's message says. It's a dried out 'pelt' of skin and spikes, picked clean by crows. Is it Tiny or the hog that was hungry for Skips? Or someone else entirely? I'll never know but I expect it has been dead for a while and was brought out into the open by rats in summer, when conditions were so dry there was no choice but to pick at long-dead things for sustenance. I also suspect it had been in the park for some time before being noticed.

I relax into being at home. Mum wants to show me her garden. When she moved here eight years ago her garden was almost completely paved, with a miserable thin strip of bare soil around the edge. Over the years she's been taking up bricks to widen the strip to make a border, and every time I visit she shows me more of what she's done. 'I have a n-n-n-n-nice new border in front of the sun room,' she says proudly. She's planted this with a Japanese maple, mahonia and other bits and pieces she's 'rescued' from the closed-down garden centre. She has a small central area in which she's planted other bits and she's removed one more brick from all around the original tiny border, which means she can plant with more depth, at a range of different heights, colours and leaf textures 'like they do in the books.'

I'm reminded of when she had her haemorrhage, that I arrived in the middle of the night to an empty house with plates and mugs used by her, unwashed, a recipe scrawled on notepaper on the coffee table. That I slept in her bed, badly, and in the morning I woke to the most amazing dawn chorus, and that the first thing I did was walk into the garden. That it was April and her espalier fruit trees, which were some of the first things she had planted in her ever-widening border, were in full blossom. I took photos of them to show her in hospital, along with other spring flowers like bleeding heart, primroses, snake's head fritillary and lungwort. When I was finally able to see her I realised it would be a while before I could show them to her, but when I did, eventually, she stared at them like a child, like she stared at us, unable to speak, unable to communicate but with love in her enormous blue eyes. I still have those photos, I can't bear to delete them. It was a good blossom year.

Today, however, she's keenest on showing me her leaves. At the end of her garden is an enormous purple beech tree, which I love. I love the grey bark of beech trees, the slender buds, the colour of the leaves when they first emerge and again before they fall. Mum has a different relationship with them: 'Bloody leaves everywhere, stopping my bulbs growing!' 'Treading on those cursed masts! Oh I could kill those masts.' And then in spring: 'Those bloody beech seedlings!'

I have never managed to time my trip to coincide with the seedlings still being in the ground. I would happily dig them up and take them home with me to make a hedge. It's a tree that deserves progeny, a tree I would like a nod to in my garden. I once nearly made it up in time. 'If you want them they're in the bin,' she said, wickedly. The tree is not in her garden but is just beyond it and I am grateful. I'm convinced she would have chopped it down if she'd had a choice.

I'm surprised then, when she shows me her 'leaves', which she has added to her borders as a mulch. 'Look,' she says proudly, 'I have read your books.' Her entire garden is a pillowy bed of the reddest, wettest beech leaves, which she has carefully tucked around and beneath plants, so as not to block light to them. It looks beautiful.

'Now who will live there?' she asks. 'Who am I helping?'

I tell her worms will slowly take the leaves into the soil and eat them underground, adding hummus and other nutrients around plant roots. I tell her moths will pupate and rest overwinter, that other critters will hunker down under this leafy winter blanket. That blackbirds will rifle through the leaves looking for morsels, that what she has done is recreate one of the oldest natural processes in the world – leaves falling on the soil to feed it and help plants grow, while providing a winter bed, and food, for many others.

'Gold star for you, Mum,' I say proudly. She then shows me her barbecue, which is a brick-built thing that resembles an open chimney with some metal shelves to hold fire and meat, beneath which she has packed yet more leaves.

'Will a hedgehog sleep there?'

'It might do, Mum!'

Many more of the leaves are in the compost heap, where they will break down with other waste and gradually become a fine material, which she can use as a summer mulch, for more soil conditioning.

'But the rest are in the bin,' she says, and we roll around, laughing. The poor beech tree. The poor, misunderstood beech tree.

Back in Brighton I set out with gloves and a bag and find the hog immediately. It's exactly where the woman said it was, on the edge of the asphalt in the children's play area. I take photos of my own, then prise its frozen remains off the asphalt and take it back to the garden, so it can be free to rot back into the earth, as nature intended, rather than the council incinerator. There's not a scrap of flesh on it, just spikes, a few ribs and vertebrae, and a skull – a tiny one, indicating that it was a young hog – but no jaw. Not much to return to the soil, but something. I lay it down on the compost heap and cover it with a thin layer of garden waste, so it, too, can work its way back into the earth. Go well, little hog.

House sparrow, *Passer domesticus*

The house sparrow is a little bird with a big *CHEEP!*
Mostly brown, the male has a black face and bib, while the
female is duller. They're scruffy things, birds of big hedges
and neglected waste ground. They eat seeds of dandelions
and other 'weeds' such as sowthistle and knapweeds. They
nest in loose family groups in holes and under the eaves of
houses, and often nest next to each other. They can have
up to three broods a year. They hang around in flocks, in
which they forage, bathe and *CHEEP!* together.

The house sparrow has declined by over 70 per cent
(that's around 22 million birds) since the 1970s, but is still the
most commonly seen garden bird in the UK. For 20 years
it's held the top spot in the Big Garden Birdwatch, an annual
bird count that takes place on the third weekend of January.
It's still common, but it's the rate of its decline that's worrying,
and scientists can't quite work out what's going on.

In urban areas it's thought a combination of loss of nesting habitat and invertebrate food, which they feed their
chicks, is contributing to the fall in numbers, with populations completely disappearing from some neighbourhoods.
Habitat loss comes from house renovations – holes are
filled in and cavity walls insulated to make them more
energy efficient, while the eaves of new and refurbished
homes are now sealed, so sparrows can't get in. The loss of
invertebrate food means fewer successful nesting attempts
– a study in Leicester blamed a lack of insects for the

number of chicks found starving in nests. It makes sense: urban spaces have less greenery than rural areas so fewer leaves for invertebrates to eat. Add to that the increase of paving in both front and back gardens, decking and plastic grass, and it doesn't take a genius to work out why the chicks aren't getting the nourishment they need.

In rural areas the situation is different, with declines linked to changes in farming practices such as the loss of winter stubbles and hedgerows, along with measures to prevent sparrows from accessing stores of grain. But studies are not conclusive. They could be declining for reasons no one's thought of yet.

The thing about house sparrows is that they're a sedentary species, which means they spend their whole lives in one territory, they don't move around like other birds. If the habitat starts to disintegrate – for example if holes in houses are filled in or there are too many paved-over and fake-turfed gardens – they just stick it out, gradually finding less and less food to feed their chicks, their house literally crumbling around them.

If you have them in your garden you probably have a lot of them – that's the nature of house sparrows, they hang out in big groups. But that doesn't mean they're not struggling and it doesn't mean you can't give them a helping hand.

In gardens they're easy to cater for. The invertebrates we have lost from urban areas are just aphids and caterpillars. Virtually all plants attract aphids, the key is to leave them where you find them and not try to take nature into your own hands by spraying them to death or rubbing them off with your fingers. They rarely harm plants and can be a lifeline for these little brown birds, which balance precariously on stems and pick aphids off them one at a time, before carrying them back to their nest. How do I know? Because

I watch them do it. Every spring I know when the chicks have hatched because the house sparrows descend on the garden and frantically take aphids from every leaf and bud. Two weeks later the fresh, fluffy chicks with gaping yellow beaks line up on the fence and tumble into shrubs and trees, not quite sure of their weight or how much space they take up. I watch their parents feed them but also teach them how to find aphids on roses, teach them where the pond and bird bath are, the feeder of sunflower hearts. At dusk they descend on the big hedge in next door's front garden and *CHEEP!* loudly until it's time for bed.

To increase numbers of caterpillars in your garden, grow native trees and shrubs, including hawthorn, beech and hazel. Let them grow scruffy and wayward or grow them as a hedge, so the sparrows can roost in them at night. Let areas of grass grow long, which will entice a variety of egg-laying moths and butterflies, along with other invertebrates such as aphids but also beetles and bugs. Having taken some of the invertebrates from the grass, the sparrows will return to take seed from the grasses and any wildflowers that have grown into the thatch.

Nesting sites are important, too. There's a pub near me, a fancy thing on the seafront, that has always had house sparrows breeding in its many holes and crevices. When the new owners bought it and the refurbishment got underway, I emailed them and explained how house sparrows lived there, how they are sedentary and likely to just stay put even if the habitat declines, that they nest communally. They responded by erecting 30 boxes on the north side of the venue. Thousands of people visit every week and never notice the house sparrows, but when I walk past them I always say hello and smile, because 30 pairs of house sparrows are raising chicks on the side of a fancy seafront pub, thanks to a couple of emails.

When I bought my house I had six nest boxes retrofitted into the cavity walls of my house, three each for swifts and house sparrows. A pair of great tits nested in one in the first year, and house sparrows often start but then abandon nest building in the swift holes. But the boxes are there for them if they need them. As they nest communally you can erect several boxes together, just make sure they have an entrance hole with a diameter of 30mm. You can buy a 'sparrow terrace', which has three boxes in one. Erect them under the eaves of your house (away from any swift or house martin nests), and keep your fingers crossed. With nesting opportunities and good chances of invertebrate food they would be foolish to stay away for long.

January

The New Year comes with yet more rain. The garden is sodden, the water butts spill over the sides and I can no longer empty them into the pond – it's all too muddy. I worry about the insects – wet winters are terrible for them because they can't hibernate properly and also because they can literally rot. I check my red mason and leaf-cutter bee cocoons in the shed and, sure enough, there's a light coating of fluffy mould on them. I brush it off and arrange them in a way that will ensure more ventilation around these precious parcels. I have never seen so much rain.

And then it turns cold again, as the jet stream wobbles to the left, forcing mild conditions south and locking cold air in the north. We are lucky this band of winds has just brought very wet, then very cold weather. In North America the jet stream delivered a 'bomb cyclone' that brought temperatures of -50°C to regions as far south as Texas, and then three weeks of rain to drought-stricken California, bringing flooding and chaos. Meanwhile

Europe has experienced one of its worst-ever heatwaves, with temperatures almost reaching summer levels in some countries. Poland's capital, Warsaw, recorded temperatures of 18.9°C on New Year's Day, more than 5°C higher than the previous record set 30 years ago. Bilbao in northern Spain reached 24.9°C and Switzerland saw 20°C. It was barely reported on the news.

Here we've had flooding, along with ice and snow, but nothing too bad, nothing 'extreme'. UK winters are always a slog, always dark and go on for too long. But this one has largely been uneventful, and I'm grateful.

I broke my toe in the first week of January and so haven't been able to do anything outside. There have been no winter runs, no frantic bursts of exercise, no New Year promises to do more, be less. Neither have there been winter treks up the Downs. There has been very little outside for me at all, save for hobbled dog walks in the park behind my house.

I have taken the opportunity to rest, to stretch out the Christmas theme of putting my feet up and eating biscuits. I repot houseplants and sow chilli seeds. I clean and refill bird feeders. I plan my gardening year, sketching out beds and thinking of what could be done better, and look at photos from last summer for inspiration. I'm distracted by summery scenes, by leaves and insects and light. I shudder at the thought of drought. I eat biscuits and watch more TV.

The constant flux between mild and wet, and dry and cold is frustrating. I worry about the hedgehogs, wondering if they keep waking up and losing energy searching for food that isn't there. Or is it there? Early one morning I walk into the garden and find mating earthworms. They, too, should be hibernating, tucked beneath the frost layer in a slime-coated ball. I keep the hedgehog feeding station out all winter, a small dish covering the biscuit bowl to stop mice from nicking the lot, but which would be no bother at all for a hungry hog to move. I check it daily and it's not been moved, nor are there any hedgehog droppings nearby. I hope they're managing to sleep.

I have seen no bees, and I am grateful for that. No butterflies or moths. Others do. Twitter is full of early bees and slow worms, of butterflies and hedgehogs. 'Will they hibernate yet?' some people ask. 'Will they be OK?' Others just write tirades of despair.

There are frogs in the pond, not in amplexus (the mating position) or showing any signs of mating, but in the pond nonetheless. I count five. Five frogs in water that keeps icing over and then melting again. I put the camera out, positioning it at one end of the pond, facing the wall, where they are congregating. On mild evenings they stick their heads out of the water, their eyes periscopes surveying the world above them. I watch cats and foxes paw at the mysterious shapes gliding beneath the surface. I watch ripples and bubbles of 'activity'. Nothing significant; when it's cold it's colder than last year; when it's mild it's 'a few degrees above average'. The frogs are later to get going this year and I'm glad. Still, I'm hopeful we are on track for a late-February spawning.

Red-tailed bumblebee, *Bombus lapidarius*

The red-tailed bumblebee is a gorgeous thing, all velvet black coat with a rusty red tail. The queens are large and have a deep buzz. Workers look like the queen but are smaller, while the males have a yellow band across their thorax and a beautiful lemon 'moustache'. Short-tongued, they feed on rosemary and dandelion flowers in spring, white clover, bird's foot trefoil, cranesbill geraniums and greater knapweed in summer. Some suggest they have a preference for yellow flowers.

They nest underground, beneath sheds and also walls, and there is anecdotal evidence that they prefer their habitats to be damper than those used by other bumblebees. It was a red-tailed queen that made her nest in the old duvet that had been thrown out in the yard all those years ago. The duvet had become damp and smelled mouldy, so it would make sense that a damp-loving bumblebee would choose it for her home.

It also makes sense that there are fewer red-tails where I live in the dry south-east than the wetter north-west. Of course, with climate change, the species is also moving northwards.

2022 was a bad year for bumblebees. Plants produce fewer flowers in a drought and flowers produce less nectar, so there was less food available for them. Also bumblebees overheat quickly and struggle to fly in temperatures above

30°C. As a result, during the heatwave, bumblebees couldn't fly for large portions of the day and when they did forage they couldn't find much food. This meant far less pollen and nectar will have been taken back to bumblebee nests to feed bumblebee larvae.

Towards the end of summer, eggs of daughter queens hatch into grubs and the workers gather food to feed them. As adults, the daughter queens and new males mate, before the daughter queens hibernate and the original nest dies. If there was less food available then fewer daughter queens would have been raised, so fewer may emerge from hibernation in spring. Perhaps the damp-loving species struggled the most in the dry weather – results from bumblebee monitoring surveys may offer some clues.

Numbers may bounce back with favourable weather conditions, although these are never guaranteed these days. But we can all step up to give them a helping hand: grow their favourite flowers and keep them watered in dry weather (save rain water in water butts and use grey water when you can). Create damp habitats for them – perhaps make a 'bumblebee nest' (find instructions online) in a damp or shady part of your garden. Like many bumblebees, the red-tail queen digs herself into the soil to hibernate. If you and your neighbours reduce the amount of hard surfaces in the area, the soils will be less likely to become waterlogged in wet winters, so more hibernating queens will survive. We can't adapt our way out of everything, but we can understand the needs of the species who live among us and give them the leg-up they need to survive.

February

I take Tos to meet her best friend Alfie in the park. I chat with his mum, Rhi, while Tos and Alf chase each other around, Tos biting his legs, Alfie weeing on hers. Another dog joins the melee – it's Twiggy! I will ask Twiggy's mum if she has a pond.

We talk about dogs for a while and then I clear my throat. 'I've been meaning to ask, do you have a pond?' She says no, and I start gabbling on about toads and how I heard squeaking from the direction of her house, and how I thought I'd ask because 'you have that lovely mixed native hedge in the front and anyone with a lovely hedge like that is likely to have a pond.' She says next door had a pond but they filled it in, but she finds toads by the shed sometimes.

'Should I bring them to yours?' she asks.

'Oh no,' I reply, 'they'll find their own way; they can smell algae from the water from miles away.' We talk about frogs and I start describing the difference between the two species and realise I have to stop now, while I'm still only just ahead. She is a nice woman, and tells me her name is Rachel. She will look out for toads for me, and let me know if she sees any.

At home I look on Google Maps and Rightmove to see if I can find the neighbour's filled-in pond in the 'sold house prices' section. I do – it's tiny! A small triangular thing wedged among a sea of decking. I can't imagine toads would have chosen to breed there. But they might have, I suppose, if there were no other options. There must be somewhere else.

Later, I bump into Johnny from over the road, and the conversation turns to ponds because he has an allotment pond that he has been meaning to clear out for the last three years but still hasn't got around to doing it (he tells me about it every spring). It's full of leaves and algae, he says, again, and he doesn't think he'll get any frogspawn this year, although he always does. But his neighbours dug a pond and got frogspawn straight away.

'WHAT NEIGHBOURS?' I ask.

'My next-door neighbours,' he says, not on his allotment but here, on this road. He tells me they had their whole house done up and as part of their renovations they made a pond with a little water fountain and got frogspawn immediately. I am delighted.

'I'm pleased, Johnny, I'm so pleased you've told me about that pond!' We chat about toads for a while and the mystery of where they came from. He says he has definitely had toads in his garden, which is currently paved but is soon to be un-paved and planted with trees and shrubs. 'We will have a hedgehog hole,' he promises. He tells me to get on to Google Earth to see where other ponds are, and I tell him I have, obsessively, and not found any. I tell him about a house I viewed on the adjacent road five years ago, which had an enormous fish pond in the back. 'It was horrible,' I say. 'All decking and then this huge pool. But it could have attracted toads.'

'Wouldn't the fish have eaten the toadpoles?' asks Johnny, and I say no, and explain that toad tadpoles are slightly poisonous and therefore usually avoided by fish. I tell him that I have looked and looked on the sold house prices section of Rightmove but not found this house and I think I'm going mad. It must have been filled in, and the decking removed. But if it was filled in and supported toads then where are the toads breeding now? This whole thing remains a mystery.

I wake early and fumble my way downstairs to boil the kettle and let Tos out. She doesn't come and I'm glad, for the door opens to a wall of sound, of frogs croaking in the darkness. I tip-toe out so as not to disturb them but I fail and they disappear with a splash into the depths of the water. Sorry, frogs. Still, by torchlight I can see the first glistening blob of frogspawn in the shallows. My heart!

I spend the day watching the pond through binoculars from an upstairs window. I count around 50 frogs, although it's hard to say exactly as they're moving around so much. It's the usual, vigorous affair: males and females in amplexus, males trying to knock other males off females, males chasing anything that moves, in big, bubbly splashes. I home in on the expanding blueish balloons the males make as they croak, at the bubbles that float and pop on the surface, on the most perfect, stripy frog legs splayed in the water. I watch couples climb on to blobs of spawn as if to claim them as their own, I watch a frog leap into the garden and land in the pond with a splash ('I'm here!'). I

watch what I think is an actual blob of spawn being laid. I
watch magic, it's all magic.

And yet there's an unease that comes with these things
these days. Last spring was so dry and this spring seems to
be going that way, too. After the sodden winter, we haven't
seen rain for weeks and the pond is already looking low. A
low pond in spring isn't normal – the whole ecosystem is
set up so there's water for frogs to spawn in, which remains
there at least until the froglets emerge in early summer. I
have water butts to top the pond up if I need to but it's just
another reminder that things are falling apart. It's hard,
sometimes, trying to enjoy natural, wonderful events, trying
to keep the clawing sense of unease at bay, trying to ignore
the new context of the story.

The frogs are also early. Not horribly so, but four days
earlier than 2022 and nine days earlier than 2021. It's only
their third year of spawning, so it's too soon to blame
climate change. But a nine-day jump in three years seems a
lot. Like the low water level in the pond, it could be
nothing, but I feel uneasy. There's still a lot of 'winter' to
go. There's still a risk of a late cold spell, of plunging
temperatures and frozen frogspawn. Frogs have evolved to
spawn in early spring, they can deal with a bit of ice, that's
why they spawn in the sunniest, shallowest parts of the
pond – the ice melts here soonest after a cold night. But
they can't cope with a deep freeze. They can't cope with
massively fluctuating temperatures; early spring one day
and deepest winter the next. They have not evolved the
mechanisms to deal with this.

I'm determined to enjoy it anyway. I battle on, watching
the spawn, watching the splashes, telling Twitter. And at
night I stick to my plan: I have lived here for four years and
the frogs have been spawning for just three, but I have
established a new 'tradition', which is to sleep in the spare

room when the frogs are spawning, so I can open the window and fall asleep listening to their croaks. I pretend everyone fell asleep listening to croaking frogs in the olden days, and that I'm channelling my inner early human.

I go to bed early so I can lie in the dark and hear them, willing myself to not sleep, not yet. My body is tense as I try to focus on the sound of frogs over people – the cars and the level crossing of the high street, the ships and horns of the port. It's only 9.30 p.m. so there are neighbours about, too, talking, putting the bins out for tomorrow's collection. Beneath this chatter and traffic is the low, constant hum of frogs. My body relaxes. I lie on my back so both ears can absorb the sound and I stay still so there are no rustles to interrupt it.

Despite my efforts I fall asleep quickly, but I wake periodically and am greeted by frogs. Unwavering, they have been spawning and calling the whole time, and in the dead of night the sounds of people are fewer and the sounds of frogs are greater. I would like to sleep in the garden in a tent but I worry about disturbing them. I would like to sleep in the garden in a tent but it's February and I would have a horrible time. So I sleep in the bedroom that backs on to the garden and I listen carefully to the croaks, to this ancient sound that belongs in my human ears. Finally, I feel good.

What other sounds have we lost? Other sounds that used to help us tell the time – of the day, of the month, of the year? Sounds that used to be so ubiquitous, sounds that we don't even know have gone? We still hear birdsong but there are fewer members of the chorus – both in diversity and abundance. What birds sang in these parts 200 years ago? Cuckoos? Nightingales? Curlews? Corncrakes? The buzz of a bumblebee, the snore of a hedgehog, it's all so quiet these days. What does a badger sound like? I don't actually know. I hate that we have evolved ourselves away from the very best of life. That we have replaced it with endless, pointless crap, and have the audacity to call this 'progress'.

I still don't know where the frogs have come from. Are there other ponds nearby they have ditched in favour of mine? Have ponds been dug and then filled in as the homes and gardens changed hands? I know of three that have been lost: the pond a few doors down that Twiggy's mum told me about, and the dumped preformed pond I found in the twitten behind my house when I moved in. Another, two roads away, that was lost a few years ago. That's the thing about gardens: the habitats are temporary. This isn't necessarily a bad thing; wild ponds are temporary, too. But if the general trend is to fill in, rather than dig ponds, then the species that use them will suffer. The frogs and the toads, but also the newts and the hedgehogs and the bats, along with the thousands of freshwater invertebrates who call garden ponds home. I haven't yet met anyone in the neighbourhood who has a living pond in their garden, besides my neighbour Kate, who dug hers a few weeks after I dug mine, and now the neighbours next to Johnny. Where were the frogs spawning before we turned up?

A hundred years ago there were ponds in the park. It wasn't a park then but a 'waste ground' left fallow after being used to mine sand and flints at the turn of the last century. Craters were left by the mines and, naturally, they filled with water. One of them was huge, over three metres deep, and was fed by a 'natural spring'. (I am interested to read about the natural spring, and wonder if it can be revived.) This area would have been rich with frogs, toads and newts, perhaps even great crested newts, as the many craters would have been used as the 'satellite ponds' that this species needs. But in 1936, some kids decided to sail boats over the largest pond in the dead of winter, and one of them drowned. For completely unfathomable reasons that I suspect had everything to do with money and nothing to do with the well-being of the local community, the council decided to fill it in, not with soil but with refuse. Imagine turning up for your annual orgy to find your party site filled with glass and early plastics, like the first disposable razor blades (I may have gone down a rabbit hole of 'refuse of the ages' here.) The poor frogs, where did they go after their home became a rubbish dump?

Sometimes I wish I had been born before the Industrial Revolution but I'm gay and a woman so I would probably have been drowned (who am I kidding? I would have died in childbirth). But I can't get past how noisy and colourful life would have been back then. How loud the birdsong and the frog croaks, the buzzing of bees. How thick the clouds of insects and bats, how full the summer skies of swifts and swallows. How many butterflies there would have been, dripping from wildflowers (how many wildflowers there would have been). How, when walking past a snoring hedgehog in summer, no one would have batted an eyelid. I could have lived in the woods! I could have lived in a little wooden shack at the edge of the woods and eaten porridge and leaves, greeted hedgehogs with big toothless grins. I could have moved frogspawn laid in puddles to my little garden pond. I could have grown herbs, a few vegetables, all to a soundtrack of song, of wild chatter. Life would have been hard, I don't doubt that, but it would have been so full of *life*.

I do enjoy bits of modern life. I'm terrible at being a consumer, terrible at being anything other than scruffy. I rarely get my hair cut or buy new clothes. But I like dancing. I like nightclubs and festivals and bowling around with my favourite idiots. I love travel (although I'm conflicted about that these days). I love sleeping in a warm bed with the window open listening to frogs, I love that I don't have to sleep in a tent. And I'm lucky. I know how lucky I am to have these privileges.

I am here and I am now on this little patch of land not far from the sea, where there were once meadows and a windmill and a fresh spring and who-knows-what-else, which is now a busy suburb of a high street, close to shops and a port. There are frogs. I have a pond and binoculars and windows. Times have changed, the weather is changing. But I can top the pond up if it doesn't rain, I can raise frogspawn indoors if temperatures plummet. I can lie in bed and listen to the ancient sounds of our oldest friends. It will never be a cabin in the woods but if I close my eyes and listen I can make myself love now. Just for a moment, just for as long as the frogs continue to sing.

The sun is yellow and the sky is blue! How can I stay away from the garden? I steal an hour outside with Tos. We open the door to light and song, to whistles and clicks and stammers and *wheeees*, to a flock of starlings on the roof. There's a blackbird nearby too, a robin and, somewhere, distantly, a dunnock. It feels like spring, it feels like hope.

Most of the garden has remained untouched since summer: it's all seedheads and skeletal remains, piles of leaves and curiously untouched berries (even curiouser is that it's just one stem of untouched berries, the rest have all been eaten). But there's a whiff of new growth and life, of daffodil, snowdrop and crocus shoots, of buds revealing themselves in the still-cold soil. 'Who are you?' I ask the buds. 'Who are you and when did I plant you and what will you become and will you look good?' I'm going to find out so soon.

I allow myself some gentle tidying, just on the sunny side, so emerging shoots and buds have room and light to grow. It's easy to come into the garden in late winter and clear everything away, but this removes shelter from hibernating insects. Gentle trimming is key, leaving plenty intact to protect the sleepy.

I start at the far end, the new border I planted in late summer. I clear old hellebore leaves to make more of the opening flowers, remove the underskirt-like foliage of foxgloves and rose campion, beneath which bulbs are trying to push through. I move, gently, towards the house, avoiding spikes of snowdrop and crocus flowers, smiling at buds of hazel and rose leaves.

I cut back stems of ice plant, catmint, penstemon and *verbena bonariensis*. I prune out rosehips that, until recently, were being eaten by squirrels but are now black and mushy and seemingly not as delicious. I weed out crocosmia shoots (there are always crocosmia shoots) and a bit of spurge but not all of it; everything is allowed to live here in moderation. The sun has finally climbed high enough in the sky to warm a few inches of soil and there I find masses of new seedlings I can't yet identify. I want them to be foxgloves or ox-eye daisies, bird's foot trefoil or clovers, plants I can use in the borders or new meadow out the front. I'll probably be disappointed. Still, I leave them to reveal themselves in time.

I would love to mulch the soil or tickle the surface with my three-pronged cultivator to make it all look fluffy and nice but that would kill the mystery seedlings, damage emerging bulbs and potentially disrupt hibernating insects. I would love to mow the lawn to make it all straight and neat. I would love to clear the shady side of the garden, too, clear leaves and sticks. I am eager for spring, for new growth, for the garden to be mine again. I resist; it's still so early, just some gentle cutting back will do for today.

While I potter, Tos helps herself to sticks. She takes fresh twiggy stems from my clippings bucket, partially composted prunings from the rough mulch I laid in autumn, entire branches from the habitat pile. She prances around with them, then lies down to chew them for a bit, and then abandons them in scatters on the lawn.

'Tosca,' I say helplessly. The new and composted prunings are soft enough but I confiscate the branches in case she splits them while chewing and splinters her mouth. She then finds a champagne cork, which, again, is partially decomposed and has come from the patch of mulch I am suddenly regretting not sieving. We play with it for a while, me throwing it for her to chase and then drop at my feet, until it disintegrates into so many pieces that it, too, is confiscated and returned to the compost bin.

'Woof,' she cries.

'I know, life's tough,' I reply.

It's not just the rough mulch where there are sticks and stems to find. The whole garden is 'littered' with planty remains. They seem ungainly now, with so little else to draw the eye, but they'll soon disappear beneath foliage and flowers, beneath the paws of hedgehogs and foxes, beneath new leaf litter, where they will slowly rot as nature intended. Tosca will find some, of course. And so will the birds: every spring I watch gulls gathering beakfuls of my sticks and flying them to the rooftops; I see house sparrows and starlings taking smaller, twiggy stems to the nooks and crannies of holey houses; magpies and crows taking them to the large sycamores in the park, the magpies returning to take pond mud to make a nice deep cup (I admit to wishing they wouldn't). Wood pigeons labouring over the perfect stick. This one? No. This one? Still no. Funny how they're so fussy with their stick picking but use them to make the most ridiculously flimsy nests.

Tosca watches me from the bench, which is now, after months of darkness, in full sun. In summer there's a bench cushion, which inevitably she has claimed as her own and she lies sleepily on it, watching me garden. She stands now on the hard wood as if to say, 'Bench cushion, please,' and I pretend I haven't noticed. I collect her discarded sticks from the lawn and return them to the habitat pile, along with my bucket of old plant stems and soggy rosehips. They go to the open heap rather than the closed bin in case they are harbouring insects, although I checked them as best I could when I cut them back. How awful it must be to wake from winter sleep to the dark, damp tomb of a closed compost bin, with no means of escape. Any insects in today's prunings still have their shelter, just a few metres away from where they intended it. When they wake they will be able to fly away or move further into the heap if they want to. They're protected from rain under the lip of the shed roof, from wind and frost and snow. They are safe there. Safe to sleep and wake and fly and simply get on with the business of being insects. Even after I've done a little tidying.

It's my birthday and I have snowdrops and hellebores to plant. I hack into frost-kissed soil with a hand fork and make space for bulbs and rootballs and fill them in and water them. Not ideal conditions but never mind, they'll be fine.

It's gone cold again, as the weakening jet stream brings more Arctic weather south of where it should. Temperatures here are dipping to 7°C (feels like 0°C), but in California again temperatures are plummeting to -18°C as ice storms bring snow and flooding to a region already hammered by 'once in a lifetime' weather events over the course of winter. Here, I worry about the frogs, about the bumblebees I have already seen out of hibernation, about the hedgehogs. Again, the up-and-down cycle of mild then cold weather is no good for wildlife. If we have a deep freeze, how will I protect the frogspawn?

There would be a lot to protect; the frogs have almost completely filled the pond now. I've lost count of the number of blobs and there's no way of knowing, congealed together as they are. After seven days there are still around 50 individuals going at it, with yet more arriving to the garden. I watch them land in the pond with a muted splash and then burrow through spawn to reach water. Mated females have left the pond already but many of the males have stuck around. This means there are now more males than females, which means mating balls are starting to form. Mating balls occur when two or more males cling to a female in the hope of being the one that gets to spawn with her. Science suggests this could be in the female's best interests, as only the strongest, most determined male will win, and she may even encourage them to compete for her. But it often backfires: in an attempt to unseat their rivals, the males make the 'ball' roll around and around, often with long periods under water. She can drown.

I see two legs poking through pondweed and spawn, which don't look right. I sit on the bench and watch. Sure enough, the legs are part of a mating ball, which is frantically being rolled by at least two males, it's hard to tell. The female is dead; it is her pale, stiff legs I spot in the water. The males, I expect, are young and overexcited. I fish her out and they quickly jump off her. She's been dead a while, poor thing, her tongue hanging out and the skin of her legs and belly rubbed clean off. What a way to go.

I think there's another mating ball but it's so hard to tell, with everything else that's going on in the water and the floating mass of spawn concealing everything. I anticipate, with sadness, fishing out more dead bodies.

I feel like the season is coming to an end, that most frogs have been and gone, that the garden is emptying of them. At night I still steal into the spare room and open the window to listen to them, waking periodically to the comforting sound of croaks. Each morning I go out and mutter expletives at the sheer number of frogs and eggs, at what the garden might look like when the froglets start leaving the pond. At the falling level of pond water.

The pond is drying out, gradually receding with every frog splash. This, so early in the year, doesn't bode well for summer. Many frogs have spawned where they usually spawn, in the far shallows where the sun hits the water first thing in the morning, but others have now spawned in what's usually deeper water. I'm keeping an eye on it; I don't want to fill the pond and interfere with the frogs' intended placement of spawn, but I don't want the spawn to dry out or freeze, either. So far I've added a bit of rainwater from my water butt, and used a rose on my watering can to 'water' the spawn gently, so it feels like rain. As the water recedes, the spawn becomes more exposed – my job is to ensure it remains just slightly under the surface.

As yet, there is no sign of toads. The next cold spell will last for a week and then afterwards, who knows? It might rain. It might be 20°C. If they don't come soon, then when?

Common frog, *Rana temporaria*

The common frog is the best-known British amphibian and is found throughout Britain and Ireland in almost any habitat where there's a suitable pond to breed in. Gardens are extremely important to frogs, and many regional populations depend on garden ponds for their survival.

They're funny-looking things, with smooth moist skin, striped legs (the back legs are longer than the front) and an angular head and body shape. They have large, goggly eyes on the side of their head and they usually have a black patch behind each eye, in which their ears are visible as black drum-like circles that pick up vibrations. They can be olive-green or brown in colour, but are sometimes found in shades of yellow, orange, red, green, brown and even blue. They can grow up to 9cm long.

They emerge early in the year, spawning from late winter, starting in the south-west of Britain, where it's milder. The first frogspawn of the year is always recorded in West Cornwall in December. In Brighton they spawn in February, but not until April in the far north-east of Scotland. Frogspawn is laid in gelatinous clumps that look a bit like tapioca. It's eaten by virtually everything, including newts, ducks and even foxes.

Frog tadpoles emerge black but soon turn brown and develop gold spots (unlike toad tadpoles, which remain black). They emerge as 'froglets' in summer, hopping about in long grass, trying to avoid the attentions of birds and other predators. Such a tiny percentage of tadpoles makes it to adulthood, there's a lot riding on those first few days out of the pond.

It's probably the easiest amphibian to cater for in gardens, as it will breed in a variety of water bodies. Frogs tend to favour small, shallow ponds (perfect for gardens!) with shallow 'beach' areas that warm up quickly in the late winter sun and mean there's less chance of the spawn being lost to ice. Unlike toads, which seem to prefer larger, deeper ponds and remain loyal to the pond they started life in, frogs are more adventurous and will try new sites that aren't always suitable – they often breed in puddles. So if you dig a pond, and you get the levels right (shallow, and gentle sloping sides are a must), you're bound to attract frogs if they're present in your area. And if they're not in your area then dig a pond anyway – frogs and other amphibians can 'smell' water. If yours is the only garden pond for miles, it could provide any remaining frogs with a lifeline, and you never know who else might turn up.

March

It was cold for two weeks. The frogs stopped their shenanigans and bedded down in the depths of the pond while we humans that could afford to turned up our central heating. Before it turned cold it was warm – really warm. I took Tos up to the Downs on Valentine's Day and wore a T-shirt. I found my first slow worm of the year and my first buffish mining bee, *Andrena nigroaenea*, feeding from snowdrops in the front garden. I saw bumblebee queens out of hibernation, the odd bursting of buds. And then it was winter again: frost on the shed roof, ice on the pond, hard, dry, ground. We can put a jumper on; what do the bees do?

While the frogs slept through the cold spell, my focus switched to hedgehogs. Suddenly the food in the feeding station was being taken, and so I topped it up properly and found it empty again the next morning, along with my first hedgehog poo of the year. It makes sense that it came to my garden as temperatures dipped, as it knew there would be kitten biscuits to make up for the sudden departure of earthworms. I put my camera out and watched footage of a chunky male hog licking his lips as he left the feeding station, and another of him coming into the garden via the back gate. It's always reassuring to see when species have survived hibernation, especially when the weather is so changeable – they can't be hibernating properly.

Temperatures eased a little for a while and the frogs started stirring again. Nothing like the vigorous parties of mid-February, but the odd blob of spawn would appear here and there, as subdued efforts to party were rekindled. But then there were reports of more ice and snow to come, of an 'Arctic blast'. It wasn't known where exactly, or for how long, but it would come. I pushed all the frogspawn beneath the surface of the water and topped up the pond to create an insulating later of water above the spawn, to give it the best possible chance of surviving. I watered plants that were already suffering from drought and which I didn't then want to succumb to the cold. I waited. On the morning it got cold I walked to the gym, and arrived with a bright-red face and no feeling in my hands. But then it got mild again, and then cold again, and mild again, and then freezing. But there was no snow. I watched the telly, bemused at all the reports of snow, and wondered if it would come here. I texted family, 'Have you got snow?' And they said, 'Yes!' and sent pics of it falling and landing in great pillowy heaps. Then one weather report made everything clear: it showed a map of the UK that was all icy blue except for a thin ribbon of yellow on the south coast. Ahh, that explains it. The Arctic blast had just missed us.

Instead of snow we have rain. Two days of glorious, life-affirming rain. I take Tos out in it, wash my face in it, open the window so I can listen to it. I rejoice at full water butts and then half-empty them again so I can water the hedge by the wall and the bit of lawn beneath the shed roof. In the front I water the pots and the rain shadow of next door's hedge, where very little grows. I stand at the kitchen window and watch raindrops land in great splashes in the pond, filling it to its absolute limit. Through binoculars I watch frogs. Lots and lots of frogs.

I count 30 frogs in the pond, just two weeks after around 50 of them had made their enormous spawn cushions. Thirty frogs leaping about, chasing each other, laying spawn. 'They're back,' I say to Emma, and immediately ban Tosca from leaping around the garden. 'They're back and they're spawning and my god, what are all these frogs going to look like in summer?'

I resume my little vigil at the bench, in the dark. It's raining and the water is running down my back. I move to the edge of the pond to make myself slightly more comfortable, and shine my torch on amorous couples, of males jumping on females, of males biting the back legs of others who were already coupled up. On a newt. A newt? A newt!

She's sitting at the edge, like she has always been there. A gravid female (full of eggs), she's ignoring the frogspawn and eating a worm. A newt! In four years and two months the garden has its first newt. For a moment everything is perfect.

It's often the way. In the wild, new ponds are formed and the frogs typically find them before other amphibians, taking advantage of fewer predators than in established ponds. They spawn and spawn and spawn, and it looks like they're never going to stop, that there's going to be too much, that there's far too much for that one pond to support. But, gradually, it all gets eaten, by beetle and bug larvae, by dragonfly and damselfly nymphs, by birds and, eventually, by newts. When the frogs started spawning in such unfettered abundance, I knew it couldn't last. 'There are no newts,' I would say to anyone who would listen. 'It's a new pond and there are no newts and they're just taking full advantage.'

It makes sense that the newts would wait for a good population of frogs to establish before laying eggs of their own. And so, after three years of absolutely enormous amounts of frogspawn and tadpoles, the frogs have met their match.

I had an inkling newts had arrived, in December. There were bubbles coming to the surface of the pond, along with flashes of movement that were too quick for me to get my eye in. So they could have been here for months. And for the first newt I meet to be a gravid female suggests there are males here, too. You wouldn't turn up to a pond full of eggs with no one around to fertilise them.

Tos wakes up for a wee at 4.30 a.m., and we let her out as she refused to go at 10.00 last night. 'I'll take her,' I say, which is only so I can gawp at frogs and newts while she finds the perfect place to pee. I open the back door and I needn't step out, there's enough to keep me entertained on the doorstep: two toads. Oh rain, how I love you and all that comes with you. Two toads on the patio, making their way to the pond, 30 frogs in the water and a newt full of eggs. It's going to be a busy few days.

The man who flew a drone at lesser black-backed gull nests last year is at it again. The peace is destroyed up to four times a day by scared, angry gulls launching into the air and crying out their piercing alarm calls. It sounds like they're saying, 'NO! NO! GET OFF! NO!' Over and over and over. They've only just returned from their overwintering sites in West Africa. They've been here five minutes and already they're being harassed. The herring gulls haven't started collecting sticks from my garden yet but they have established their territories and both species have returned to the same nesting sites as last year. Which means they're in trouble. The same people in the Facebook group are up in arms. 'I'll dig out the number of the PCSO I spoke to last year,' says one. 'I've got more footage!' says another.

I decide this year not to take a back seat, not to read without comment. I post on the page: 'Hello, would anyone like to meet up to discuss if we can work together to help the gulls?' Three people say yes and two can make it for a drink in the local pub. I meet Lorna and Lin. Lin tells me to 'look out for a tired old goth,' while Lorna I recognise as she often stops to chat when I'm in the front garden. They bring photocopies of emails and I take my notebook. We assign tasks, swap information, give the man a nickname: Drone Bastard. I confess that I don't actually live on their road and feel like an interloper. They don't seem to mind. 'Can we call ourselves Gulls Allowed?' I ask, and they laugh. I will try to fight this man with humour and love; I will try not to be upset by him. I will try to get the police to turn up. They have one job – for the love of all the things, please, just turn up.

I haven't seen my little gravid newt since that first night, but I have been putting the camera out and the hedgehogs have set it off while the frogs have been croaking so I've been able to gawp at chubby hedgehogs while listening to frogs. It's a nice life if you can get it. In one of the clips, above the snuffling of the hedgehog and the low croaks of the frogs, I could just make out the squeaking of toads. Or one toad? Naturally, I aim to find out.

I've seen three toads in the garden so far this year. They're small, warty things, standing still for ages. Males only. They seem less eager to get into the pond, less frantic and desperate than the horny frogs. Watching leaping frogs through binoculars from the bathroom window was extremely amusing. Toads, by comparison, seem almost prudish. Perhaps they're young, perhaps they're shy. I really hope the females turn up this year and show them what's what.

Twiggy's mum, Rachel, said she would keep an eye out for toads for me. She seemed open to the idea of me inspecting the twitten at night with a torch. Bits of rain are forecast now for the next few days, so more shy, prudish toads will be on the move. I will be on my bench in the dark, waiting for them.

Mid-March and it finally feels like spring. The sun is shining, there's a gentle warmth out of the wind. There are hairy-footed flower bees fighting over lungwort, the first *Eristalis tenax* drone fly basking in the sunshine. A bald wet alien climbs up a daffodil stem and later reveals itself to be a newly hatched narcissus bulb fly. There's a chiffchaff on the shed roof, the first tadpoles in the pond.

I sit in the front garden and marvel at my new meadow. It's nearly looking good: daffodils provide colour and height, above the snowdrops my sister Ellie gave me for my birthday, and the first of the bright pink lungwort flowers. There are large clumps of grass I can't yet identify, which looked out of place a few weeks ago but now seem less so as everything has grown around them. There are clumps of other things emerging, too – somewhere some of the 50 snake's head fritillary bulbs I planted in autumn, along with what looks like alliums I must have missed when digging up the herbaceous plants. (They might look out of place in a native-ish wildflower meadow but I can always cut them for the vase.) There's purple toadflax, which seeds itself in and provides leaves for the caterpillars of the toadflax brocade moth, along with nectar for dozens of bees, butterflies and moths. There are primroses, which haven't quite done anything yet, and primulas, which must be somewhere. There are the first lush clumps of mountain cornflower, the first new leaves of evening primrose. There are strappy leaves of greater knapweed, splayed-out rosettes of shepherd's purse. I'm pleased to find the wall bellflower, *Campanula portenschlagiana*, is finally growing in the wall – after four years of trying I had almost given up hope. The sweet rocket is putting on growth and should flower for the first time this year. Above it is a large gap in my side of next door's hedge, where I've planted winter honeysuckle and ivy, in the hope that something might thrive there. Eventually, I would like them to outgrow the forsythia and Japanese spindle. Just a little bit. Just enough so they still provide support for the ivy to grow up.

When I moved the meadow from the back to the front, I planted things into the rain shadow of the hedge to see if anything would survive. I've been emptying the previous night's hot-water bottle on to it daily for the last few weeks and my efforts are paying off – the ox-eye daisies are putting on growth, along with the red clover and some sowthistle that had self-seeded. That area will always be drier than the rest of the garden and I'm hoping I can work out which species will not fare so badly there. There's plenty of room for other things to seed in if they want to, otherwise it can just become an additional habitat for mining bees, many of whom nest in dry, sparse soil.

We often forget, as gardeners, that every single thing in the garden has the potential to be a habitat, like the leaves that were blown into the pond, which provided a microhabitat for tiny new tadpoles that sit in them and eat algae from them. The rain shadow in the front garden, where plant growth is limited because the hedge stops rain falling beneath it, could therefore be celebrated as a habitat in its own right. Rather than trying to encourage things to grow, rather than emptying endless spent hot-water bottles on to it, perhaps I should leave it bare and see which invertebrates use the expanse of soil, which plants seed in that can cope with the dryness. There's another mini habitat here, too, a little pile of stones and earth beneath the gas meter that mining bees might nest in or a frog might take shelter beneath. Along the far side, beneath the hedge, is a tiny wall where the render has started to come off, revealing a mass of bricks with no pointing. Perhaps hairy-footed flower bees nest here, and there will be other insects and spiders taking advantage of the sunny crannies, too. Literally everything is a habitat.

The pots along the front path are coming along well. The tiny strawberry tree that will never be a tree, the mint and oregano that will soon be ready to harvest. The agapanthus, the lavender. Everything is so full of promise.

In the back I steal an hour to do some gardening. There's not much to do so I sweep the patio and pull up the remains of last year's sweet peas, and put the table and chairs back out. I cut back fern leaves, beneath which new fists of growth are punching through the soil. I pull out crocosmia seedlings and sweep bay leaves off emerging primrose flowers. I transplant clumps of grass that have seeded into the border to some bald patches of lawn, and use a fork to scratch the remaining bald patches to sow seed into. Rain is due tomorrow so I'm hoping the combination of moist soil, mild temperatures and a dog that hates being wet might just encourage germination.

The pond has turned bright green with algae but I can't do anything about it now there are tiny tadpoles. Besides, what do tadpoles eat? I hope nature will sort itself out and not let me down. I tickle the soil with my cultivator and wonder, still, who everyone is that is popping up to say hello. Little red buds, little green leaves. I scrape hedgehog poo off the feeding station and clean the bowl before refilling it with biscuits. Then the gulls start crying and I look up to see the drone flying low above the rooftops, scaring them off their nests.

I grab my phone and stand on the bench so I can get a better view, take a better video. The drone moves purposefully – starting at one end of the row of houses and working its way to the other end, stopping periodically at what I can only assume are gull nests. I watch it dip down and then rise again, move on to the next nest, dip down and then rise again. I can see that, despite wanting to stop gulls nesting only on his roof, Drone Bastard is also disturbing the gulls on the roofs of nearby houses. Gulls that Lin and Lorna have told me nest there every year and have names. Gulls that are part of the fabric of this neighbourhood. Gulls that belong here. I make a few videos and then text the Gulls Allowed group, who tell me he's had the drone out five times today. Is there no law that will stop him?

Another visit to Dad and Ceals and I'm thinking of curlews. I have Tosca with me this time. She gets me up at 5.30 a.m. and we head out into the dawn, crossing the road to the path that will lead us on to the marshes.

It takes ages to get off Dad's estate. Tosca is beside herself with excitement – she hasn't been here before and every bit of grass, every lamp post, every boring-looking piece of pavement is a new world of things to sniff.

'But curlews!' I say. 'Come on, you'll have all the sniffies of the most wondrous things you never dreamed existed, in just a few minutes!'

'But this bit of manky puddle,' she says. 'This old leaf.'

I let her off the lead so she can sniff to her heart's desire while I make my way to the path – she can catch me up when she's ready. She's soon at my heels again. 'Sorted?' She huffs. We cross the empty road to the path. Tosca stops to sniff the broom, the bracken, the soil, and then catches me up in great, leaping gambols. She is a sausage.

The dawn gives way to a beautiful spring morning. There's a big yellow ball rising into a cloudless blue sky and only a whisper of wind. The dawn chorus has shifted a gear and I can hear great tits and chaffinches, blackbirds and wrens. It's been a long time coming, this spring. There's no hint of the marshes yet; the path is surrounded on either side by heathland. There are posters warning of adders but it's too early in the day to worry about them biting an excited dog's nose, and besides, despite her excitement, she knows to stick to the path. I think of all the things she might be smelling now. What do weasels and stoats smell like? What do adders smell like? Can she smell hares or hedgehogs or badgers? She can't contain herself. She's running around in circles, from one smell to the next, pausing only to catch up with me. Her face tells me everything I need to know: that this path is the most exciting path EVER, that these bushes and bracken are FULL OF ALL THE SMELLS. But then it ends. Just as suddenly as crossing the road from Dad's estate on to the heathy path, we leave the bracken and broom and my boots sink into mud – the outskirts of the marshes. We briefly join a clay, puddly bridle path that leads to a metal kissing gate that opens on to the estuary, and as I click open the latch I hear a bubbling overhead. A curlew!

It's the only curlew I hear this morning, a brief call as it comes to land or takes off. We're entering their breeding season and I wonder if they breed here as well as overwinter, or if they move on to somewhere else.

Instead I tune in to oystercatchers and skylarks, to ducks and geese that I can't identify – perhaps the wigeon from November. There are no cows on the marshes today. We walk along the old railway line, which is only slightly drier than the boggy grass around us. On one side is short grass and puddles, which is usually where the cattle graze, and the other side has long grass – perhaps a crop of rye – and reedbeds in the distance. We stick to the short grass and the path, so as not to disturb any wild things, me throwing treats for Tos, who runs up and down the banks in excited scurries, splashing in puddles and stopping for yet more sniffies. The sky echoes with oystercatchers.

The wind picks up and the oystercatchers land and quieten, and I tune in to a different sound, an eerie sound I've heard only once before in a sound recording of marshland, which I thought was feedback from the recordist's equipment. It sounds like a synthesiser, like aliens have landed. It's brief so I can't follow it to locate its makers. But I'm enchanted again, as I was in autumn with the curlews. What other secrets do these marshes hold?

We head onwards, the dog and me, over the estuary bridge on to Walberswick Nature Reserve. The marsh recedes to heathland again, and with it return the posters warning of adders. The sun is higher in the sky now, and there are grassy patches where there might be nesting – or resting – birds. I put Tosca on the lead and we stick to the main concrete path that takes us to Walberswick village, which, we both decide, is only slightly less interesting than bowling among the bracken. She makes me stop for every last sniff; I make her stop for birdsong.

Every tree has a chiffchaff in it, every third tree has a yellowhammer, and as we walk past one particularly chunky broom, I jump to my first booming Cetti's warbler since last summer. Oh, my heart. It's still only 8.00 a.m. and my whole body rings with the sound of a thousand wild things. Why must mornings like this be so rare?

We walk into the village, say hello to the swings I used to play on as a child, marvel at beautiful houses I couldn't begin to dream of living in. We loop around the church and head back on ourselves, back to the bridge and the ridge, the puddles and the oystercatchers. I marvel at the footprint patterns of wading birds in the sand. I listen out for the eerie sounds again but the wind fails to bring them to me.

Back at Dad's I message Stephen, who made the sound recording where I mistook living beings for electrical feedback noise. I find his clip with the noises and identify the eerie sounds at 1 minute 42 seconds. I confess my ignorance and ask him, 'Do actual birds make this noise?' I feel stupid but there's no point in pretending to know things you don't know, and I'm a city girl after all. Besides, he's used to my questions. It was Stephen I chatted to about curlews back in November, Stephen who suggested what time to head out to hear them, Stephen who explained how they live. If anyone is to join me for my marshy awakening it must be him. 'I'm ever so sorry to bother you again,' I say.

He tells me they are lapwings. Lapwings, the birds with the black-green and white markings and the crest, birds I have seen and known (or thought I have known) for years. I've spotted them flying overhead, watched them land to feed in fields. During a particularly cold spell recently, there was one that ended up in Brighton city centre, which was rescued by someone from the bird rescue group I follow on Facebook (it had a terrible neck injury and died, sadly). I know lapwings. I thought I knew lapwings.

I remember being told that they are called peewits because of the strange sounds they make, and of not really paying attention because *peewit* isn't such a remarkable sound when said phonetically by a human. Stephen sends me another recording, this time only of lapwings, and I am transported into another world, a world of the most wondrous sounds, of wildness, of loss.

The lapwing has declined by 55 per cent since 1967, due largely to the intensification of agriculture. It's no real surprise that I've never heard one – I grew up in the suburbs just outside Birmingham and have seen them only a handful of times. 'You will have seen them out of breeding season,' says Stephen. 'That sound is only what they make on nesting territories in the spring.'

Like the curlew, the lapwing is a ground-nesting bird, and subject to the ravages of farmland machinery and the absence of 'fallow' land that used to be commonplace. I read that they nest from mid-March to June, and realise I have caught them at the very beginning of this year's breeding season. I read that the collective noun for lapwings is a 'deceit', which seems mean, although they did convince me they were electrical feedback noises rather than actual birds. I read that they nest on short grassland and grazed farmland, and that wet pasture is an important source of food for them. No wonder they like Walberswick.

The next morning I wake again to my furry alarm. 'Shall we go and see the lapwings?' I ask. 'Woof,' she replies.

The wind is stronger today and I tune in to fewer songbirds as we trudge along the path to the marshes. We walk together on the lead, just in case there's a stray lapwing on the short grass, along the old railway line and over the bridge to Walberswick. There are fewer chiffchaffs and yellowhammers, there's no Cetti's warbler. We do meet a redshank, though, as we walk back along the estuary. It has been spooked by something that is neither me nor the dog, and it cries out, loudly, taking refuge on a boat. A predator, perhaps. A stoat?

There are no distant alien sounds today, or none that is carried on the wind. But, as we head back, I loop round to another bit of path beyond a mound, from which yesterday's noises came. I have no binoculars with me but I can just make out a deceit of black-and-white birds near a stretch of water in the distance. 'Lapwings!' I tell Tosca. She is busy tracking the scent of something.

We plan to return, with Dad's binoculars, the following morning but we don't make it. Tosca treats me to a lie-in until 7.00 a.m. and we stay in bed for cuddles while the wind and rain howl around us. I am more prepared for wet weather than I was the last time I visited, but it's still not enough to persuade me to head out. And Tosca hates being wet. So we stay in bed and play 'Cheeky Monkey', which involves me grabbing her paws and asking 'Are you a cheeky monkey?' while she lies on her back and growls. Sometimes that's all you need, along with nice a cup of tea. But the curlews and the lapwings, and the other new marsh friends I have yet to meet! I'll be back for them, perhaps, without the dog.

From Dad's I head to Emma's mum Anne's, where Emma has been for the last couple of days. We spend the weekend celebrating Anne's 70th birthday and then return home after nearly a week away, tired but happy to have seen everyone. I open the back door and squat down in front of the pond.

'What are you doing?' says Emma.

'I'm looking for toadspawn. I can't believe there isn't any,' I reply, wondering where they are breeding because there was a couple in amplexus last week and it would be odd, although not that unusual, that they would get together in my pond and then swan off somewhere else to actually lay their eggs.

'It's here, you plonker,' she says, 'it's bloody everywhere!' and suddenly I see it, tramlines upon tramlines of the stuff, ribboned through the curled pondweed and wrapped around submerged stems of marsh marigold and even a thin, underwater branch of one of the bits of wood I placed at the edge, which doubles up as a dragonfly perch. Just as it should be. 'Toadspawn!' I gasp. 'So it is!'

At night I let Tos out for a wee and crouch down by the toadspawn. There are several males, but at least one couple in amplexus, along with a mating ball that I think involves a frog. I laugh, and then see my little newt (or one of my little newts?) pawing through the pondweed into my torchlight. 'Hello toads, hello frog, hello newt,' I say. After a few days in the countryside among Cetti's warblers and lapwings, I was worried I would have fallen out of love with my little city garden. But how can I? I sit on the bench as toads squeak among their eggs, as a hedgehog crunches kitten biscuits, as this little patch of Earth wakes into spring. 'Hello, hello, hello!'

In a stable climate, temperature and rainfall records are rarely broken; the highs and lows fall within established, constant parameters. But in a destabilising climate records are broken all the time, and so it is that after the driest February since 1934, we are closing in on the wettest March in 40 years. I'm grateful for the full water butts and pond but am itching to get outside and do some gardening. I watch the outside from inside: my rambling rose 'Frances E. Lester' has come into leaf, as have my spindle and guelder rose. Daffodils are still going strong although they're being battered by wind and rain. There are primroses, lungwort and cowslips in flower. Every night I fill the hedgehog dish with kitten biscuits and every morning I watch videos of hedgehogs coming and going from the garden, entering the feeding station or pushing each other out of the way. What I'd give for a calm, sunny spring day.

The winter robin has gone and the spring and summer robin has taken his place. I don't know this, really, I'm just guessing. They could all be the same robin for all I know. This new or not-so-new robin has brought a mate. I watch them from the kitchen; they hide in next door's wisteria and take it in turns to visit the hanging bird feeders, which 2022's summer robin didn't do. Perhaps this is the winter robin who has defeated his rival and decided to stay? There's no way of really knowing.

There are two robins and I like them. One morning, Tos gets me up at 5.30 a.m. and I stand in the kitchen, looking out. The robins are inspecting the robin box and its vicinity. I watch them fly to and from it, fly to the ivy growing around and beneath it, hop among the guelder rose branches that grow next to it. The female sits in the box and splays her wings as if to say, 'Let's choose this one!' I text Emma and tell her the robins have been and she tells me she has seen them 'opposite the bench, yes?' She has seen the robins together in the garden and not thought to tell me, and I would be annoyed if I wasn't so delighted. We might have baby robins!

Later, I bump into Helen, who lives in the house behind mine and has had robins nesting – unsuccessfully – in her garden several times.

'Have you seen much of them this year?'

'They're around, but I don't think they're nesting yet.'

I tell her about the splaying behaviour and the box and the ivy. 'That's exciting,' she says. She tells me she had a conversation with another neighbour about hedgehogs recently, and that my efforts to rewild South Portslade are working. 'Excellent!' I say, deliberately not spoiling the moment by asking if the hog was seen out in the day. We both agree to keep an eye out on the robins, and keep each other posted. I LOVE having these chats with my neighbours.

Speckled wood butterfly, *Pararge aegeria*

The speckled wood butterfly (*Pararge aegeria*) is a butterfly of woodland glades, of dappled shade and hedgerows but also gardens, including very urban ones. It was one of the first butterflies to arrive in my garden, although I'm not sure if it's breeding here. It's brown with a series of spots, which are cream-white if you live in the north of Britain but cream-orange if you live in the south. It rarely visits flowers as it prefers to drink aphid honeydew from high up in the tree tops but it's a strong flier and males are territorial – look for spiralling fights as they chase rivals off their patch.

If a female happens upon a male's patch she will fall to the ground and, after a brief courtship, will mate with him. She lays her eggs in long grass – specifically cock's-foot (*Dactylis glomerata*), common couch (*Elytrigia repens*), false brome (*Brachypodium sylvaticum*) and Yorkshire-fog (*Holcus lanatus*). These will naturally seed into your 'lawn' if you let them. As in my garden, it's usually the first butterfly to arrive to new meadows but others may follow suit, including meadow brown (*Maniola jurtina*), gatekeeper (*Pyronia tithonus*) and ringlet (*Aphantopus hyperantus*), which all breed in long grass.

The speckled wood butterfly is unique among British butterflies as it can overwinter as both a caterpillar and a chrysalis (pupa). This means you'll find adults at different times in spring, with some emerging as early as March and others not on the wing until June. They have two or three generations per year, depending on the weather, and adults of later generations are generally darker than those from earlier in the year.

To garden for them is easy: they need long grass, areas of shade, and somewhere for their caterpillars or pupae to shelter in winter. The fresh green chrysalises are usually attached to the underside of a grass stem or piece of dead leaf. I often worry that cutting meadows to the ground in autumn is bad for speckled woods, as the caterpillars may still be using the grasses or the pupae may be attached to a stem that is cut – I've found them only when cutting long grass. One of the reasons I've moved my meadow into the front garden is that there will be less incentive to cut it right back at the end of summer, that I can leave it long and scraggly for winter. I'll cut it back at some point, but I'll leave a few inches above ground as a 'buffer' and let the clippings rest on the surface for a few days so anything eating the cut blades can simply drop back into the thatch. You could do this too: let grass grow long but let some of it stay long (or at least tufty) all year round. It won't be long before a cream-spotted brown butterfly lands in a sunny spot and claims it as his territory. Fingers crossed a female will fly past and drop down to join him.

April

I was expecting little nephew Stanley to have forgotten about the pumpkins I promised he would be growing at his new house this year, but he told Mum he was excited about getting them ready for Halloween. No pressure, then. I turn up with a multi-cell tray of compost that I promise has seeds in it. 'I didn't label them, though, so they might be butternut squash,' I say.

For three months we have had a plan: Stanley goes out with his dad while Mum fixes up the greenhouse for tomato growing and Ellie and I work on the garden. We all meet up for a curry later.

It doesn't work out like that, though. Ellie, full of pregnancy hormones, decides Stanley would be better off with us in the garden, while Mum makes a start weeding the path.

'Do we have time for path weeding today, Mum?' I ask as gently as I can.

'Well, it's very weedy,' she says. I make further gentle mutterings about the greenhouse and the tomatoes she's been talking about growing since Ellie first mentioned going to look at this house over a year ago, and she mutters back something about a special path-weeding brush she needs to retrieve from her shed.

'OK, off you go then.' I crack on with the pruning, and wonder if I'll have time to do the greenhouse myself.

We find Stanley jobs to do. After destroying a few sacrificial tulips, he makes an excellent daffodil deadheader, and shows his mum the difference between a new tulip and an old daffodil.

'Told you he's a gardener,' I tell Ellie.

We work hard, Mum on the weedy path, Stanley on the deadheading, Ellie on keeping Stanley occupied, me on the roses. The previous owners must have loved their roses; I count 20 of them growing into the sky, which I use loppers to bring back to head height. There's a honeysuckle, too, which I tame and bring back to the garden. My arms hurt and I'm tired. But I carry on, we have only one day. Mum eventually starts work on the greenhouse, clearing out old pots and what she calls 'unusual finds', and then pots on the three grafted tomato and sweet pepper plants I bought her for Mother's Day. Eventually, I'm satisfied she will have room for her growing plants.

I have no time to make a vegetable bed but I fill an old recycling box with compost and cover it up, leaving instructions on when and how to pot on the pumpkin plants when they emerge. I have a feeling that, between them, Mum, Ellie and Stanley are not going to manage this. But we'll see. At least I pruned the roses.

Back home and finally the sun comes. We're treated to two days of it. Two days of blue and yellow. Two days of cheerfulness and laughter. 'It makes such a difference, doesn't it?' says everyone, 'a bit of sun'. And they're right, of course, but I think back to how I spontaneously started singing in the park when the rain came after the drought, how it's not sun specifically but the right balance of sun and rain that we crave, that's somehow wired into us. Wired into us, I suppose, because sunshine and showers make the food grow – too much of one or the other and life becomes hard. Somehow, instinctively, our bodies know this.

I garden gently. There's a cold wind but I can just get away with a T-shirt if I keep moving. I sow 'hard-wearing' grass seed on hard-worn patches of bare earth, and cover them with frames and cloches to stop the dog, the hedgehogs and the foxes walking on them. They butt against the edge of the pond and I wonder who – me or Tos – will be the first to slip and fall into the water. I tend the new border at the back, selectively weeding out some of the creeping speedwell, chickweed, cleavers and young nettles, while letting plenty remain. I'm pleased to see one of the globe artichoke heads that I rescued from a bin in autumn and fixed to the trellis as a sort of bird buffet (which was then ignored) has yielded seedlings. I untie the seedhead from the trellis and chuck it down where I think I might like a globe artichoke to grow, hopefully recreating the soft landing a fallen stem might make in the wild. I remove little clumps of grass from the border and transplant them into the lawn, I remove figwort seedlings from around the pond (the figwort is allowed to live at the back of the garden only). I remove spent daffodil flowers and compost them. I check on new growth that has pushed through the soil since I last looked. I find a home for my new bird bath, which I bought second-hand from the man at the end of the road. I greet my first dark-edged bee-fly of the year – 'Hi!' – and lie on my belly and gaze into the pond.

The water fizzes with new life. There are masses of tiny things – little nymphs, or midge larvae, perhaps, that have been laid in the pond recently. I spy water hoglice eating algae off leaves, water snails slithering over stones. There are tadpoles, of course, thousands of them. Despite the recent cold, some of them are quite big already, it won't be long before they develop legs. Others are small, just recently hatched. I watch seething masses of them in various clumps, frantically eating. The pond is coming back to life.

Some of the tadpoles are eating the toadspawn. I suspected they were doing this a few days ago but dismissed this because toads, their larvae and their eggs, contain a toxin called bufotoxin, which makes them slightly poisonous and distasteful to predators. This means they're not eaten by newts or fish; indeed toads seem to prefer to spawn in ponds populated by fish, presumably because the fish eat the competition (the newts and the frogs). But frog tadpoles? What are they doing?

Lying on my belly with my head close to the water I can see that they're just eating the jelly that surrounds the egg. The bufotoxin is present in the egg only, so the crafty tads are getting their fill of the protein-rich jelly and leaving the eggs without protection. The jelly is there to insulate the eggs, to protect them while they develop into tiny larvae. It's then the first thing the young tadpoles eat before finding other food in the pond. Without it, it's unlikely these eggs will survive.

Oh precious toads! I have waited so long for them and they are being destroyed by other things I love. This is too cruel. It's too late to save them now; the eggs float in the water like words spilled as jumbled letters off a page. Some of them seem slightly half-developed, will they make it? I don't know. And then I realise, of course, there is a way to find out.

I retrieve a glass bowl and a small jar from the kitchen and return to the pond where the toadspawn is. I try sinking the jar into the pond but come away with a few eggs and lots of tadpoles. I change my tactic, honing in on dense clumps of the stuff and using my fingers to shovel it in. This works better – there are still tadpoles, of course, you couldn't retrieve anything from this pond at the moment without tadpoles – but there are more eggs. Gently, I tip the jar so the eggs spill into the bowl while the tads swim to the other end, where the water remains deepest. Then I release the tads back into the pond.

I don't collect much, just enough to see if it develops. I inspect my newly decanted quarry and fish out two rogue water hoglice that I suspect are also partial to a bit of spawn jelly. Some of the spawn is still intact; the eggs are encased still in small amounts of goo. They're at various stages of development; there are tight little balls that look like they'll never do anything, but there are little nuggets, too, little half-formed things that are neither egg nor tadpole. It's these I've got my eye on.

With less jelly to feed on they will need something else to eat, so I return to the kitchen and retrieve fish flakes from under the sink. These I will feed to my tadpoles as they get bigger, when they start getting a taste for meat. I put a few in the water and watch them disintegrate into it. There will be plenty of nutrients for them to eat, for now. Lastly, I dig out my trusty caterpillar mesh tent from the shed and lower the bowl into it, to keep marauding birds at bay. Then I move the whole kit to the side return, which gets very little sun, so they don't overheat.

The garden is transformed again. Each time I go out, there is something new to gawp at, something shiny to marvel. Today it's all primrose flowers and unravelling fern fronds, mitten-like leaf buds and the promise of blossom. Little details reveal themselves as I walk around: hints of fresh green hawthorn leaves against blood-red uneaten berries, the first chequered blooms of snake's head fritillary, the fattest of hellebore seedpods.

I'm pleased to see there are masses of flower buds on both the guelder rose and spindle. In previous years these two native shrubs have borne only one or two little blooms but now, in their fourth year, they're about to flower their socks off. I can't wait to see which pollinators visit them. I can't wait for guelder berries and bright orange and pink spindle fruit. Who will eat them? How will they look against the rest of the garden? It's all so exciting.

I need to go over the borders again because there are things popping up all over the place that shouldn't be there. Alliums that somehow worked themselves into shady corners, things I've planted too close together or that have grown into the space intended for something else. Grass seedlings everywhere except, of course, the lawn. I'm sad to see there are ominous empty spaces where there should be things – there's no sign of regrowth from the penstemons; have I lost my penstemons? It's silly, I know, but I loved them, and I planted them next to the buddleia so the wine-red of their bell-shaped blooms would complement the fresh purple of the buddleia's panicles. It was a flower combo that looked smart and sumptuous, something someone scruffy, like me, would never normally be able to pull off. It was a combo that was accidental at first, borne from plunging something at the back of the border because I had no space elsewhere for it, but which I couldn't stop staring at once it got going. As the flowers started to fade and the display lost its mojo, I added a second penstemon, from the front garden, so there would be two flowering among the buddleia, with agapanthus, nepeta and cranesbills in the foreground, plus a splash of white from the Shasta daisies. Now, in the year where I would finally see them looking their glorious best, the penstemons have gone and died. Looking at the border now, I can't make out the Shasta daisies, either. It makes sense; both can suffer in winter wet, especially on clay soil. And if there's one thing we had this winter it was wet. I haven't quite given up hope but it's not looking good.

I can't tell the difference between honesty, charlock and garlic mustard seedlings but there are masses of them all over the garden. Is it honesty? I think it is, but I've been caught out before. I don't mind charlock and garlic mustard at the back of the borders but not centre-stage, not bang in the middle of my display. I look them up and check them against the clumps of heart-shaped leaves. I think it's honesty. Or at least some of it is. Most of it is. Maybe.

I'm pleased to see the greenest of ivy leaves, the newest of climbing hydrangea foliage. The gaps between the ivy plants are closing now. I grin at the thought of an ivy-clad fence, with climbing hydrangea growing among it, and of all the things that will live in it. I post about it on Twitter and men tell me my fence will fall down.

The hops and golden clematis, *Clematis tangutica*, on the trellis are coming into growth. Normally I cut these back in early spring but I have left them this year so as not to put the robins off. Instead, I cut the clematis stems back to the base of the trellis but leave last year's stems in place. *Clematis tangutica* is a Group 3 clematis, so flowers on new growth only. So if you don't cut it back hard every spring you end up giving your neighbours free flowers, while you are left staring at a tangled mass of old stems. I'm happy with a tangled mess but I'd like the flowers to stay here, so I cut the stems at the base of the trellis but I don't remove the old growth so it remains to provide shelter for birds until new stems grow into its place. The hops, too, can stay tangled. The robins, of course, have decided to nest elsewhere but one day, perhaps, they will take a chance on the garden, and maybe they won't need the box, maybe there will be home enough for them in the climbers.

The tadpoles in the pond are getting big and swimming strongly. It won't be long before they have legs. I scatter fish flakes over the surface and watch the tads gulp them up with little clicking noises. The toad tadpoles in the bowls are little commas now, so they are growing after all. I add fresh water from the water butt and move the bowl around a bit to give the illusion of moving water. I have absolutely no idea at all if they will like this but it feels appropriate to try.

The front garden is coming along, I think. There's a lot of grass, but among it are primroses and cowslips, lungwort and snake's head fritillary. There are clumps of things that will look nice, I'm sure: ox-eye daisies, greater knapweed, red clover, ribwort plantain. It's a meadow, of sorts, but it's odd-looking, for now. I need to get in to see if there are yellow rattle seedlings. I might see if I can cut the grass a bit, to give things a chance. I need to trim next door's hedge so it doesn't steal more light than is necessary from the things I want to grow. It may yet prove itself beautiful.

We are having a proper spring and I'm grateful for it. We get sunshine and showers, frosts and the odd bout of above-average temperatures that allow us to dream, hopefully, of summer. There's a fair amount of wind, of wobbly jet stream, of hot and cold and wet and dry and Christ-will-you-just-make-up-your-mind? But it feels, largely, normal, perhaps on the cool side of normal. Spring-like. Not like 2022 when the ground was cracking already due to lack of rain. There's plenty of time yet for cracked earth; I'm just grateful, now, for full water butts.

Our gulls are nesting now. I hear them mating, see them gathering sticks, watch them sit on eggs with a contentedness I can only dream of having myself. A lesser black-backed gull on a roof against a blue sky is the most beautiful thing. To think that Brighton and Hove is full of them – full of gulls on rooftops, gulls mating in the most ungainly and noisy fashion, gulls gathering sticks to live in the sky. I love them. We are so lucky to have them.

They're still being harassed by Drone Bastard and we are running out of ways to stop him. The RSPB has confirmed that what he's doing – disturbing active nests with a drone – is illegal, but we're not sure if they've been to see him this year. The RSPCA has been to see him but has decided what's he's doing isn't illegal, and they have told him so (helpful, thanks). I spoke with the man who paid him a visit and he was absolutely confident that flying a drone at active birds' nests isn't illegal.

'If he goes on to the roof and removes nesting material, that's illegal,' he says. 'But dive-bombing nests with a drone? However unpleasant that is, it's not illegal. Plus, for what it's worth,' continues the man, 'he's wasting his time. He won't stop them nesting.'

'But what if there are chicks in the nest?' I ask. 'What if he's causing eggs to break and preventing the parents from feeding their chicks?'

'Not illegal,' he says, and tells me to get footage of the man climbing on to the roof to destroy nests, which of course we won't get now because he knows we're on to him.

'Please be very careful what you say on your Facebook group,' he says. 'Please don't misquote me.' I tell him I have 33,000 followers on Twitter but I won't tell them.

'Thank you,' he says.

'I'll write about it in my book instead,' I say.

Our local councillor comes round and we take him to the warehouse, where we find Drone Bastard using his drone to dive-bomb gulls. We watch him for a while, and then the councillor goes to speak to him while we hide around the corner. 'Be careful,' we tell him, and sure enough, the man frog-marches him off his property and shouts until he's blue in the face. At least he can see what we're up against.

Finally, we think the police pay him a visit, or at least speak to him (annoyingly they won't give us details). Everything goes quiet for a while and we four members of Gulls Allowed tentatively book an evening in the pub to celebrate. But then it starts up again. He's bought a new drone, an enormous thing and the way he uses it now is even more menacing. Once again, three, four, five times a day, the peace is ruined by crying gulls, flying off their nests and eggs to get away from this new and unfamiliar threat. It's absolutely devastating.

At this point, I realise he's spending more money on drones than he would need in order to have his gutters regularly cleared, which he claims is the root cause of his issue. This is the third drone we've seen him use; he must be spending thousands of pounds. To have someone clear your gutters once a month during nesting season – £300?

The sun is shining and I take a break to trim my side of next door's hedge, which is largely Japanese spindle and must be cut at least twice a year or it will eat my house. I check it thoroughly for nesting house sparrows, even though I know they're not nesting in it because the hedge is outside the window, in front of which is the sofa, where I sit. The house sparrows nest in holey houses, not in the hedge, and not in the expensive nest boxes I installed in my wall cavities for them, either.

I cut it back gently, starting at the base and then using the step ladder to climb to the top, to stop it growing into the guttering, which is already living on borrowed time. Next door's uncut half sticks out like a sore thumb and, for the first time in four years, I knock and ask if they would like me to cut their side, too. They almost bite my hand off. 'Yes, please! Please cut my side of the hedge, please do it, yes!' I laugh. They bring me a little chocolate egg, which I give to Emma, and for me I take their clippings to feed my compost bin (for all that I hate it, Japanese spindle composts beautifully). It's the day after Storm Noa and it's comparatively calm and sunny, a good spring day. I watch house sparrows fly to and from holey houses, hairy-footed flower bees chase each other around pulmonaria. I'm wearing a T-shirt with a big bumblebee on it, and feeling some semblance of hope, except there are very few bumblebees about. Late, perhaps, due to the recent cold snap. As I trim the hedge, one sparrow remains inside and chirps gently, keeping me company, and I feel happy that I'm not disturbing it or causing it distress. But then the gulls start crying, and I look up to see the enormous drone, looking like some sort of plane, flying low over the rooftops and pausing over nests to dive-bomb them. I can't tell you how much I hate Drone Bastard.

The other three members of Gulls Allowed live closer to the action and have a good view of the nests he's attacking. They say there are several pairs of lesser black-backed gulls who have not been put off nesting and are currently sitting on eggs. They say the gulls rise and try to attack the drone before, eventually, settling back down again. They say the gulls should be OK – it looks like the man from the RSPCA was right.

But it's not the point, is it? It's not enough that the gulls should just about manage to raise chicks despite the efforts of one man who wants to stop them. They should be able to nest safely and peacefully, to sit on eggs against a blue Brighton sky, to raise squawky gangly things that fall off roofs and get into scrapes because they're BABIES and they're ridiculous. Imagine a drone flying at your head every time you try to feed the dog or change your baby's nappy. Imagine putting your child to bed and having someone constantly trying to stop you. I'm not convinced Drone Bastard is well, and I feel sad for him. But he's got to stop tormenting these gulls.

I look on Facebook Marketplace for a drone. I have never flown one before and don't really know what I'm looking for. I chat with a man who's selling an old one for £30. He promises it works but it doesn't have a camera. Is that enough to do what I want with it? And what do I want to do, really? I fantasise about sending up my drone every time he sends up his, and flying it over his stupid head to distract and intimidate him. I would need a camera for that, certainly. What about using it to fly at his drone and chase it off the gulls' nests? Or using it to attack his, like some sort of robot war? That, too, would disturb the gulls.

I'm so angry with him. He's clearly been spoken to by the police and the RSPCA and he's responded by buying a bigger drone, by parading it around to show all of us who have complained about him that he's in charge. I want to throw dog shit into his warehouse. I want to empty tins of paint over his vans. I want to graffiti the words *GULL KILLER* all over his precious business. I can't do any of those things because they are illegal and the law is firmly on his side. I hate everything.

Back in the house I stand at the kitchen window and stare into the garden. The robins are trying to get to the bird feeder but the house sparrows are in the way. They take it in turns to fly at the feeder and hover beside it for a few seconds, presumably with the hope of persuading a sparrow to shift or at least budge up, which none of them seems interested in doing. They fly back and forth, between the hawthorn and the feeder, eventually unseating the sparrows. They take a couple of sunflower hearts but seem to lose interest in it after the other birds have gone. Hmm. I've got my eye on you, robins.

I watch them for a while. I'm sure they're not nesting in my garden but they still seem quite attached to the area where the robin box is. I watch them fly around a bit but always lose them when they get to that spot – which I think is the ivy growing up the fence beneath the box. I'm pretty sure I would have noticed them nest building, as they would have been flying to and from the spot determinedly, with nest material in their beaks. Perhaps they are nesting elsewhere but are regretting it? Perhaps they are a few doors down but feel sad they are not here. Perhaps one is nagging the other, 'We really should have nested at Kate's.' More realistically, I wonder if Storm Noa destroyed their existing nest and they are now reconsidering their options. It's a possibility, I suppose. Maybe they haven't started nesting yet? It seems late, mid-April, but it has been cold and perhaps they are young and this is their first coupling. Perhaps they don't know what they're doing, and are taking their time over their decision, although I'm terrified at the thought of them nesting on the ground behind a measly bit of ivy. 'Have you heard of cats?' I mouth to the robins through the double-glazed kitchen window. If they start nesting on the ground beneath the robin box I shall never sleep again.

The 'honesty' is garlic mustard. Of course it is. All of it. I walk around the garden and laugh at every single plant I have lovingly dotted around in ones and threes, each one developing little white flowers at its tip rather than the larger purple and white blooms they're supposed to have. I've planted them so well. If they had been honesty the garden would be a flowering mass of purple and white right now.

'It's a shame you're so bad at gardening,' says Emma.

There is some honesty but it won't flower until next year. The seeds I threw around the beds in autumn have germinated and the plants are growing strongly. I make a note of where they are so, when I transplant them around later in the year, I'll have a chance of moving the right ones.

The garlic mustard is looking beautiful, actually. As yet untouched by insects, its leaves are fresh and green, with a little ring of reddish foliage around a central head of the whitest flowers, so bright and full of promise. They will grow to around a metre in height and look handsome in my shady woodland borders and around the pond, but not among poppies and agapanthus and buddleia and catmint. I do have limits. I weed them out of the pollinator border and leave those growing on the shady side, along with some others around the pond that will also get some sun. I laugh a bit more. Maybe I am really bad at gardening?

I introduced garlic mustard a few years ago. I had hoped to attract orange-tip butterflies, although I've never seen one in the garden, let alone a caterpillar. Garlic mustard, cuckoo flower and, to a lesser extent, honesty and sweet rocket, are all food plants for the orange-tip butterfly, whose eggs and young caterpillars are orange, in a nod to the male's beautiful wing tips (the female's are black). Every year I check the stems and leaves for eggs and caterpillars, and every year I'm disappointed. Maybe this year, the year I have a lot more garlic mustard than I bargained for, will be the year of the orange-tip butterfly.

In the front the meadow is developing nicely. There are large grassy patches, which I intend to cut back in stages, as if I were a highland cow grazing on an open piece of native hay meadow. This would create microhabitats that don't exist at the moment, while enabling wildflowers to get a step ahead of the growing game. The beauty of the front-garden meadow is that it's small so I can channel my inner highland cow on my knees with a pair of scissors.

It's still looking odd. There's a huge angelica that's growing tall and developing its flower head, just in front of the window. It's been in the ground for nearly three years now. A biennial, it was supposed to flower in 2022 but, like many plants, it simply refused to bloom in the drought. I'll whip it out as soon as it's set seed, find somewhere for its children to grow next year; it can't live in the meadow, it's too big and ungainly. There's also a tired old perennial wallflower, which I haven't the heart to remove because it usually flowers all year round, although is not doing so at the moment. The hedge shadow is its usual bald self, which irritates me, but probably, hopefully, provides a home for mining bees.

I'm pleased to see the ivy I planted in the gap in the hedge is not yet dead. This fills me with hope that, one day, it will take hold and not only fill in the gap but grow through it, increasing the biodiversity of the hedge and perhaps even limiting the growth of the Japanese spindle. I have other rooted ivy cuttings sitting in water in the kitchen, some of which are earmarked for my back fence but others which could be added to the little gaps in the hedge. It's a long game, waiting for ivy to take hold, but I'm here for it.

Without honesty, the back garden is looking flowerless, green and almost lush but not quite ready for the season. The guelder rose and spindle are in full leaf but have not yet flowered, while the hawthorn is just coming into leaf and the rowan is not far behind. By the end of the month there will be blossom and light, blooms on which my eyes and bees' tongues can feast. It's a shame about the honesty, but if the garlic mustard brings butterflies it will be a mistake worth making.

I stand in the kitchen and watch rain fall on to the garden. There's no wind and the water falls in straight lines, landing on leaves, on the compost bin, in bubbles on the pond. I can hear the gentle trickle of water filling the butt beside me, the drips as it lands in puddles on the patio. I watch my new bird bath fill up, which yesterday I saw sparrows bathe in for the first time.

The garden has a lushness I haven't known before. The grass is full and thick, the ivy is bunching up. The rowan and hawthorn are just about in leaf now, the rowan's leaves with a hint of blue that you only see in the first flush of spring growth. A bit of warmth and there will be blossom – not just in the trees but in the guelder rose and spindle, too. I still can't wait to see them.

The below-average temperatures have preserved spring flowers but delayed those of summer: there are still primroses and cowslips, hellebores and snowflakes. But everything else is taking its time. I want to see them, I want the bees to wake up. But I still want this rain – I want it all.

The robin flies into the garden and heads straight to the ivy, into which he dives because he can now, because it's thick and strong enough to support him. He seems to find something, and then struggles to tug it out, and I don't see what he takes off with. He's not nesting here, I know that, but I'm confident he will one day. For him, the garden is just becoming good enough.

Sparrows, which always seem more bothered by rain than most, as if clamouring to shelter beneath an imaginary umbrella, land on the feeder but give up and retreat. A field mouse dashes between the habitat pile and the hedgehog feeding station, its mouth full of stolen biscuits. There is a stillness and serenity to gentle rain, and I am grateful for it.

The new border at the back has flowering red geums, which look beautiful with the marsh marigold in the foreground, a plant combination I hadn't realised when I planted them at the time. Soon there will be foxgloves and cranesbills, catmint and ornamental poppies. Red campion, viper's bugloss, roses and clematis. Will plants flower better this year? Will there be ruddy clover and lamb's ears? A large clump of red clover blocks my view of the pond and I realise that it, too, should be moved to the front meadow.

I am irritated by plants growing too closely together, by garlic mustard that should be honesty, by the summer pollinator border that looks terrible in spring. I make mental notes to fix these when I can, to make everything prettier. I eye up large clumps of primrose that I can divide when they've finished flowering, at snowflakes that could be used to fill gaps. A gardener's work is never done, but that's more than half the joy of it.

Some of the most important pieces I've read in recent months have been from climate protesters explaining how they got into doing what they do. They post on social media, addressing those who sit at home wanting and feeling that they ought to be helping the cause, but not quite being able to do so. They say things like, 'It takes a while to work out how you can be useful.' They say, 'Everyone wakes up in the morning and looks for a million excuses not to protest.' They tell you it's OK to turn up for an hour and stand at the back, they say you don't have to do anything you don't want to do. But they also say, and this is what chimes with me the most, that for those who are feeling despair and lack of hope about the climate crisis, getting out and being surrounded by people who feel the same is incredibly uplifting. It's the doing versus not-doing, they say, the finding of your people. 'Don't just sit at home and cry while doom-scrolling,' they say, 'get out there! You will work out how you can be useful.'

I've never been much of a protester. I've spent my life going to Gay Pride events – I've marched two or three times, watched the parade a handful more. But mainly I head straight to the party. Beyond Pride, I've done a bit. Back in 2000, as a green first-year university student and new member of the student union LGBT group, I took part in small protests about Section 28, Thatcher's hateful local government Act that prevented homosexuality from being 'promoted' in schools. The Act was in place from 1988 to 2003, for almost my entire school career. In reality, it meant gay children, like me, who had never really had to think about who they were, were suddenly plunged into the despair of being wrong, of being 'other'. It meant being bullied for being gay while teachers turned a blind eye. It meant listening to teachers being openly homophobic, it meant my local newspaper dedicating a whole page to the vitriolic outburst of the husband of one of my teachers (who I adored), in which he argued that gay men were paedophiles and suggested they shouldn't have access to the NHS (I was 16 when I read this and it broke my heart). It meant entering adolescence, suddenly alone, with not a single adult having my back.

While discussions took place to repeal the clause, a privately funded campaign was set up to keep it. Part of this campaign was a poll funded by Brian Souter, founder of the Stagecoach travel company. Along with others in my university LGBT group, I boarded Stagecoach buses and handed 'Repeal Section 28!' leaflets to bemused passengers. I was also an active filler of envelopes with paperclips, which were then sent by Freepost to the Keep the Clause campaign, to waste their money. I remember being cold, standing at the bus stop waiting for buses. I remember feeling awkward and exposed as I handed people leaflets, the discomfort of stuffing envelopes while kneeling on a hard, dusty floor. But I'm glad I was there. Section 28 was finally repealed in 2003. I'm glad I was part of that piece of queer history. (And no, I still won't travel by Stagecoach.)

I didn't protest Brexit, I didn't attend any of the women's marches. I did march against the Iraq War and former President Trump's state visit to the UK. I've been on a few School Strike for Climate marches, rallies for Palestine and local Extinction Rebellion events (if there's a local event I'm more likely to go). But that's about it; I struggle with the big London ones, they're big and noisy and involve a much greater effort to go, and I would always rather be in the garden. Still, that piece of queer history, that momentous repeal that means today's queer kids have an easier time in school? I was there. It feels good knowing I was there.

I get Extinction Rebellion emails. I've joined Zoom meetings and chatted on the phone with Just Stop Oil volunteers. I sign up to talks and open calls and then don't bother attending. There's a wall, a stumbling block, that has so far stopped me from being properly involved. I want to be a part of it but, I suppose, I'm scared. I don't want to be kettled, I don't want to get into trouble with the police or lose any work. I certainly don't want to be cold. But I do want to be there. For the birds and the hedgehogs and the elephants and for my nephew Stanley and his little brother on his way. For me and my mental health. For literally everything we live for and love, all of us.

Extinction Rebellion recently announced it was moving away from disruptive tactics, to 'prioritise attendance over arrest and relationships over roadblocks.' Along with Greenpeace and 200 other organisations, they organised The Big One, a three-day peaceful protest in London, where they pleaded with people to come but to 'leave the locks, glue and paint behind'. Would more people turn up? People like me?

Different groups with different interests arrived on different days. Saturday was 'Biodiversity Day', where wildlife people marched to lament the loss of life both here and across the world. But I went on Sunday, with my friend Abigail. Both of us have chatted about wanting to do more, wanting to be there, wherever 'there' is, because it matters.

There were no marches on the Sunday but lots of stalls, demos and activities where you could write messages to the world and make a paper boat with a plea to the Home Secretary to open safe routes of passage for refugees, which would be floated down the Thames to Westminster. We watched Amazonian tribespeople speak of the threats to their cultures and land, we wore stickers, we chatted to scientists. We even cheered on the London Marathon, which ran through a part of Parliament Square and I was so happy to see that no one attempted to disrupt it. Then we went for a pint before making our separate ways home. It was nice to have some company, it was good to go with a friend. And I'm so glad I did it.

The world needs us in whatever way we can give ourselves to it. And we must. We must give ourselves to the world and the climate crisis. To the people of the global south, to our children, to all of the species that face extinction. Now, in whatever way we can. We all need to step up and do more, to show those in power that we won't tolerate them reneging on the 2016 Paris Agreement. As I type, our prime minister, Rishi Sunak, has just approved the licences of 100 more gas and oil projects in the North Sea, while he continues to fly around the country in private jets and helicopters. Sunak is not interested in the climate crisis, he's made that abundantly clear. But he won't be in power for ever and the next government needs to know that its people won't stand for more gas and oil. We won't stand for further destruction of natural habitats, of the near-death of rivers, of the stifling of the right to protest, of the continued mistreatment of refugees, many of whom are coming to our shores because of climate change. If we stay home and cry while doom-scrolling, how will we tell them?

Emma knows that if I am pottering in the kitchen and then suddenly go quiet, I am looking through the kitchen window. She used to call out, 'What are you doing?' But now she doesn't need to. Now she knows I am looking at leaves and flowers, tracking growth, planning which things to move or divide and imagining what the borders will look like when my dreams and plans have been realised. Or

I might be looking through binoculars, at frogs in the pond or mining bees in the lawn. I might be ogling a blackcap in the hawthorn tree or a chiffchaff on the roses, or greeting my first-ever black redstart.

(Actually, no, I did a fair amount of squealing when I saw the black redstart.)

Today I am watching the robins, which, of course, are now gathering nest material and taking it back to their favourite patch of ivy. So they were intending to nest here after all, they just hadn't got around to it. It's late, nearly May. I wonder if this is their first time nesting or if they have been assessing the availability of invertebrate food and didn't want to start until there was plenty to feed their young. Or if they have attempted nesting elsewhere and it's not worked out. I will never know but I'm so glad they're here.

I've never understood how people don't notice birds nesting in their garden, because nest building is very obvious and deliberate behaviour. It's the female robin that builds the nest, which is cup-shaped and made using dead leaves and moss and lined with hair. They're typically found on or near the ground in any number of situations, including climbing plants and log piles, as long as they're completely obscured. I can't see exactly where they're nesting and that's the point – I'm not supposed to. But I watch her gathering leaves from the habitat pile and the borders, and disappearing with them in the general direction of the ivy, back and forth, back and forth.

I tell Emma we can't use the garden now.

'But we live here,' she says. I tell her Tos has to do her business out the front.

'Tosca also lives here,' she says, as she opens the door to let her out for a wee. 'The robins have been hanging out in the garden for three months. They know us, they have decided we're safe. Don't go changing anything now.'

I huff and grumble, as Tosca comes back in and they return together, to the sofa. I close the door and continue looking out.

The robins have fully claimed the garden as their own and I love it. On either side of the shed is a water butt with a small plastic lid that I have positioned upside down so it collects water. I thought the birds might like these as extra bathing spots and I was right, our robins seem to have taken to bathing in the one on the left, which the small hedge has started to grow around and partially hide from view.

Robins are flighty. They abandon their nests easily – they don't like it when disturbed or 'discovered'. Later, we sit on the patio with our Friday beers, catching the last of the day's sun, and I see the female struggle with our presence. She stops short of going into the nest, she drops her beakful of leaves. We look away and she resumes her activities, but as soon as we look at her again she retreats. I'm worried she will abandon it, late as she has left her nest-building efforts. I worry the garden is too small for us and the robins, that it is we, not them, that should stay away. At least while they're nest building. But, as Emma says, we live here. We have to rub along together.

In the morning I stand in the kitchen again and look out. I have come to know that I need stand only for a minute or two before a robin turns up, that if they are still nest building, the female will soon appear with an old leaf. I wait. They've abandoned it, haven't they? I wait. Then, quickly, the male shoots into the garden, grabs a sunflower heart from the feeder and shoots back out again.

Tos wants to be let out for a wee and I open the door and go out with her. She heads straight to the ivy and sniffs

– she too knows something is happening here – and I shoo her away. I walk past it, as I do every day, to the hedgehog feeding station, to see if the hogs ate all of their dinner (they did), and to retrieve the camera from in front of the bird bath. I wonder if I can fix the camera in front of the nest to watch them without disturbing them, or if the act of positioning it there would be disturbance enough. Perhaps they've abandoned it already.

I head back upstairs with tea, feeling deflated. And then I realise – what if they are wise to me standing in the kitchen? What if I can watch them another way? I should be able to see them from the bathroom if I get in the bath and open the frosted window, which – I suppose – might act as a sort of bird hide. I may as well try. I climb into the bath, open the window and wait, heart in mouth.

There are sparrows being noisy in the cherry trees a few doors down. A wood pigeon *coo-COO-coo-coo-coos* from somewhere else. There's no sign of any robin but I can hear the faintest *pip-pip-pip*. A robin? I wait, barely breathing as I tune in to the tiny sound almost obliterated by sparrows. It falls silent again and I relax. I wish I had my binoculars, I could laugh at the sparrows in the meantime, look for other things – chiffchaffs maybe, in the cherry trees.

Pip-pip-pip-pip. I look down and see nothing. Still, I wait, squatted as I am in an empty bath, in my pyjamas. I wait.

The female appears suddenly on the trellis, carrying a leaf. She's still nest building! Phew. She doesn't notice me and heads straight into the ivy, and back out again to the habitat pile. I breathe a thousand sighs of relief, close the window and vow to leave her alone. It takes a robin up to six days to build her nest. We are on at least day two, so that's four more days of staying out of the garden. Can we do that?

Red-tailed mason bee, *Osmia bicolor*

Also known as the snail-shell-nesting bee, *Osmia bicolor* is unique among British bees in that it nests in empty snail shells, typically on chalk and limestone grasslands but also in quarries and brownfield sites. I've met them only once, on a chalky snail-shelled slope near Cerne Abbas in Dorset, where I spent a few hours watching the females stock their nests.

Similar looking to the red mason bee, females are not strictly 'red-tailed' but have a black head and thorax and orange-red abdomen. Males are slimmer and pale brown all over.

They emerge from hibernation in spring and quickly get on with the business of mating, after which the female seeks out the perfect empty snail shell to lay her eggs in. She rolls the shell into the correct position, then makes up to five individual cells within the shell chamber, which she seals with leaves and chalky soil, and even shell particles, chewing them into a sort of pesto. She stocks each cell with a store of pollen and nectar, before laying an egg. Once she has filled the shell she plugs it with an extra-thick layer of pesto, and sometimes goes on to 'plaster' the outside of the shell to camouflage it into the landscape. She then flies off in search of grass, which she chews into manageable pieces and carries back to her shell to further hide it.

Only when she is happy with the positioning of the shell, the plastering of the pesto and the extra camouflage provided by the clump of severed grass stems does she move on, often to find a second snail shell to lay eggs in. Are there enough empty snail shells for the snail-shell-nesting bee? You would think not, and I know people who collect shells and drop them off at known snail shell nesting sites, in case they may be of use. Inside each shell the eggs hatch into grubs, which feed on the store of pollen and nectar their mother has left for them. They then spin a cocoon and pupate into an adult, living in their sturdy home until the following spring, when they mate and make pesto and cut grass and lay eggs.

Red-tailed mason bees visit a range of flowers, including trefoils and vetches, and blackthorn and hawthorn blossom. They're mostly found in southern and eastern England, although there's some suggestion they're moving north. They're not a garden species, so there's not much you can do to help them unless you live close to a colony and have an abundance of snail shells to drop off for them to make use of. I just wanted you to know that such a creature exists in this fragile landscape we all call home. Such a wonderful creature exists.

May

The robin nest, as far as I can tell, is wedged behind some hop stems, against the north-facing wall, just beneath the trellis. It's also behind the shrub rose, which is prickly. This means it won't be troubled by wind or sunshine and heat, and is surrounded by thorns, which will make predation hard for cats. Well done, those robins.

I still worry about squirrels and magpies. There are crows, too, which steal in each day to gobble tadpoles. Tosca chases them out of the garden – they're big enough to be invaders of her territory – but they always come back when she's inside. The cats don't, there are definitely fewer of them since Tos arrived, but the combined threat of predation is a hard one to bear. I know how few robins there are in this neighbourhood. I know the future of these chicks is, partly, in my hands. Suddenly I want to spend more time outside, not less. I want to guard the nest with my trusty, barking canine. I want to help secure the future of those baby robins. I want there to be more robins.

Helen, who lives in the house behind mine, told me they have nested with her a couple of times but always lost their eggs to magpies or squirrels. Another woman in the next road has said the blackbirds nesting in her garden suffered the same fate for three years before they gave up. When I moved here four years ago there was one dominant blackbird and three sub males (his sons?) who sang each evening from the top of Helen's house. They're all gone now. The last time I heard a blackbird was in March; he had been singing his dawn chorus alone since January. One day he stopped and I haven't heard him since. There are some about, in the next road maybe, but I rarely see a blackbird in the garden.

Two common bird species that are almost absent from our landscape. Two common species that should be singing from every other rooftop but are struggling to live among paved and plastic gardens, in conditions that provide advantages for magpies, crows and squirrels, where every other home has a cat. Can we please do better for our birds?

Nest building took around five days. Since then all has gone quiet and I have avoided the area. I'm not avoiding the garden completely, though, as I realise – and as Emma suggested – the robins chose us for a reason. Perhaps the dog and the gardener are integral to their plan? Perhaps they know I will protect them? I'm assuming the female is now sitting on eggs, that they are being discreet so as not to alert the magpies, cats, crows and squirrels. The female lays up to six eggs, at a rate of one egg per day. She lays in the morning while the male sings from the cherry tree five doors down, defending his territory, which spans several of our small gardens. I would think she has laid all of them now and is sitting on them, quietly waiting for them to hatch. They should hatch within two weeks, when the sound of hungry chicks will alert all of the predators. I check the dates in my calendar, for when I can anticipate noisy nestlings. Can I clear it? It's Chelsea Flower Show that week and I have to go to press day. But the rest of the week? Yes, clear it. I buy a parasol for the table so I can work outside. I don't want to interfere with the nest, I don't want to do anything to poke or get in the way of these birds and their young. But if I'm working away at my makeshift outside office, the dog sunbathing on the grass, then surely the magpies and crows, the cats, squirrels and foxes will stay out of the garden? And the robins will have a chance of success. If we — the dog and I — can get them to fledgling stage that will be something. At least we can get them to the point where they leave the nest. It's got to be worth a try. In the meantime, we pack our bags for a mini-break in the New Forest, leaving the robin to sit on her eggs in peace. I hope upon hope the predators don't notice her.

In the woods we are dusted with the glitter of goldcrest song, as shafts of light bend time and space and the world around us becomes taller. Who sings above us? Goldcrests and firecrests, redstarts, coal tits, blackbirds, robins. Everyone. Autumn's leaves crunch underfoot as we make our way through the trees but I stop and stop and stop, and listen to birds. I want to sit beneath a tree and soak it all up. I want to bring sandwiches and spend the day being washed with birdsong. I want to…

'Kate!'

Emma throws a ball for Tosca, who gambols about, high on woodland smells, and begs her to throw it again. We are on a woodland walk in the New Forest, day three of a five-day mini-break, where every day is the same: we get up, we go for a walk, we return to our cottage and read books or pop to the pub for a pint and a packet of crisps. We eat dinner and watch TV before going back out to look for nightjars. The dog goes bonkers over new smells, I moan about not living here permanently, Emma can't work out which of us is more delighted. Every day the same. It's wonderful.

Here I am less anxious. There's a robin and blackbird on every roof, along with tits, house sparrows, dunnocks and goldfinches. There are bees, albeit small ones (a sure sign of a cold, wet spring), there are some butterflies and other insects. I wouldn't go as far as to say the insect life here is abundant, but it's better, noisier, than at home. There are new birds to meet: on the heath I find stonechats and meadow pipits, plus curlews and lapwings I can get to know better. In the woods I meet firecrests and marsh tits, woodlarks, common redstarts. At 4.00 a.m. I wake to the dawn chorus against a backdrop of churring nightjars. All around me there are new sounds. New sounds that aren't new but are old, ancient and mostly forgotten. New sounds for my ears – here, ears, take them, they're good for you! Take them and hold on to them. Bathe in them. I want to dig myself into the sand and drown in a high tide of firecrest glitter, of birdsong.

It's easier, here, to forget what's happening, to lose sight of the collapse of insect and bird populations, of the increase in temperatures and the flooding and fire that barely makes the news but which I see each day on Twitter. I feel calm here. There are pregnant donkeys and horses with tiny foals; nothing bad can come from a place with such delights. The donkeys try to get into the garden but the woman who owns the cottage won't let them in.

While we're away the news breaks that we'll 'probably' reach 1.5°C of average global warming by 2030; indeed, the World Meteorological Organization says we have a 66 per cent chance of reaching this 'limit' by 2027. The BBC stresses that reaching this milestone will likely be temporary, but makes no mention of tipping points, such as the thawing of Arctic permafrost that would release huge deposits of methane into the atmosphere, leading to further 'runaway' heating. No mention of when we are likely to hit 2°C (by mid-century) and what life will look like then (horrendous, if climate scientists are to be believed, which, of course, they should be). Still, I am grateful the report actually makes the headlines, although only for a few hours before Prince Harry and Meghan Markle are involved in a car chase and I wonder what schemes are at play to keep the masses from the truth.

We walk for miles: on heathland and in woodland, on beaches and along rivers. We are recharged. And then we go home again, to empty flowers and a dawn chorus of just one robin, to Drone Bastard flying his drone at gulls. I try to stay positive. I stand in the kitchen and look for robins. Where are they? There's no sign. I feel glum, wondering if they laid eggs, if any eggs have been eaten by squirrels, if the robins themselves have managed to avoid the attentions of cats.

'I think the nest has been abandoned,' I tell Emma.

'Oh dear,' she says.

'Do you think I should check?' I ask.

'I don't know,' she says.

I look online for guidance of such things. I want to find an article entitled 'Paranoid? Here's how to check on your robins without disturbing them'. Instead, I find a nest-watch survey on the British Trust for Ornithology (BTO) website, which actively encourages you to check nests but to do so in a careful manner that doesn't interfere with the birds. Then you report your findings for 'science'. It tells me I can check the nest but only when I know both parents are not present, and to quickly look or take a photo and then retreat. OK! But there are no robins. Are there robins? Where are the robins?

I spend more time looking through the kitchen window. Of course, the robins are still in the garden, they are just keeping themselves to themselves, as robins do when they're not fighting or protecting territory. I'm so relieved. I watch them dart about, the male bathes in his favourite water-butt bird bath while the female perches on her favourite rowan branch (they have a branch each, which is a delight). Then they swap – him drying off in the rowan, her taking a bath. An evening shower after a long day of, what? Sitting on eggs? Feeding young? Laying eggs to replace those that have been eaten by squirrels? They fly off, in the direction of my neighbour Kate's garden, and I know this is my time. I dash out, excitedly, nervously, and fumble to use my phone to locate the nest. I don't know where it is exactly, but know it's somewhere in the hops. It doesn't take long to locate it. Through the viewfinder I home in on a little grassy bowl holding six eggs. Six eggs! I take a photo and dash back to the house to look at it. The photo is blurred and so I have to return, stealthily, to get another, which I make sure is in focus. I run back into the house again and shut the door. Phew!

Six eggs! They are beautiful, perfect. Cream-speckled brown with a matt finish, laid in two neat rows of three. Some are lighter while others are more brown. I write everything down for the BTO, including the time of day, the height, aspect and overall description of the nest. The six eggs. Six eggs!

The nest is marvellous, built on a ledge of hop stems just beneath the trellis. It's entirely hidden by hops but also right against the wall, so is protected from wind. They have been enormously clever. I look back at my notes and realise I first noticed them looking for a nest site in early March; this event has been two months in the making. I am so in awe of them.

I return to the kitchen and watch to make sure they return to the nest. They do, or at least the female does – I don't know what the male does while she sits on her six eggs. I see him on his little rowan perch, bathing in his makeshift bird bath. He is part of this garden and I love him, I love them both. This place has nothing of the magic of the New Forest but it has the potential to have six more robins than it had a few weeks ago. I'm absolutely determined that it will.

We had, perhaps, not factored in the possibility that Mum had forgotten how to grow tomatoes. She used to grow them every year but stopped when she had her haemorrhage and hasn't tried since. It has been at least five years. I try to direct her from Brighton.

'Show me photos,' I say on the family group chat. She keeps forgetting, tells me she's tired from (still!) weeding the path and watering. I'm worried she's overdoing it, that she's taken on this task and is giving it too much, that the weedy path is distracting her from the tomatoes. Eventually, after much nagging, she sends me images of plants in too-small pots, supported by enormous bamboo canes that are very loosely tied to not very much at all. Ah. I suggest she repots them into slightly larger containers, pushes the canes into the compost rather than leaves them loose, and sends me more regular updates.

As well as the tomatoes and sweet peppers, she is also growing basil. She was going to grow it from seed before I suggested she buy a pot of basil from the supermarket and then divide up the rootball, potting each young plant up separately. Supermarket basil is actually lots of plants crammed into one pot together; they have few roots for the amount of leaf and don't live long (they're not supposed to). But if you remove them from the pot, separate the individual plants and pot them into containers of fresh compost they will develop more roots and grow into strong plants. It's a much easier way of growing basil than from sowing seed. However, these too are looking straggly and sick, and are also being supported by bamboo canes. I suggest she cuts them back and waters them a bit less often. 'OK!' she says.

All but one of the pumpkin plants has been eaten by snails.

'Have you thought about removing slugs and snails from the greenhouse, Mum?'

'Great idea!' she says. I tell her I'm worried Stanley won't have any pumpkins for Halloween.

'Right,' she says. 'Well, I'm very tired.' I can tell it's all a bit too much for her and feel bad for nagging about the pumpkins. But really, Mum, have you considered not weeding the path?

She does her back in and needs to rest. We all agree this is a good idea. Ellie takes over watering duty and, once again, the basil plants are drowned. I decide to take a break from nagging about the pumpkins; it's the last thing anyone wants and it won't be the end of the world if Stanley doesn't get his Jack-o'-lantern. There are bigger things to worry about.

It's dry again. Amazing how quickly things can change from too wet to too dry. It hasn't rained for weeks, the ground is starting to crack again and my four water butts are empty.

Again.

The garden is OK, for now. I'm more prepared this year; I've been watering and keeping the pond topped up (hence the empty water butts) and I've already moved the mop bucket into the shower to collect grey water to reuse on the garden. But it's nesting season and the birds are struggling – in the park, I watched an exhausted blackbird follow volunteer gardeners as they weeded the rose beds. He left with a full beak of worms but what will he do now the gardeners have gone home? How are he and his chicks now?

The robins are flying back and forth with bits of this and that – the eggs must have hatched. I look through my binoculars at beaks of tiny worms and other morsels. I'm pleased to see there's some food around for them, but there's not much. The flowers are still devoid of bees, there are few flies, I'm still not seeing anything like the abundance of even 2022 – where are they all? Where are the red mason bees, who started nesting in my bee hotels and then abandoned ship? Where are the butterflies? By this time in 2022, I had found three batches of small tortoiseshell caterpillars. Where are the mining bees, the plasterer bees? I planted angelica for the wasps but the flowers have gone over and I didn't see a single wasp or even one insect on the blooms. What's going on? I see similar reports on Twitter, whole patches of wildflowers empty and quiet, people in despair. Where are the insects? Was it last summer's drought or the fluctuating winter temperatures? Was it the cold, wet spring? Are the insects dead or just late? All of the above, probably. I watch a robin take a sunflower heart from the feeder and 'rinse' it in the bird bath for moisture before taking it back to the nest. Oof, that's not good.

Nestling birds don't drink. They get all of the moisture they need from caterpillars, worms and other grubs. Or so they should. Twitter is full of people crying over starving chicks in their nest boxes, of a new 'Silent Spring'. Rinsing sunflower hearts to feed to baby chicks surely means my robins are struggling, too. What if the chicks are dehydrated? What if they're not getting enough moisture?

I wait for my moment to steal a photo of the nest and take it when both parents fly out of the garden. I find three fluffy things with gaping beaks. Baby robins! I run back to the house and look at my photos closely. I think there might be more among them. There were six eggs, could there be six chicks? I make a plan. They are finding some natural food at the moment but it can't be easy and they're obviously substituting it with sunflower hearts. Plus, the starlings and house sparrows have fledged and the garden is full of hungry chicks, putting even more pressure on precious resources. How can I help? I can water the garden, of course, encourage worms to come to the surface. What else? The robin chicks are tiny, so small morsels are better than anything big; it seems too early to introduce mealworms. But I have a compost bin of soft, moist brandling worms, of course! When it gets hot they climb to the top to escape the heat and I find piles of them when I lift the lid. Would they like a tablespoon of brandling worms? I open the lid and they are gathered obligingly in little piles on the ridge. I'm so sorry, brandling worms. I fetch a spoon and load them on, and then drop them at the end of the garden, near the robins' favourite bird bath. I return to the kitchen with binoculars and wait.

It's a long wait; the robins are suspicious of me and I worry that the worms will just work their way away and not be found. But sure enough, eventually, one of them stops at the meaty pile and takes a worm and eats it, like a human might test food before giving it to a child or sprinkling milk on to the back of their hand to make sure it's the right temperature. Once satisfied the worms are not poison, it then picks up a couple and takes them back to the nest. Yes!

It's dry and there are few insects but the robins have a garden with some availability of natural food and a couple of tablespoons of brandling worms each day. There's a hanging feeder of sunflower hearts that I usually take down at this time of year but which I know is helping to fuel them as they search for better food (I'd like them to stop feeding sunflowers to their chicks, though). There are full, fresh bird baths for them to bathe in. I will take photos of the nest only every few days so as to not disturb the parents or the chicks, and the dog and I will shoo cats and crows out of the garden. I can't do much better than that for now, but I hope I can make a difference. I'm not going to give up on these robins.

The swift spends its life in the big blue sky, airborne except when breeding. It flies here each spring from the rainforests of Africa, lays eggs, raises young, and then leaves again. As the chicks get ready to fledge, they prepare themselves for a whole lifetime of living above us, by doing 'press-ups' in the nest.

The swift has declined by 50 per cent in the last 20 years. I dare say there were even more of them 20 years before that, and I try not to think how few of them there will be in 20 years' time. They used to nest in tall trees but we chopped them all down, and now they nest in buildings, although we're making that hard for them too. They eat insects, which some studies suggest have declined in abundance by 75 per cent, and they have to navigate fires and storms on the way back to the Congo in summer (and yes, there's less and less of the Congo rainforest each time they return). Now, in parts of Europe, their nests get so hot the chicks jump out of them prematurely, to their deaths, although lucky ones are saved and raised in rescue centres only to starve or be caught in a storm a few months later. Every single year the number of swifts arriving in Brighton seems smaller and every year another piece of me dies. Could I witness their extinction in my lifetime?

We can help them, to a point. They need nest sites, positioned on the north side of buildings so their chicks don't fry. They need food to feed themselves and their young, so they need insects, which means they need meadows and ponds and trees and gardens, an absence of pesticides, paving and plastic. They need good weather, which is to say they need a stable climate. They need a stable climate.

It takes a lot for me to get in touch with strangers and ask them if they would consider putting up swift boxes. It seems like an imposition, like an inconvenience – surely the last thing they would want to do while having work done to their house. But, sometimes, I overcome this fear and ask anyway, although I haven't done so since writing the letter last autumn to those with the scaffolding and the new roof, who ignored me completely. I still take their rejection personally but I must remember that this isn't about me, it's about swifts. And they don't have a voice.

So it is that, when a man posts about his scaffolding on a public group on Facebook, I comment to see if he would consider putting boxes up. He lives on the next road and has a wonderful pitched roof, where I have actually seen swifts 'banging' or searching for new nesting opportunities. If he put boxes up, there would be a good chance that the 'bangers' would return and find them and thus would help expand the colony of 'bin lorry' swifts from the other side of the main road. It might even encourage them to nest with me.

He writes back with a resounding yes, and invites me round. Oh!

I head over on a sunny but windy Saturday afternoon, to find him halfway up his scaffolding, muttering over a downpipe. His name is Peter and he's nearly 70 but he's doing all the work to the house himself, which includes fixing the guttering and downpipes, re-rendering bits that need rendering, something about stress fractures and finally a new coat of paint.

'This is the only time I'll have scaffolding up so you timed your request well,' he says. He invites me to climb his scaffolding and I reluctantly agree, taking deep breaths while trying not to look down.

'You get used to the height!' he says, as he warns me not to bang my head on scaffolding boards while I climb a wooden ladder. Funny, at the top of his four-storey house, with 30mph winds whipping around us, this is of no comfort to me at all.

I tell him about swifts and show him precisely where I saw them banging, taking pleasure in being able to touch the wall they have scouted. I tell him that they seem to love a pitched roof, that I've seen them banging all along this strip of houses and that I'm sure there is one nest nearby but that the majority of them live on the other side of the main road. He tells me he has a mate who builds swift boxes and that he intends to fit a few, both at the front and the back. I am delighted.

I don't ask but wonder if his immediate enthusiasm for erecting swift boxes had anything to do with The Feather Speech, Hannah-Bourne-Taylor's campaign. Conceived on the hottest day the UK has seen to date, Hannah's idea stole the nation's heart. The aim was simple: to get 100,000 signatures on a petition to ask that swift bricks be made compulsory in new-build homes, which would mean the issue would be discussed in Parliament. How would she achieve this? She would take her clothes off, of course – how else do you get attention for a serious issue?

The Feather Speech took place on Hyde Park Corner one autumn afternoon in 2022. Hannah wore nothing but a thong, boots, and body paint naturally depicting swifts and the three other endangered cavity-nesting birds that the campaign sought to help (house martins, starlings and house sparrows). With support from the RSPB and

Rewriting Extinction, she gave an impassioned speech to launch her campaign. I watched on social media, agog, wondering if she would get her 100,000 signatures. No one had done anything like this before.

Over the next few months, Hannah appeared on television and radio and in newspapers and magazines. Piers Morgan and Channel Four News interviewed her. She attended an event at the National History Museum wearing a gold taffeta dress decorated with paper cut-outs of swifts. She encouraged people to sign her petition in the street, on the tube, on social media. She didn't give up. She didn't once stop. She never focused on rejection or used it as an excuse not to stand up for swifts. As her campaign grew, I realised that she was a force, a power among the nature community and that she would not let this go or ever let the swifts down. In the end, she got more than 100,000 signatures; of course, she did. She also made sure the issue would be debated in Parliament (apparently it's not guaranteed) and secured the support of several MPs and Lords. All of that got even more media attention, and I lost count of how many national news items I watched where people were discussing homes for swifts. The outcome of the debate was an unhappy one; despite impassioned pleas, Parliament denied the requests. But suddenly, everyone was talking about swifts, and people were putting up nest boxes where they had scaffolding. Suddenly, I had renewed confidence in asking a stranger if he would put swift boxes up, and suddenly, he said yes. Suddenly, a little corner of our world looked a little wilder.

I want to tell the swifts about The Feather Speech. I want them to know that the tides are turning, that years of habitat theft are finally yielding a new kindness, new ways of learning to live among other species. Not just for them but for everyone. 'Can you hold on?' I mouth to the sky. 'Can you keep going for another few years? We have plans for you, little swifts, and we are doing everything we can to save you. Don't give up on us yet. Don't ever give up on us.'

In the pet shop I buy sunflower hearts and mealworms. I take them home and fill a new, clean feeder with sunflower hearts, and add a few mealworms to the robins' favourite bird bath on top of the furthest water butt, in the hedge. The chicks are bigger now – there are five of them, with grumpy downward smiles, semi-open eyes and pin feathers. It's time: if they can thrive on rehydrated mealworms they may yet fledge successfully.

I don't know how old they are. I read up on different stages of robin development to see if I can anticipate when they will fledge, at which point I will need to keep 24-hour guard for cats and crows. I learn that they start opening their eyes on day 5 and have fully opened their eyes by day 8, and that they fledge on day 13. I checked the nest for the first time last Saturday, when I found six eggs, then there were fluffy things three days later, on Tuesday. Today is Monday, so if they hatched on Sunday they are eight days old, but if they hatched on Tuesday they are six days old. And did they all hatch on the same day? I'll never know. Today's photo shows three with open eyes and two with shut eyes – it's clear three are stronger than the others. The female robin lays one egg a day and starts incubating them only after the last egg has been laid so they hatch at around the same time, but the first eggs still have some developmental advantage over the later ones, and it looks like the sixth egg didn't hatch at all. The three with their eyes open must therefore be from eggs one, two and three, and the two with their eyes shut will be from eggs four and five. Phew! Open eyes means day eight – they hatched on Sunday. Perhaps the weaker two hatched a day later.

You can buy live mealworms, but rehydrating dried ones in water is fine and far less gruesome. Other birds love them too but, so far, don't seem to have noticed where I've put them. They are bad for hedgehogs so I'm deliberately leaving them up high and out of the way – there's more wildlife than the robins to think about.

As with the brandling worms, I stand in the kitchen with binoculars and wait for the robins to find their quarry. This time the wait is much shorter – a robin pops to the bird bath, takes one, eats it and then takes another and flies back with it. My plan is working! I'm reading too many reports of chicks starving in their nests this dry, cold spring, but I refuse to let that happen here. I'm still leaving out brandling worms but now they have mealworms, too, which I will drop into fresh water each evening so they have moist things to feed their chicks in the morning. These birds will not starve on my watch, I will make sure of it.

The parents fly out of the garden for other morsels and I take my chance again for another pic. I grab it and go, retreating back inside to coo over the details. I can't believe how much they've grown, the little darlings. Such grumpy-looking things but with real feathers. They grow up so fast.

The doorbell rings. Through the frosted glass I see a woman carrying a box. I open the door, 'Hello!'

'Hello, I know you like frogs.'

I laugh. 'Erm, yes? Have you brought me a present?'

'I found him under the tarpaulin in our front garden,' she explains, 'can you take him?'

The frog is a female, already gravid with next year's spawn.

'She's a she,' I explain, 'you can see her belly where the spawn is developing.'

'Oh,' the woman says. 'Do you think she wanted to spawn in my tarpaulin?'

'No,' I reply, 'it's late, they would have done that in February.'

'February? Gosh.' She looks distantly in the direction of her tarpaulin, as if imagining a pool of tadpoles she had somehow missed.

She tells me where she lives and points to her house and her husband. The husband and I wave to each other. I want to ask if hers is the front garden that has tarpaulin laid over the whole space, which has been there for at least a year, and if she has plans for making it nice (this seems a bit rude so I don't). I also want to ask her if she or any of her neighbours has or had a pond in the back garden, where my toads might have come from. But I don't manage to get the words out.

Neither do I ask why she was so determined that the frog should live at mine when it was clearly happy beneath the tarpaulin. Many frogs are found beneath such materials, where they remain cool and moist, and where they might find food such as small slugs and worms to eat. As much as I hate plastic pollution and the locking away of land that could be used to grow plants and provide habitats, a wet-skinned frog could do worse than shelter beneath tarpaulin during a dry spring. But no matter. I take the frog through into the garden and pop it gently among the herb Robert in the shade; if it liked the tarpaulin so much it will be back there tomorrow. Before she leaves, the woman laughs and says again, 'I know you like frogs.'

'I do,' I reply, 'I like them very much.'

The tadpoles in the pond are coming along nicely, although there's so much duckweed I don't often get a good look at them. If I sit beside the pond I can see little divots in the surface where they pop their heads up to eat something, or if a sparrow has a bath and has left a 'window' in the weed I can see them swimming beneath. I keep meaning to remove the weed but it's such a delicate operation when tadpoles are present, as you have to check each clump you remove, for swimmers. Larger tadpoles may be able to wriggle their way back into the water if the weed is left on the side, but smaller tads won't. So I leave it until it gets to such a point that I just can't anymore. Besides, it hasn't rained, so the duck weed will be reducing the amount of pond evaporating into the sky, and it also makes hunting more difficult for crows. Both of these things I am grateful for.

The pond is nearly full but only because I've been topping it up. I am now using tap water, which I decant into a water butt for a day, removing the lid so the chlorine and other nasties can evaporate, before releasing it into the pond. I don't like using so much tap water but I don't like the garden drying out either, and after the heartbreak of 2022, I am mindful not to let it dry out completely. Plus we had a wet winter so there is more in the taps to go around. The backswimmers still haven't returned, neither the adults nor their tiny nymphs, which normally appear at some point in May and grow from tiny, wingless boats into large, silvery synchronised swimmers. When pond dipping I've always found masses of them. They are so huge and majestic and I miss them so much. I wonder where they went last summer when the pond dried out; the wingless nymphs will have been eaten by birds and hedgehogs but the winged adults will have tried to find more watery habitats. Canals? Rivers? A garden pond that someone was topping up?

There are no dragonflies or damselflies, either. No papery exuvia left on plant stems, which is the sign that a nymph has climbed up before finally metamorphosing into an adult. I'm hoping they will recolonise the pond but I have seen few so far this year. It's early, though, there's still time. What else did I lose? I don't even know. Mayflies, perhaps, although numbers have decreased since they first colonised the pond four years ago. Those little brown beetles, the non-biting midges, the mosquitoes. Surely there are mosquitoes? Perhaps the duckweed is putting them off, or the tap water isn't as free from nasties as I thought it was and is too much for the more sensitive aquatic larvae.

It's hard to know what to do for the best; just yesterday I had a rare visit from a frazzled-looking blackbird, exhausted from another season of trying to raise young without rain. He stopped for a drink and a bathe, a bit of shade, before disappearing again. The pond needs topping up for the birds and hedgehogs, the tadpoles, the missing species that I hope will return. When it's full the garden feels alive. It feels cooler, more relaxed, green. Perhaps my four water butts aren't enough, perhaps I need to bite the bullet and erect an ugly rainwater tank in the side return. Perhaps it will rain soon.

I check the forecast: nope, not for another two weeks at least.

Maybe it's the duck weed, then. Backswimmers locate water at night, they're known for landing on silvery car roofs by accident, which they mistake for water. The duckweed has turned the pond green, which means they won't be able to see the water, so it must be stopping them from being able to recolonise it. Of course. I take a cushion from the bench and drop it at the side of the pond to kneel on, and use my hands to finally scoop the weed out. I check each pile carefully for tadpoles and drop any I find back in the water. The weed I leave in little piles on the edge so leeches and water hoglice can make their way back. I spend half an hour on the job, which is about as much as I can bear.

Common pipistrelle, *Pipistrellus pipistrellus*

The common pipistrelle is the smallest and most common of our 18 bat species. It's the one that flies above my garden and is most likely to fly above yours. All British bats are nocturnal but most emerge around half an hour after sunset. In summer I drink wine outside and wait for my one pipistrelle bat to fly in a big loop that takes in my garden and the houses behind it, over and over again.

Pipistrelle bats are so small they can fit into a matchbox, and so they eat midges, tiny moths and other small flying insects, which they find in the dark using echolocation (a series of shouts, which then echo or bounce back from prey so they can home in on them). One pipistrelle bat can eat 3,000 midges in one night. There are three types of pipistrelle bat: common and soprano, which were discovered as separate species only in the 1990s, and Nathusius's pipistrelle, which is slightly bigger.

They roost in tree holes, bat boxes and the roof spaces of houses, often in small colonies. In summer, females get together and form maternity colonies, in which they give birth to one pup each. They feed their pups milk for three weeks until they are able to take them out on foraging trips, where they teach them to become independent. They hibernate together, too, in north-facing boxes that aren't warmed by the sun, and in gaps with no draughts. This ensures they remain, hopefully, undisturbed.

To garden for pipistrelle bats is to garden for insects. Let grass grow long, grow plenty of native plants, shrubs and trees, which are more well used by insects than those from further away. Grow flowers for nectar-feeding moths. A pond works well for bats, too – at dusk midges appear from nowhere and dance above the water, before my pipistrelle arrives and gobbles them all up. You could put up a bat box or let an old tree remain old, where holes and crevices will provide opportunities.

In the UK, bats are one of the few species to be fully protected by law; it's illegal to disturb a bat roost. If they live in your roof consider yourself lucky, they are some of the few species that have learned to live among us.

June

Little nephew Bert has arrived. I take the train to Birmingham to meet him and he sleeps for most of the day. He is tiny and precious, he fits in the crease of my elbow and I have to keep reminding myself he's there. He has milk spots and puffy eyes, the most perfect little hands, which he clasps together like an old man. He looks like Ellie, pale with a shock of bright yellow hair. When she leaves the room I style it into a Mohican.

Mum pops round to water the tomatoes, which are finally growing strongly. She takes basil leaves for her lunch, marvels at the beginnings of peppers.

'Are you feeding them?' I ask.

'Yes, I am feeding them and watering them and staking them and all the things you told me to do,' she says. I think she's enjoying the process, hard work though it has been for her. I think I will give her plants again next year.

The squash plants all died and the big bin of compost remains in the garden, unplanted. Stanley will not get his pumpkins; it was too soon for him and everyone else has a lot going on. I'll try again in a few years. I'm there for just 24 hours but I manage to feed Bert, tickle Stanley, catch up with Ellie and Gareth. The morning before I leave I actually sit down and do the crossword with Mum and Pete. We are shockingly bad at it. I get the first clue wrong (I suggest 'cache' rather than 'stash'), but Mum can't spell, follow instructions or, it seems, read a complete sentence.

'Darling, I've had a brain haemorrhage!'

'This is abundantly clear.'

We laugh, a lot. We are lucky. We are very lucky.

The robins should fledge today. I don't know what to expect – do they fledge in the morning? One by one or all together? The chicks are so big now I can see them poking out of the nest from the lawn.

'Look at their little beaks!' I say to Emma as we sit on the lawn and peer through binoculars at five chicks among the hops and roses. They are fidgety and flighty. I daren't nip in for a photo in case I force them out sooner than they are ready.

Besides, I can't get in now. Over the week I have become more and more anxious. Both the crows and the magpies have been bringing dead starling and sparrow chicks into the garden and butchering them in the bird bath, before taking them back to feed to their own nestlings. I find the gruesome remains of bones and pin feathers in the water. They're also soaking bread in the bird bath, along with an entire pie and what looked like the contents of a packet of Nik Naks. It's clear the dry weather is affecting them, too.

Crows and magpies aren't stupid, and I have convinced myself that they have been waiting for the robin chicks to become big enough to be worth taking – why not let the parents do all the hard work so you can give your own young a bigger meal? The crows come in every day and sit on the fence above the robin nest, of course they know what's going on.

Our barky little canine does a good job of keeping cats, crows and squirrels away during the day but what about at night? I see cats on the night camera, and there's nothing to stop foxes helping themselves to the nest while we're still in bed.

So I built them a cage.

I have an old rabbit run, which I bought second-hand for the purposes of looking after poorly hedgehogs but which I have used only once. I have considered getting rid of it but it's useful for other things: keeping the dog and pigeons off germinating grass seed, placing over a bit of border that has suffered too many playful foxes. But now it's being used for another life-saving mission: I've fixed it around the robins' nest. It's supposed to be built into a rectangular, roofed frame but it's collapsible and has five panels, so I have joined these together with twine to make a roofless, fenced-off area. It covers a fairly large space, meeting the fence to the left of the hazel and to the right of the shrub rose (with the guelder rose in the middle), with three panels at the front, on the lawn. It's high enough to stop cats and foxes getting in and tight enough to ward off crows, which seem to struggle navigating small spaces. It's probably not squirrel proof but it's a barrier for cats, foxes and crows, at least.

I built it in stages as the robins left the garden, to cause as little stress to them as possible. They don't seem to mind it, they know the cage – it was on the grass protecting germinating seed when they started building their nest – so I already know they can fly between the bars. They continue to feed their chicks constantly. I like to think they also know what I'm trying to achieve; it's been so long since they had a successful nest.

In bed, I lie awake trying to work out how a predator might get in, and sleep better knowing most of them can't. When the dog gets us up at 4.30 a.m., I let her out for a wee and then leave the back door open so she can patrol her territory. The robins don't mind Tosca, they haven't once let out an alarm call when she's been in the garden. They tolerate Emma and me as long as we don't get too close to the nest, and they absolutely hate next door's cat. But they're fine with Tosca, they ignore her and she ignores them.

I get up at a more reasonable time of 6.00 a.m. and spend as much time outside as I can. I potter gently while the dog alternates between sleeping in the sun and sleeping in the shade. We both chase crows. Emma comes home from the gym at midday and makes herself comfy on the sun lounger – we three protecting the robins although staying away from the vicinity of the nest. In distant parts of the garden I dig up an ornamental poppy that I've been waiting to go over so I can move it. I divide and replant cranesbills and trim grass at the lawn's edges. I tidy the shed. I sow lettuce seed and water potted hazels, all as far away from the nest as possible. Eventually, when I have finished all the other jobs, I try to do something with the new border around the pond.

The robins continue feeding their young. They are calling to them now, making beautiful twittering noises that the chicks are responding to – practice, perhaps, for when they have fledged and will still rely on their parents to feed them. They are taking a good number of mealworms and I top them up, with fresh water, to keep them going. I also spot the male return with an enormous caterpillar and a tiny snail, proof that there is some natural food out there for them despite the continued lack of rain. I dig up an earthworm and throw it near the nest and the female swoops in immediately. I feel bad for the worm but the fizzing sound of excited chicks 20 seconds later more than makes up for it. Besides, how else will robins get worms in this weather? The ground is baked. All day we hear twittering and fizzing. We watch the many routes the parents make to the nest, the different food items they bring back to their chicks. We listen to the calls they make: the 'Here I am' *deets*, the soothing twittering, the warning whistle when I get too close to the nest and the frantic alarm calls when next door's elderly cat pops out for a snooze in the sun. By the end of the day I can almost speak Robin. Emma takes Tos out for a walk because I refuse to leave the garden, and instead I lie in the sun and read for a bit before falling asleep to the sound of happy birds. They won't fledge today but they will soon, and we are one step closer to success.

I meet friends and family for drinks and catch-ups and find myself withdrawing into myself, away from them. They say the most ridiculous things. No one knows what's going on. Over the last two years I have been accused of trying to scare children, of not being present, I have been told none of what I fear will happen in my lifetime, that everything will be OK because 'someone will invent a machine'. There are scripts, among deniers, that are churned out religiously.

There are fewer of them these days but they are still about: full deniers who say the climate has always been changing, that pseudo scientists have exaggerated it all and besides, don't you drive? We can't return to living in the Dark Ages, they say. 'Stop using fossil fuels? Preposterous.'

Most people accept it's happening but refuse to believe it's a problem. They are 'partial deniers' and claim the fossil-fuel industry is in the best place to find a solution to the climate crisis because they 'have so much technology and resources'. They don't understand that the climate crisis is more than atmospheric levels of carbon, they claim governments simply won't let the world end, they hail the invention of a carbon capture machine that doesn't yet work at scale. (The machine actually works very well if you realise its intended use was only ever to buy more time for the fossil-fuel industry.)

A mate asked me if something was going on, if something was wrong, because she'd seen so many butterflies lately. 'Is there a plague of butterflies?' she asked. I responded by asking her what the butterflies looked like, how many, exactly, she had seen. 'They were white,' she replied, and she'd seen no more than 20. But seeing them had surprised her so much that she'd thought something was wrong, that there was an invasion, that there was something going on that needed to be controlled. I could have wept.

It terrifies me that we are so disconnected from the natural world. That people don't understand the very basics of how life works. I've had friends tell me we're going to be OK because climate change 'isn't going to be as bad here, is it?' To which I ask where their food comes from, and if they've considered where those fleeing inhabitable countries are going to try to live. They look at me as if I'm speaking a foreign language.

'We're going to move abroad when the kids finish school. I just want to live somewhere really hot, you know?'

'Let's all get a timeshare in Spain!'

'But you can't think like that. Just don't think like that.'

'Hahaha, my great-great-grandchildren are so fucked.'

'I just think food security is far more important than saving bloody bees.'

'I'll be dead by then.'

'Just focus on the now and the people in your present.'

'Well, I like the mild winters and the longer summers.'

'Darling, look out of the window! Everything's fine!'

You can't see the quietness of everything, the disappearing of the life, on which Earth depends. You know we need that rain (but not too much of it)? We need that soil? We need those plants?

Isn't it funny how nature has always been something to conquer and control? The aphids on our beans, the mice in our house, the midges around our face? With every generation we have moved further away from it, from life itself. We live in houses, take hot showers, deodorise and sanitise. We entertain ourselves at the cinema and gigs and festivals and the theatre. We watch TV and read books and listen to the radio. We dance, oh we dance. And it's wonderful, it really is. But, for most of us, Nature is 'other' to all of those things. It lives outside and preferably far away. Where does it live? In our gardens? Sometimes. In the countryside? Barely. In the forests and woodlands we have yet to chop down? Just about.

When I talk to people about climate change they either laugh, stare at me blankly or appear to take what I'm saying as a personal attack on them and their freedoms. 'It won't happen' is the most common response I get, 'they're just not going to let it get that bad.' (Who are they?) But it is that bad, it's already happening. As I type, temperatures in Pakistan have reached 49.5°C. There are record-breaking temperatures across Asia, Africa, South America, Australia. Twitter is full of wildfires and floods, of death and human suffering.

But they won't let it get that bad.

For us, do you mean? Perhaps the people of Pakistan don't matter, or the fact that 49.5°C is no temperature to work, live or grow crops is irrelevant to you. Perhaps you haven't thought about where the world's wheat and rice grows, where the people of soon-to-be-uninhabitable countries are going to escape to. At what point will climate change matter? At what point will it be so bad that you, finally, have had enough of it? When the fire and floods are at your door? When you're hungry because the crops have failed? At what point do we, as a nation, as a continent, as a global community decide enough is enough and really pull together to lower emissions, which, as I type, are still increasing? At what point do we realise that no good can come from ignoring this? Why, when we live in a stable climate that feeds and nourishes us and that is full of such incredible beauty, would we deliberately risk everything? What good is money when you can't leave your home because of wind? When you don't have a home because of fire or flood? When your plate is empty? When entire nations of desperate people escaping literally everything are knocking at your door?

At the time of writing, not one G20 country is anywhere close to meeting the targets laid out in the 2016 Paris Agreement. Imagine if they were – together, the G20 emit nearly 80 per cent of the world's emissions. Local news reports tell us runway expansions and post-Covid holiday booms are a good thing, while reports of Amazon deforestation due to beef farming, of the devastation caused by wildfires, of the Earth-altering loss of ice, are ignored. If I could wish for one thing, it would be that governments the world over took the climate and biodiversity crisis seriously, actually listened to scientists and worked together to solve this problem. Humans are problem-solvers, after all. We could do so much!

It makes me so sad that most people don't understand that loss of nature and climate change are essentially the same thing. That 'biodiversity' means life on Earth, that we can't just suck CO_2 out of the atmosphere and continue destroying the world's life systems. Systems that absorb and store carbon and water, systems that provide homes for insects that pollinate our food, and others that eat 'pests'. Systems that ensure we have clean water, healthy soils to grow food in, breathable air. To think we are above these systems is completely bonkers when we actually rely on them for life. Our life. Everyone's life.

When I'm old I will sit at the window and look at the garden. My knees will have finally given up, the rest of me creaky and stiff but I will sit, with tea and maybe the crossword, like Mum, and I will watch my world grow wilder without me.

There's no shame in letting your garden go as you age. There's no harm in setting it free. There's a beauty, I think, in watching your patch of land grow as you fade. My garden is wild enough as it is but I am always in it, with secateurs and twine, tying bits in, trimming, controlling. I mowed the lawn this year and I liked it. But when I'm old? I will let it go, all of it. I will let ivy take my house, let the pond silt up, let the hedge grow tall and wayward. The frivolity and freedoms of youth, long gone for me, will be realised outside, in one final, out-of-control party. What new species will turn up? Who will make nests? I am almost looking forward to it.

The old people in my neighbourhood are stewards of special places. Of stepping stones, of spaces for wild beings to breathe. They don't venture out, they can't keep it tidy. And so these gardens return to nature in a way most of us wouldn't allow if we had the bodies to do something about it. Wildlife deserves to live without the constant threat of humans and I'm grateful for these near-abandoned gardens, these urban patches of complete wilderness.

When I'm old we will have passed 2°C of average global warming and could well have reached 2.5°C. By then there will be more food shortages, more migration, more war. There may be lockdowns due to heat and wind. The sun may be too intense to be out in. No rain, too much rain. We may lie in bed at night listening to the wind howl, worrying about our roofs. Will we still have a Gulf Stream, an Amazon rainforest? Will the continents of Asia, Africa and South America still be habitable? Will southern

Europe? Will people be living in the Arctic to escape the heat, trying to grow food in soil that has been permafrost for thousands of years amid storms, drought, a lack of pollinators and everything else an unstable climate throws at us in a formerly uninhabited part of the world?

Will I even make it to old age?

Where will the people go? Where will the customs, the cultures, the traditions, the histories go? Where will the love and friendship go? What will be passed down to future generations, what will be taught? Letters, photographs, lockets, rings, stories, laughter, gardens. Caught in a storm and blown around the Earth as dust for the rest of time. And the wildlife. What will be left? Will there be robins?

I will sit at the window and watch the garden, a little refuge in a shrinking city. By then, more people will have woken up, more people will have taken up their plastic and their paving, returned their gardens to nature, voted out ineffectual governments. People will guerrilla-plant trees to absorb CO_2, dig ponds, fight for wildflowers. Our homes will be clad with plants to deflect heat, there will be more solar panels, more insulation. We may have finally managed to decrease our CO_2 and other greenhouse gas emissions. But it will still be scary, too late for millions of people and other animals, caught out in a drought or a storm or flooded or hungry or just too hot to breathe.

I will hobble out to top up bird baths, I will try to feed the hedgehogs. I will have finally given up on the astilbes. Will the ivy have taken the fence down? I must remember to tell the Twitter men. Will Drone Bastard still fly his drone at gulls? Will there be robins? I will wait, each year, for the swifts to return, I will never give up on the chance of seeing one again.

I will love it, with all my heart, whatever has managed to remain, whatever is left. I will hold its hand until the bitter end, I will love it. I will never give up on this space, on this world, on the little things I can do every day to keep this all ticking over. With every ounce of my fading being, I promise to never stop loving it.

The dog shifts in her bed and gets up, shakes her head with a flap of the ears and stands at the door waiting to be let out. I sigh and open my eyes. It's 4.30 a.m., the day's first light shifts beneath the curtains. Time to protect the robins.

We travel downstairs together, her getting under my feet, as she always does, huffing excitedly at the thought of being back in the garden. Still blurry-eyed, I open the kitchen door and watch her run to the far end before I return to bed, leaving her out there. I know her routine: she checks the exits first – the back gate, the habitat pile that foxes jump up on to climb next door, the two hedgehog holes. Who has been in and out? Tosca knows. She works her way around the garden, then, tracing hedgehog trails and fox wees, the lingering scent of cats, which she always responds to with a low, rumbling growl. How cruel we are for denying her the chance to patrol this space 24-7. There would be no cats on Tosca's watch.

I join her an hour later, as the sun sparkles over the rooftops and is mirrored on heavy dew drops at the tips of grass stems. I sit on the bench with tea, less blurry-eyed but still sleepy. Wet feet. I am travelling to London today to see friends and I have just a few hours in the garden before my train leaves. What shall I do? Perhaps I'll tackle more of the pondweed, which has thickened up again since I first started removing it. Maybe I'll weed the patio, removing grassy clumps to transplant into the lawn. Or I

could just lie in the sun and read my book, it's Sunday
after all.

I sit on the bench, nursing tea. The robins are up and
about, the male perches on the bee hotel and bubbles to his
young in the nest but the female is in the habitat pile. I
watch her dart around the top and inspect the robin box
fixed to the shed wall. She seems agitated; is it me or Tos?
There are no warning calls. I call Tos back to me anyway
and she jumps up beside me on the bench. The male
continues to bubble and receives responding pips from the
chicks. But the female… she flies back around to the water
butt where the mealworms are and takes one, then returns
to somewhere within the habitat pile. Then I hear it, the
fizzing of a chick being fed. There's a chick in the habitat
pile, they're fledging!

As I turn back to the nest two fly out in a flurry of
frantic and unexpected flapping. 'Yes, baby robins you can
fly!' One clings to the bars of the rabbit run, shocked,
while the other lands on the back of the bench behind us,
also shocked. Tosca leans in to sniff it, gently, before looking
at me as if to say, 'What have you done now?' Bench robin
flies back to the other side of the garden and buries itself
among the herb Robert, and the other launches itself into
the gap between mine and next door's trellis, which is
thick with rambling rose.

'C'mon, Tos, let's leave them to it.' We head back inside
and close the door but I watch, for ages, as the parents fuss
around their chicks, which are becoming fledglings before
our eyes. Fledglings. We did it!

I have come to learn so much about robins. I have
learned that they talk to each other, that the bubbling
from the male was gentle encouragement to the chicks to
leave the nest, the returning pips were the chicks nervously
deciding whether they were going to or not, or perhaps

egging each other on. The female is frantic because she's organising the flock – at least three are out of the nest, which means one or two remain. Does she settle them down, as a mother would: 'Here, take this mealworm, stay hidden in this patch and call me when you need to.' Does she see to one before moving on to the next? They are such good parents, tackling this, as with every other process of nesting over the last few weeks, with military precision and care. They've really thought this through, or at least it seems that way. From nest building to feeding to this amazing process that's unfolding before my eyes, they have done such a brilliant job. Perhaps it's instinct or maybe years of losses to predators that has made them such amazing parents, willing to take no chances. There's one in the trellis – check; one in the herb Robert – check. I take Tos for a walk before the heat of the day makes the pavements too hot for her paws, and when we return two hours later the parents are still herding their young, still bubbling and pipping, still frantically feeding. I watch the last fledgling cling to the trellis, having presumably just left the nest, before it flies off to a distant garden. I open the door and walk into mine, as the bubbling and pipping rolls into the next street. Gone, just like that. I can't go to London today, I don't want to miss this.

I leave my friend Andy a garbled voice message about needing to be here for this momentous day. He is remarkably understanding, says he gets it, he knows how much this means to me. Emma comes home from the gym and I explain that I need to be here, and does she mind, had she planned a special day alone with Tos? 'Of course not,' she says, although I suspect she probably had.

The robins largely stay out of the garden. Emma takes me plant shopping and buys me foxgloves, Mexican fleabane and plume thistle (*Cirsium rivulare*) to fill gaps and

plant around the pond. Back home, I start arranging and
then planting while she plays ball with Tosca. Then I send
her out for provisions so we can have beers in the garden
followed by burger and chips when we get hungry, just like
we might if out with friends. We don't listen to music, our
ears are cocked for the distant pips from the most excellent
robins. We have a happy day, the happiest day. Our precious
world is home to five more robins.

When they first dispersed I thought that might be it,
that I wouldn't see the chicks again, but they're not too far
away. There's one behind the shed and another in the log
pile in the twitten just outside the garden. I listen to their
calls throughout the day, watch the parents return to check
on them and feed them, reassure them that they're still
being cared for in the big wide world. 'Are you alright? Do
you need anything?' The garden is still the parents' territory
too. They still perch on the bee hotel, still take mealworms
from the water-butt bath. I am terrified about the chicks'
first night unprotected from cats, squirrels, foxes and crows,
but I've done my bit. I can't wrap them in any more cotton
wool, I have to let them be wild. But to have helped them
reach this stage is huge, after at least three years of failures.
In a spring of few insects and dry soils, in a neighbourhood
plagued with high densities of cats, squirrels and corvids, I
have helped five little robin chicks fledge their nest. It's
quite something, even if I say so myself.

I've been in the garden for most of the day, for most of
the weekend. As the sun retreats behind the trees I dismantle
the cage around the nest and finally take a closer look at
where the chicks have been growing for the last two weeks.
How did they fit in it? It's small but so perfect, the most
beautiful grassy bowl. Of course, it's not quite empty – the
sixth, perfect egg sits there, unhatched. I reach in and pick
it up, the tiniest ball of speckled treasure.

Epilogue

I never found out where the pond was that the toads came from. I asked more neighbours but got nowhere. Eventually, after searching Google Earth and finding no leads, I found a local history page on Facebook, the type of group where old people reminisce about sweet shops and post photos of roads and buildings in days gone by.

'Does anyone remember Woolworths?'

'Ooh yes, we used to go for penny sweets after school on a Friday.'

'Does anyone remember the rag 'n' bone man with his horse and cart?'

'Oh yes, I broke my foot once and he gave me a lift to hospital!'

It's a nice group, soothing, amid the noise of everything else. And full of people who might have remembered toads.

I ask if anyone who lived in my road or neighbouring roads remembers a pond. I tell them I know there was a pond in the park until a child drowned and it was filled in, but that I don't know where toads might have been breeding since then.

People write back, mostly to say they don't remember anyone having a pond in the neighbourhood but confirming that there was a pond in what's now the park.

'My dad was best friends with the kid who drowned.'

'My uncle tried to save him.'

I start to think I may have opened a can of worms.

But then I get more. I'm told a nearby road is named after a brook that used to run all along here from the Downs, that there were farms with ponds where car dealerships now stand. I don't get dates but I'm beginning to build a picture of the landscape of the area before today, when life was a lot wilder. If there was a brook, a large pond, a farm with ponds, this area would have been wetter than it is now, with plenty of opportunities for toads and their frog and newt cousins. As the patchwork of habitats was gradually taken, they would have been squeezed into ever-tighter habitats but somehow, remarkably, the toads have survived.

I'm always upset when I hear of rivers and streams that have been buried underground; living things that no longer see the light of day. Where are the fish that used to spawn in its pebbles, the dragonflies that used to lay eggs in the weed? Were there kingfishers along this stretch of water, were there otters and beavers and swallows? My toads have a space to breed now but they deserve a better landscape, they deserve a proper home. Come the revolution I will be there, with my pickaxe, fighting to reclaim the old East Brook.

Gulls Allowed continues. We meet for drinks and make plans for how to deal with Drone Bastard next year. Lin has written to our MP and we are looking at trying to get the law changed, so that those who fly drones are not allowed to use them to deliberately disturb wildlife. I suspect we'll need a change of government to see this through but we will wait, we're not going anywhere. (Neither, sadly, is Drone Bastard.)

Happily, despite his efforts, the gulls on the factory roof successfully raised their chicks. And Lin has recruited me as a gull rescuer. She texts me when she hears of gulls that have fallen off roofs and we head out together, me with oven gloves and her with an umbrella to protect us from their dive-bombing parents, and help them out of the road and back on to a roof. Sometimes I have to go on my own and I have further recruited neighbours with loft conversions so I can lean out of their Velux windows and deposit chicks directly on to roof tiles. Sometimes, if the weather is bad, they have to stay with me for a few hours, much to the irritation of our ever-patient Tosca.

Pete from my local rescue centre has asked me to show him how to raise butterflies and I've asked him to teach me how to rehabilitate birds, like robins, when they fall or are taken from their nest. Our nature-loving community, like my ivy, continues to knit together and grow.

Acknowledgements

Thank you to my wonderful agent, Jane Turnbull and my editor Julie Bailey. Once again, they took a chance on a half-formed idea and gave me the time and space I needed to work with it. Thanks especially to Julie for working so tirelessly to make everything shipshape and on time – I was so pleased to work with you again. Thanks to my patient copy editor, Elizabeth Peters, who asked all the right questions, and to Charlotte Atyeo for proofreading. To my illustrators, Abby Cook and Jasmine Parker, who have brought the book to life, and to Rachel Nicholson, Lizzy Ewer, Katherine Macpherson and Sarah Head at Bloomsbury, who have given my book wings and sent it out into the wide world. This book would be nothing without the amazing work of this team of brilliant women.

Thanks to my fact checkers: Emily Robinson (amphibians), Richard Comont (bumblebees), Richard Fox (1976), Ann Winney (hedgehogs) for your time and advice, and to Alex Lees, Hannah Bourne-Taylor and Susie Howells for making sure what I said about your respective projects was exactly right. Thanks to Choel for letting me write about the hedgehogs. Thanks to the many neighbours for letting me mention them and for Pete and Gayle Foggon at Sompting Wildlife Rescue and Ann Winney at Hurst Hedgehog Haven for trusting me with precious hedgehogs to release into the garden, and for letting me write about them, of course.

Thanks to my gull friends for the laughs. If one good thing has come from the activities of Drone Bastard, it's been getting to know you.

I am so grateful for Emma and Tosca, who make me laugh, and for the emotional support of friends Andy, Jo, Eli, Becky, Helen and Humey, who were happy to talk, or not talk, about my bloody book. Extra special thanks is due to the wonderful human that is Melissa Harrison, who took time to read the whole manuscript while busy on her own projects – the book is so much better for her input. And to my family: thank you for letting me continue this strand of our story.

This book has been challenging to write, and I wrote myself into many ridiculous dead ends. One day, by chance, Kath Moore phoned me as I was staring out of the window wondering if I should just tell Bloomsbury this had all been a mistake, and said, 'I want to know what you're doing.' I want her to know that those words changed the course of the book and its journey to where we are today. I'm not sure I would have continued writing it had I not picked up the phone.

30 Million Gardens
for the Planet

We live in one of the most nature-depleted countries in the world thanks to years of agricultural intensification and a demand for cheap food. Since the turn of the last century two of our bumblebee species have gone extinct, along with 97 per cent of our wildflower meadows (go figure). Since the 1970s we've lost 67 per cent of our common moths and 40 million birds. Some 80 per cent of butterflies are in decline, while a conservative assessment of insect numbers generally suggests 60 per cent have disappeared in the last 20 years alone – this, I feel, is very conservative: when did you last clear insects from the windscreen of your car? There are efforts to re-establish hedgerows and field margins to give space back to nature, rewilding projects that aim to return landscapes to the living habitats they once were. Good things are happening. But, on the whole, we continue to slash and burn. We continue to bulldoze through ancient woodland and greenbelt, to fill rivers and seas with human excrement, pesticides and pollution. Still we transform little pockets of living space into joyless car parks. Still we ignore the needs of hedgehogs and countless other wild species, to the detriment of all of us.

Climate change and habitat loss pose the biggest ever threat to life on Earth. Most species can't adapt quickly enough to the changes that are happening and we will see many extinctions in our lifetime. These extinctions represent a heartbreaking and completely avoidable loss, but also they will make life harder for those of us who are left. All species on Earth are part of a series of ecosystems that keep life ticking over: the pollinators that provide food while ensuring the next generation grows the following year; the earthworms and other soil fauna that keep the soil healthy so we can grow food in it; the beavers that keep rivers clean so we may drink the water. These are some very basic examples of the amazingly complex webs of life that have evolved on Earth over the last 12,000 years, which we are destroying with our collective reluctance to transition away from fossil fuels.

Climate change is a global issue, but we must stay focused on what we can change here, at home. It has not been caused by us but by big business, by oil giants, by capitalism itself. But it's us who are sleeping through the destruction, us who are letting it happen. We need to educate ourselves more on what is really happening, which goes far beyond seeing what's reported in the news – and fighting against it. And we need to fight hard.

While we fight with all of our might to force politicians to make the changes we need for a liveable future, there's a lot we can do at home. The UK's 30 million gardens represent 30 million opportunities to create green spaces that hold on to water and carbon, create shade, grow food and provide habitats for wildlife that might otherwise not survive. It might not look like much but that little patch of land outside your back door could help species survive the assaults of climate change and habitat loss; it could be part of a corridor that allows wildlife to travel north in search of cooler temperatures; it could provide food and water when there's little in the wild; it could offer a windbreak that simply enables bees to land on the flowers they need to feed from. We can do this, one garden at a time, one allotment, one balcony, one patio, one windowsill at a time. Don't have any outdoor space? Join your local park group – we have 27,000 public parks – as a few extra habitats here and there will further add to the survival rates of certain species and make life easier for us, too. Don't forget that all of these extra plants we'll grow and the habitats we'll create will mean there will be less CO_2 in the atmosphere, less water flooding the streets, less heat, less wind. It's not one garden against the world, it's 30 million gardens, 27,000 parks and countless balconies and roof gardens *for* the planet.

Where to start

Ultimately, whatever space you have, look at growing more plants in it. Cover your walls and fences with climbers and plant up bare spaces so the whole site is greener and more alive. All of these plants will absorb CO_2 while providing habitats for a huge range of species.

Grow flowers for pollinators, specifically single flowers, where you can see the central part of the bloom, and flowers of different shapes so they attract the widest range of insects. Keep them well watered so they produce nectar, even in a heatwave. Also grow more drought-tolerant plants such as Mediterranean herbs, catmint and chives, which don't need so much watering but still produce nectar. (Grow honeywort if you dare!)

Grow leaves for leaf munchers, including caterpillar food plants. These are nearly always native plants – native shrubs and trees like hawthorn and hazel but also 'weeds' like dandelions, grasses and bedstraws. Look at growing near-natives for those arriving from the Mediterranean. Easy starting plants include fennel and carrots, which are used by the continental swallowtail butterfly, and cleavers and bedstraws for the hummingbird hawk-moth.

Plant a hedge, which will filter and slow down wind, rather than a fence, which wind will smack into, giving it energy to do further damage along your street. Birds will roost and nest in it, hedgehogs will shelter beneath it, butterflies and moths will lay eggs in it. In autumn, when its leaves fall to the ground, leave them there. Worms will take them into the soil and, along with fungi and bacteria, will break them down into food that's returned to the roots of the hedge they came from. A mixed, native hedge planted with hazel, hawthorn, wild roses and guelder rose is best for wildlife but all hedges will slow down wind, absorb water and lock away carbon.

Dig a pond, which will absorb and hold on to carbon while providing drinking and bathing water for birds and mammals and breeding opportunities for aquatic invertebrates and amphibians. Get to know the wildlife that uses it, including the backswimmers and whirligig beetles, the pond skaters and the huge great diving beetles. Sit by it and feel peaceful by it. Hang around at night and wait for bats.

Make hedgehog holes on either side of your garden and chat to your neighbours about creating a 'hedgehog highway'. Look at your garden not as a small, private space outside your back door but as part of a wider landscape, a network of habitats that could save lives and save species. If you have plastic grass, decking or paving then there has never been a better time to take it up.

Be wilder by letting areas of grass grow long, leave fallen leaves where they land and stop sweeping away the pile of debris that accumulates behind your pots. Let seedheads and berries feed the birds they are intended to feed. Be nice to weeds, for they are nice to wildlife. Please stop using pesticides. Please avoid using peat.

Save water when it's wet so you can use it when it's dry. Currently we seem to have wetter winters and drier summers, so we can plan ahead to ensure we have water to feed plants, top up bird baths and keep ponds full all year round. Buy the biggest water storage container you can afford and connect it to the downpipe of your house so it fills quickly when it rains. Look on your local council website, where there might be a discount on water butts, or visit your local tip, where water butts are often given away for free or for a few quid. Get as many as you have space for. If heavy rain is forecast, empty your water butt into the garden so it refills and prevents some water from reaching the sewers. If it's dry, use that water to keep your garden alive, your flowers producing nectar. If you live in a flood-prone area then consider making a rain garden, which will take all the water from your gutters and hard landscaping and hold it in the garden, where it will slowly seep into the ground.

Grow food to connect you more with the land. The greater connection you have, the more you will understand about the natural systems that aid food security. Start with easy crops like courgettes and climbing beans. Compost your kitchen and garden waste to feed your soil and the invertebrates, bacteria and fungi that keep it alive. Rejoice in the many living things – frogs, slow worms, beetles, hedgehogs – that will live in your compost heap while it breaks down. These species will return the favour of you providing them shelter in your garden by eating the slugs, aphids and caterpillars that would otherwise eat your crop.

Put up bird boxes to help birds. Swifts and house sparrows are particularly in need of nesting sites but starlings and songbirds need them, too. If you have scaffolding up, erect swift or house sparrow boxes beneath the eaves of your house. The two species don't get on with each other, so keep nest boxes separate to avoid conflict. In the garden tit boxes are readily used. A dense mass of foliage is perfect for robins.

Keep an eye out for caterpillars on nettles or other foodplants in communal spaces, such as your local park. If you find caterpillars, ask yourself: will they be safe? If not, move them to a spot that will be safer (perhaps away from the path or in a wilder area of the park, or your garden or allotment). Always move them on to the same foodplant you found them on; they simply won't survive if you put them on a different plant. If none of the above options is available, you could take them home and raise them yourself. You'll need a mesh cage (known as a butterfly cage) and a daily supply of fresh foodplant leaves. Please only do this if you can commit to feeding them every day and be around to release the adults safely when they are ready. If you're a beginner, start with just a few and work your way up to caring for larger numbers.

Leave water for hedgehogs and birds to drink. If you see birds struggling to find food for their chicks in spring then leave out mealworms – you can rehydrate dried ones in a bird bath or similar. Mealworms will be taken very quickly by all birds so you may want to put a cage around them so only smaller birds can access them, which will prevent hedgehogs from eating them, too. But, whatever you do, open your eyes and take action. If birds and other wildlife are going hungry then feed them. You can save their lives.

Feed grounded bumblebees that have emerged from hibernation but haven't found nectar in time to give them the energy to fly. Gently pick them up and pop them on a suitable flower, such as a crocus or primrose, making sure you watch them drink before you move on. If they don't drink, find them a better flower (remember you need to see its centre) or mix a teaspoon of sugar with a teaspoon of tepid water and see if they will drink that instead. Wait for them to buzz and fly off.

Rescue hedgehogs you notice are out in the day during winter. In summer, it's normal to see hungry mums with young in the nest come out during the day to find food and water, but at other times of year a hog out in the day is poorly and, usually, close to death even if it looks OK. Find details of your local rescue centre and call them, tell them what you see. Is it tiny? If so it won't be big enough to survive hibernation. Is it walking in a circles? Not moving? Remember that hedgehogs never 'sunbathe'. If you can quickly get it to a rescue centre, you may save its life.

Get to know and record wildlife to help track the movement of species. Growing plants and creating habitats is only half of the story. It will help so much if you get to know who visits your garden. Buy a bee book or a bird book or a butterfly book or a frog book. Read it, marvel at the wonderful things you learn and use that knowledge to better understand the needs of those living in your garden. Long-tongued bees need flowers with long flower tubes; frogs and toads need different types of pond (or different habitats within the same pond); birds have a range of food and habitat requirements that change from winter to autumn. Get to know who visits you now so you will know who arrives in the future and who stops visiting you, too. It's important to know. Take photos of species and log your sightings on irecord.org.uk, which will help ecologists track population movements, including declines, increases and arrivals.

Reading List

Beebee, T. 1997. *Frogs and Toads (British Natural History Series)*. Whittet Books, Totnes.
A joyous read about frogs and toads. What's not to like?

Bradbury, K. 2019. *Wildlife Gardening for Everyone and Everything*. Bloomsbury, London.
This will give you a solid foundation on which to build a wildlife garden.

Carson, R. 2000 (first published 1962). *Silent Spring*. Penguin, London.
Where this all began. Read it and weep.

Durrel, G. 2016 (first published 1956). *My Family and Other Animals*. Puffin, London.
Because we should all be more like Gerald.

Falk, S. 2018. *Field Guide to Bees of Great Britain and Ireland*. Bloomsbury, London.
Hands down the best field guide to bees there is.

Harrison, M. 2021. *By Ash, Oak and Thorn*. Chicken House, Frome.
Three little people set out on a journey to save themselves. A story for all of us.

Majerus, M. and Kearns, P. 1999. *Ladybirds (Naturalists' Handbook Series)*. Richmond Publishing, Totnes.
A great little book on the lives and species of ladybirds.

Monbiot, G. 2023. *Regenesis: Feeding the World Without Destroying the Planet*. Penguin, London.
This book is so important. It's not written for the home grower but it has changed the way I grow my food.

Morris, P. 2015. *Hedgehogs*. Whittet Books, Totnes.
All you need to know about hedgehogs, in a really simple and engaging book.

Sladen, F.W. L. 2014 (first published 1912). *The Humble-Bee: Its Life History and How to Domesticate It.* Cambridge University Press, Cambridge.
I have all the bee books, and this is my favourite. A lovely bit of bumblebee history. Sladen writes of his time as a 16-year-old, travelling round Kent in his horse and trap, and digging up bumblebee nests to keep in his parlour. Considered the first in-depth study of bumblebees in Britain, it's a must for anyone who loves bumblebees.

Tree, I. 2019. *Wilding: The Return of Nature to a British Farm.* Bloomsbury, London.
The story of Knepp, one of the most hopeful places on the planet.

Helpful Websites

Bat Conservation Trust
All about bats and how to help them
www.bats.org.uk

The British Hedgehog Preservation Society
On helping hedgehogs
www.britishhedgehogs.org.uk

Bumblebee Conservation Trust
Learn about bumblebees and how to help them
www.bumblebeeconservation.org

Butterfly Conservation
Find out how to help butterflies and moths (and their caterpillars)
butterfly-conservation.org

The Feather Speech
All about Hannah Bourne-Taylor's campaign for swift bricks, and how
you can get involved
hannahbournetaylor.com/the-feather-speech-campaign-for-swifts/

Froglife
Get involved in the conservation of frogs and other amphibians
www.froglife.org

Heal Rewilding Charity
A brilliant idea: collectively buying land and giving it back to nature
www.healrewilding.org.uk

Hedgehog Street
Learn more about hedgehogs and how to set up your own 'Hedgehog
Street'
www.hedgehogstreet.org

iRecord
Start recording the wildlife you see in your garden or local park
irecord.org.uk

Knepp
Visit this magical place and see what nature restoration looks like on a
larger scale
www.knepp.co.uk

The Mammal Society
For the protection of Britain's mammals
mammal.org.uk

The People's Trust for Endangered Species
Studies and campaigns relating to many garden species
ptes.org

The RHS
The UK's leading gardening charity
rhs.org.uk

The RSPB
Lots of gardening advice centres on all wildlife, not just birds
rspb.org.uk

Swift Conservation
All about swifts and how to help them
www.swift-conservation.org

Wildlife Gardening Forum
A collaboration between the RHS and The Wildlife Trusts, the forum
provides a hub for wildlife lovers who want to make their gardens
better for wildlife.
wlgf.org

The Wildlife Trusts
Wildlife gardening pages to help you start creating habitats
wildlifetrusts.org/gardening

Index

aphids   56, 106, 131, 147, 163, 179–80

backswimmers   22, 91, 94, 95, 127, 266, 267
basil   255–6
bat boxes   23, 268
Batman hoverfly   147–9
bats   24, 268–9
bee-flies   54, 225
bee hotels   23, 30–1, 110–11, 257
bees   27–8, 30–1, 81–2
   bumblebees   17–18, 27–8, 82, 106, 171, 185–6, 205, 295
   hairy-footed flower   27, 28, 82, 210, 212
   leaf-cutter   31, 183
   mining   24, 28, 54, 80, 205, 211
   red mason   22, 28, 30–1, 183, 257
   red-tailed mason   247–8
   wool carder   22, 110–11
Big Garden Birdwatch   178
biodiversity crisis   15, 18–20, 290–1
   lack of understanding about   275–8
   see also declining species; habitat loss
birds
   birdsong   120, 131, 193, 195, 215
   black redstarts   158–61
   blackbirds   250, 256–7, 267
   chiffchaffs   24, 130–2, 143, 210, 215
   curlews   156–8, 214
   declines   57–61, 163, 178–80, 217, 259, 290
   diseases   162, 172
   feeding   161–4, 172, 235, 257, 258–9, 263, 264, 295
   gulls   38–41, 66–8, 69, 80, 208–9, 213, 231–2, 233–4, 286–7
   house martins   132
   house sparrows   35, 55–7, 103, 130, 161, 163, 172, 178–81, 233, 235, 239, 258
   lapwings   216–17, 218
   nest building   244–6
   nest predation   165, 166, 249–51, 272–3
   nesting materials   198–9, 244
   nesting success   165–6, 178, 250
   robins   164–6, 220, 230, 235–6, 239, 244–6, 249–51, 253–5, 257–9, 263–5, 272–5, 282–4

   scrub and   143
   starlings   35–6, 40, 55–6, 196, 258
   swallows   132
   swifts   57–61, 259–63
   willow warblers   24, 131–2
black redstarts   158–61
blackbirds   250, 256–7, 267
Bourne-Taylor, Hannah   261–2
brandling worms   258, 264
British Trust for Ornithology (BTO)   253, 254
brown tail moth   73
bufotoxin   226
bumblebees   17–18, 27–8, 82, 106, 171, 185–6, 205, 295
butterflies
   declines   64, 83, 290
   drought and   105–7
   gardening for   221–2
   holly blue   34, 36
   large white   106–7
   orange-tip   236–7
   parasites   83–4, 89
   pupation   75, 83–4, 85, 86, 89, 221–2
   raising   65–6, 72–6, 83–7, 89–90, 295
   small tortoiseshell   64–6, 72–6, 83–7, 89–90
   speckled wood   221–2
butterfly cages   65–6, 75, 86, 90, 107, 227, 295

carbon stores   12–13
Carson, Rachel   19
caterpillars   24, 80
   as food for birds   163, 179, 180
   food plants for   34, 124, 180, 236–7, 292
   hummingbird hawk-moth   124
   parasites   83–4, 89
   pupation   75, 83–4, 85, 86, 89, 124, 221–2
   raising   65–6, 72–6, 83–7, 89–90, 295
   small tortoiseshell   64–6, 72–6, 83–7, 89–90
chalk aquifers   97
chestnut-leaved holly   88–9
chiffchaffs   24, 130–2, 143, 210, 215
climate change   11–16, 169–70, 219, 279–80, 290–1
   chiffchaffs and   131–2